A TOWN'S PRIDE

Victorian Lifeboatmen
& their Community

by Rob Blann

Published by

Rob Blann, Worthing, West Sussex BN11 5JL, England.
To benefit the
Royal National Lifeboat Institution.

© Rob Blann 1990

Ist Edition 1990

Blann, Rob

A Town's Pride: Victorian Lifeboatmen and their Community.

ISBN 0 9516277 0 8

Cover illustration Richard Marsh,
depicting the *Henry Harris* Lifeboat and Crew
returning from service to the *Indiana* in 1901.

Printed in England by Amherst Offset Ltd.
Ferring, Worthing, Sussex.

A dramatic and informative insight of a seafaring community during the latter half of the 19th century, in which true stories reveal the lives and times of fisherfolk in a close-knit neighbourhood.

Featuring a lifeboat station from its inception, *A Town's Pride* takes the reader through every exciting rescue mission, describes each lifeboat parade, and details sailing regattas.

The author endeavours to show how a sea-going community lived in one particular town — Worthing — eleven miles west of Brighton, on the Sussex Coastal plain.

Nationwide progress of the R.N.L.I. is traced throughout the period, 1850 – 1901. This is the first of a trilogoy. Two further books will cover the period from 1901 to the present day.

Part of the proceeds from 'A Town's Pride' will be donated to the Royal National Lifeboat Institution – an organisation relying entirely upon voluntary contributions for saving lives at sea.

Other books available or in preparation by the same author

Pulling Together (2nd book in Trilogy)

Foreword

Michael Ashley, R.N.L.I., Regional Organiser, South East of England.

For anyone with a love of the sea and a desire to learn of their local nautical heritage then this fine book created with personal pride and great feeling by Rob Blann is something to read and to cherish. It is also a chronological record of the lives and times of Worthing people, of seafarers and of lifeboatmen.

Spanning just 50 years this most comprehensive and immensely readable record preserves for all time the history of Worthing's gallant lifeboatmen. The happy days when men are plucked from certain death; the sad days when nature's terrible force prevents even the bravest of men from achieving their goal.

'A Town's Pride' brings to us the lives of those people, men and women, dedicated to the cause of saving life at sea. Even now, when Worthing no longer boasts its own lifeboat, the author, the great great grandson of Tom Blann, one of the crew of Worthing's first lifeboat, continues this tradition as a member of the Worthing Fund Raising Branch Committee of the R.N.L.I.

Introduction

Eric Cockain, Conservation Officer, Worthing Borough Council.

The author is full of enthusiasm in all that he tackles. In 1988 he tried, unsuccessfully, to re-unite an historic lifeboat with an equally historic lifeboat house on Worthing's seafront.

Now he is Chairman of the Joint Committee of Conservation Groups known as S.W.O.T. (Save Worthing Old Town), set up to save historic buildings, including the unique Dome Cinema Complex, in a redevelopment area which has become affectionately known as the Old Warwick Quarter.

His eagerness to record his family's illustrious connections with the lifeboat service spurred him on to complete laborious researches, and enabled him to converse with other descendants of lifeboatmen in an easy and frank manner. The story is, therefore, a gossipy one and easy to read.

These inimitable compulsions and connections allow him to recapture the spirit of a time when earning a living for some of the town's inhabitants was made bearable or desperately difficult by the whims of a sometimes kind but always unpredictable sea.

This book is a chronicle of a lifeboat service born out of catastrophe, a chronicle spanning half a century of Queen Victoria's reign. A future book will continue the story into the 20th century.

Great occasions are described in great detail. Annual events are reconstructed in a tradition many a sportsman will know as an essential part of the day, the pub post-mortem. Throughout, the readiness of the lifeboat crew to serve, and the keeness and pride of Worthing's lifeboat supporters are abundantly apparent.

Some of the illustrations used are breathtaking. Each lifeboat can be imagined and many of the characters in the text can be recognised in the photographs.

For those who are not conversant with all the technical vocabulary there is a glossary of terms. I hope the book will be attractive, not only to locals who bemoan the loss of lifeboat activity but to a wider public who share in, and regularly support everything associated with the clever boats and brave crewmen who give our coast its glorious and still vibrant mantle of care.

Contents

List of Illustrations

To my wife, Josephine

Worthing beach on a reasonably calm day

Preface

In 1988 when Worthing's old lifeboat house came up for public auction, I, a descendant of a line of Worthing lifeboatmen, initiated a campaign to raise money for its purchase.

An arduous and exhausting task ensued, coupled with wide coverage in the media, with the objectives of restoring the lifeboat station, returning to it an historic contemporary lifeboat, and opening it to the public with a display of artefacts.

If the will had existed Worthing could today have boasted a unique tourist attraction - an original Victorian lifeboat house, built by the Royal National Lifeboat Institution (R.N.L.I.), containing an ex-R.N.L.I. pulling and sailing lifeboat.

But apprehension and indifference prevailed, and the lifeboat house was sold for conversion to a three-bedroomed house.

As the Worthing lifeboat service was such an important part of our heritage I felt compelled to reveal its emotional and colourful history. Immediately after my campaign I commenced the mammoth task of putting together this, my first ever book, enabled by my family links to view, in a special way, a whole era of the town's history which might otherwise have been lost forever.

Centuries ago Worthing was a tiny fishing hamlet in the Parish of Broadwater, and one mile distant from that village.

Worthing grew from only 22 listed inhabitants in 1086; its population approaching 1,000 towards the end of the 18th century.

Throughout time, fishing developed into a large industry here, and, without the early fishermen, Worthing would not be the thriving Sussex seaside town that it is today.

My history of Worthing watermen, who volunteered as lifeboat crew, begins in 1850 when 5,000 people lived here, a mere 5% of today's residents.

Fishermen boarding their boats on a rough day

Ch. 1

Eleven Souls Expose A Need. 1850

In the early hours of Monday 25 November, rough weather struck along the south coast. Soon after daybreak Worthing fishermen congregated on the beach, braving the biting, strong south westerly wind; their salty eyes searching the huge waves of the frenzied sea for any sign of a vessel that might have been caught in the storm.

On the horizon, about three miles out, they spotted a distress flag flying from a mast. Through the haze they could just make out that it was a barque with only two of its three masts still intact. The crew had cut away the main mast in desperation to stop the ship keeling over in the gale. All of her sails had been blown away and she ran a risk of being driven ashore, where she could be battered into submission and destroyed by the powerful foaming breakers.

These brave watermen felt it their duty to try and save their fellow mariners from the stricken ship that was at the mercy of the wicked elements. They were all experienced: the best sailors and fishermen in Worthing. The risks were high, the weather conditions appalling, but their willingness to help others in distress shone through.

It was low water and impossible to launch a large fishing lugger that would have been capable of riding the mountainous sea; immediate help could only be given in an open boat; the best on the beach was the ferry boat, belonging to Sydney Beck, an innkeeper, capable of carrying 20 to 30 men in very heavy seas. The fishing community had turned out in force and there was no shortage of help in dragging the boat across the sand to the water.

Four members of the Newman family clambered into the boat: Jim, his two sons Jimmy and John; and his brother Harry. The brave and fearless Newmans were joined by two young bachelors, Bill Wicks and Harry Slaughter.

Tom Blann, my great great grandfather who was only 17 years of age, struggled to board the boat; but his fiance's father John Louis Belville stopped him and insisted: "Not you son, you're too young". Tom reluctantly accepted the decision of his future father-in-law and made way for the two mature 40 year old twin brothers, Steve and Jim Edwards who, with Bill Hoskins and Harry Bacon, completed the crew.

Young Tom was among those from the close-knit fishing fraternity who waded into the foaming surf to help launch the ferry, called the *Britannia*, but nicknamed *Lady Lump* because of some peculiar characteristic in its construction. The 11 courageous crew, pulling double-banked oars, three on either side with one man to each, succeeded in putting off shortly after 8 a m. After they had got through the crashing breakers they hoisted the foresail from the main mast, a mizzen sail astern and a topsail from the topmast, which Tom could see bobbing up and down in the swell for some time as they kept a fair course towards the stricken barque.

People were coming from all over Worthing to share the excitement of 'the wreck' and concern for its crew and rescuers. The crowds that filled the beach in both directions had to move back as the tide had turned and the sea was flowing strongly.

The gusting south westerly was becoming more powerful and the heavy sea getting worse the further the volunteer crew sailed out under light canvas. They reefed the foresail and partly rolled up the mizzen on the floundering ferry boat. Then, as the boat neared the ship , Tom, watching from the shore, found it difficult to see clearly because of the great distance and the high swell. The onlookers were only just able to make out that the distress flags that were flying on the barque had been lowered; and it looked as though the ferry boat had reached the distressed vessel. As I understand it, the crowds were enthralled and hopes were running high.

Suddenly the signal colours were being raised again in great haste as if expressive of more urgent distress! The perplexed crowd strained to focus their eyes as they searched the horizon for the distant boat. What had happened! Sydney Beck, proprietor of the *Wellington Inn* (later known as the *Pier Hotel*) at the sea end of Marine Place, recalled later, "I watched the boat with my glass for some time, and then came up into the town; and on my return, about five minutes past nine, I could see nothing of the boat."

Becoming extremely concerned about the fate of their 11 comrades, 20 or so more Worthing fishermen decided to brave the wicked sea. The tide was on the turn and it was now possible to launch a larger boat.

I know that this latest brave crew, which included Tom and his brother Ed (Edwin Blann), set off in one of their heavy two-masted fishing luggers which these deep sea fishermen would sail for some hundreds of miles, to the best fishing grounds off the east coast or sometimes off Cornwall. Without fear and notwithstanding the terrible thoughts of the previous crew's fate that were agonising their minds, they rowed nobly on. When they were about 50 yards from the dismasted barque, whose anchors had held, they could find no trace of the ferry boat or their colleagues. As the 35 feet long lugger rode up on the crest of each enormous wave, Tom could perceive that the name of the ship ahead was the *Lalla Rookh*, a trading vessel of around 700 tons. I can tell you that two of the ship's crew made repeated attempts to cast a rope into the lugger as they came alongside, but failed, apparently from weakness. At length, the captain, by dint of great exertion, succeeded in getting a line to the fishermen and they were hauled in close enough to shout to each other above the howling wind.

Ed, whose twentieth birthday was in a fortnights time, asked the *Lalla Rookh's* nine crew, who were apparently in a state of great exhaustion, as to the fate of his 11 fishermen companions. Captain W. H. P. Hains, mustering a loud voice to be heard above the tempestuous storm, informed him that the raging sea had swamped the small craft and that all were lost! "I started to send a boat to their assistance," he said, "but I saw that I should lose my men and do no good, and so I ordered them in again."

I dread to think how their hearts must have sunk to the bottom of their waterlogged leather boots on realising their friends' fate. Every one of them gone! What an unprecedented tragedy!

The crew told them that the boat had reached within 200 yards of the *Lalla Rookh*, when it capsized. Four or five of the unfortunate fishermen had clung to the upturned craft, and had drifted past too rapidly and too far away for their own crew to render the slightest assistance, even if they had had the energy.

The barque *Lalla Rookh* and the approaching ferry boat overturning in tempestuous conditions

The sea was excessively rough, and it was exceedingly dangerous for any boat to run alongside the large vessel. The captain told Ed that he required 12 or 14 hands; but transferring them was difficult and dangerous. He talked of tying a line round each of the men and hauling them aboard one by one, but the fishermen would not agree to this in the cold and wet slippery conditions. They thought it better for the crew of the barque to lower the open jolly boat and raise the men up in it.

The lugger dropped down clear of the vessel's quarter to leeward just astern. A boat was then lowered from the stern davits of the vessel, and as soon as it touched the water Ed Blann, his younger brother Tom and his cousin J. Burtenshaw, jumped into it from the lugger. The boat was hauled up and again lowered for Jim Benn, John Teasdale and George Steere. This process was repeated for John Tester, Harry Head, Tom Coppard, 34 year old George Wingfield[1], Bill Marshall[2] and Jim Searle, until 13 or 14 men had been shipped. With the extra help, Captain Hains and his crew were able to rig up some fresh canvas on the two remaining masts; and the East Indian trading ship struggled to finish its voyage from the Brasils to its home port of London, laden with rum and sugar.

The eight crew remaining on the lugger had to face the arduous task of sailing the lugger back to the beach in such evil stormy weather. There was great excitement among the watching crowds as they saw the lugger heaving up and down in the heavy swell as it drew nearer. The relations and loved ones of the 11 fishermen of the ferry boat were hoping that by the grace of God some of them may have been saved. The lugger managed to reach the shore safely and it is my belief that these men must have been suffering not only from sheer physical exertion but also from the anxiety created by the loss of their 11 mates and the terrible thoughts of breaking the disastrous news to their families who were in suspense. The eight crew were Alex Churcher, John Collier, Ed and Pete Edwards, Steve Parsons, Bill Field, Bob Hills, and Harry Wingfield[3]. They slowly dragged themselves out of the lugger as if shocked into a trance, while their downcast eyes and averted looks revealed something terrible.

"All are lost!" was uttered and pandemonium broke out with screams of disbelief and sorrowful wailing from their mothers and wives. The scene was so distressing, with everyone so full of grief and sorrow, that many could be heard sobbing aloud. The distress and agony of some of the widows and fatherless children was truly heartrending.

Bill Hoskins aged 37 who resided in West Buildings, left a wife and four children. Harry Bacon aged 48 who left a wife and six children was so poor that he possessed not even one penny when he embarked on the fatal expedition. John Belville at the age of 49 left behind a wife and five children including Tom Blann's fiance Fanny. Bill Wicks and Harry Slaughter were both 28 year old batchelors. Bill's ageing parents outlived him while Harry was survived by his elderly father.

Harry Newman[4] who was 47 years of age left behind a widow and eight children. His brother Jim, aged 51, the eldest member of that fated crew, lived in Marine Place, where he had been rather better off financially than the other men. Jim's wife, on hearing of the melancholy fate of her husband and two sons, was struck speechless; being unable to utter a word or even cry for some time to come; having, by his death, become solely responsible for bringing up her remaining seven children. The wife of her son John, aged 26, who was expecting their first child was confined that same morning, and the extremely sad news of her husband's untimely end was kept from her. John's brother, Jim junior, a batchelor of 21, was the youngest of the ill-fated crew.

My research shows that Sydney Beck's doomed ferry boat was washed ashore, bottom upwards, near Hove Gap that afternoon. The mainmast with broken topmast, which was also washed ashore at Hove, had evidently been cut away to relieve the vessel whilst attempting to ride at anchor near the *Lalla Rookh*.

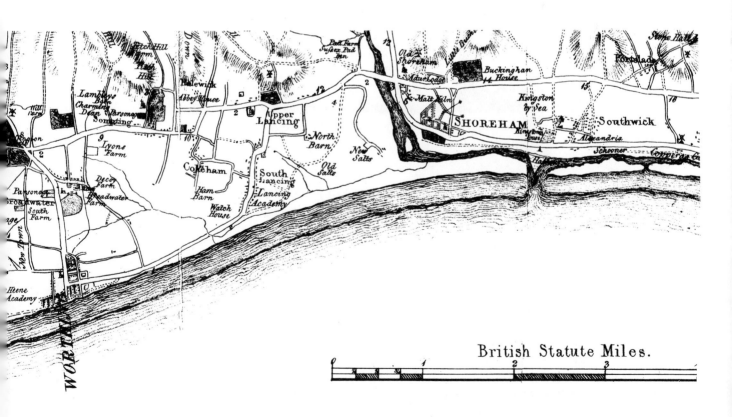

British Statute Miles.

Worthing and its environs to the east

The body of Steve Edwards[5], aged 40, was picked up from Hove beach at 7.30 the following morning by Tom Batt, a master mariner of Hove. Steve's four children were left fatherless, as were the two children left by his twin brother Jim.

The inquest on poor Steve Edwards was held before Inigio Gell Esq., the Deputy Coroner, on Wednesday 27 November. Tom Batt testified that when he was at the bottom of Hove Gap with Captain Spearlock, he saw the body of the deceased washing about in the sea weed about six feet from the shore, his head towards the beach. He and Joseph Mash, who was also on the beach at the time, dragged the body ashore. Although quite dead, blood was still oozing from a cut on his forehead, which must have been caused by striking against the boat or rocks. Tom Batt continued, "I should not think the deceased had been dead a great while. With the help of Mash I brought the body on a plank to the Ship Inn. The deceased's trousers and drawers were down when we found him. He had a blue guernsey frock and a check shirt on. I do not know who or what the deceased was."

After formally identifying Edwards, Sydney Beck, of the *Wellington Inn*, deposed, "I have seen the body of the man just now visited by the jury. It is that of Stephen Edwards of Marine Place. I knew him well. My impression is that when the rest of the fishermen were washed out of the boat within 200 yards of the barque, Edwards must have come very near the shore before being washed out." The jury returned a verdict of accidentally drowned.

The Chapel of Ease pictured here on the right and later called St. Paul's.

The Rev. William Davison, Minister of the Chapel of Ease, Chapel Road, set about ascertaining the financial position and needs of the bereaved families; resulting in a public meeting on Thursday 28 November, three days after the disaster, at the Town Hall (by the present-day taxi rank at the bottom of Chapel Road.) The notice convening the meeting was signed by the Rev. Peter Wood, the Rector; Mr Edward Braby, Guardian; Messrs. Charles Ballard and George Cortis, Churchwardens; Messrs. George Heather and William Penfold, Overseers.

At the meeting Rev. W. Davison, of Broadwater, gave the names of the sufferers, and the number of their dependants: stating that the total number of fatherless children was 36; children now independant, 8; dependant on the mothers, 28; and under 14 years of age, 14. Also among the bereaved were parents who partially depended on three of the single men who had died.

It was suggested that the Rev Davison had been slow in not arranging a meeting before, but the names and numbers of the bereaved persons had to be obtained; the previous day was bench day, and this was the first vacant day since the melancholy event.

A newspaper of the time reported, 'It had been urged that the sympathies of the public would wax cold, but he (Rev Davidson) well knew that the sympathy of the people of Worthing would not wax cold in a day; it would not pass away like steam.'

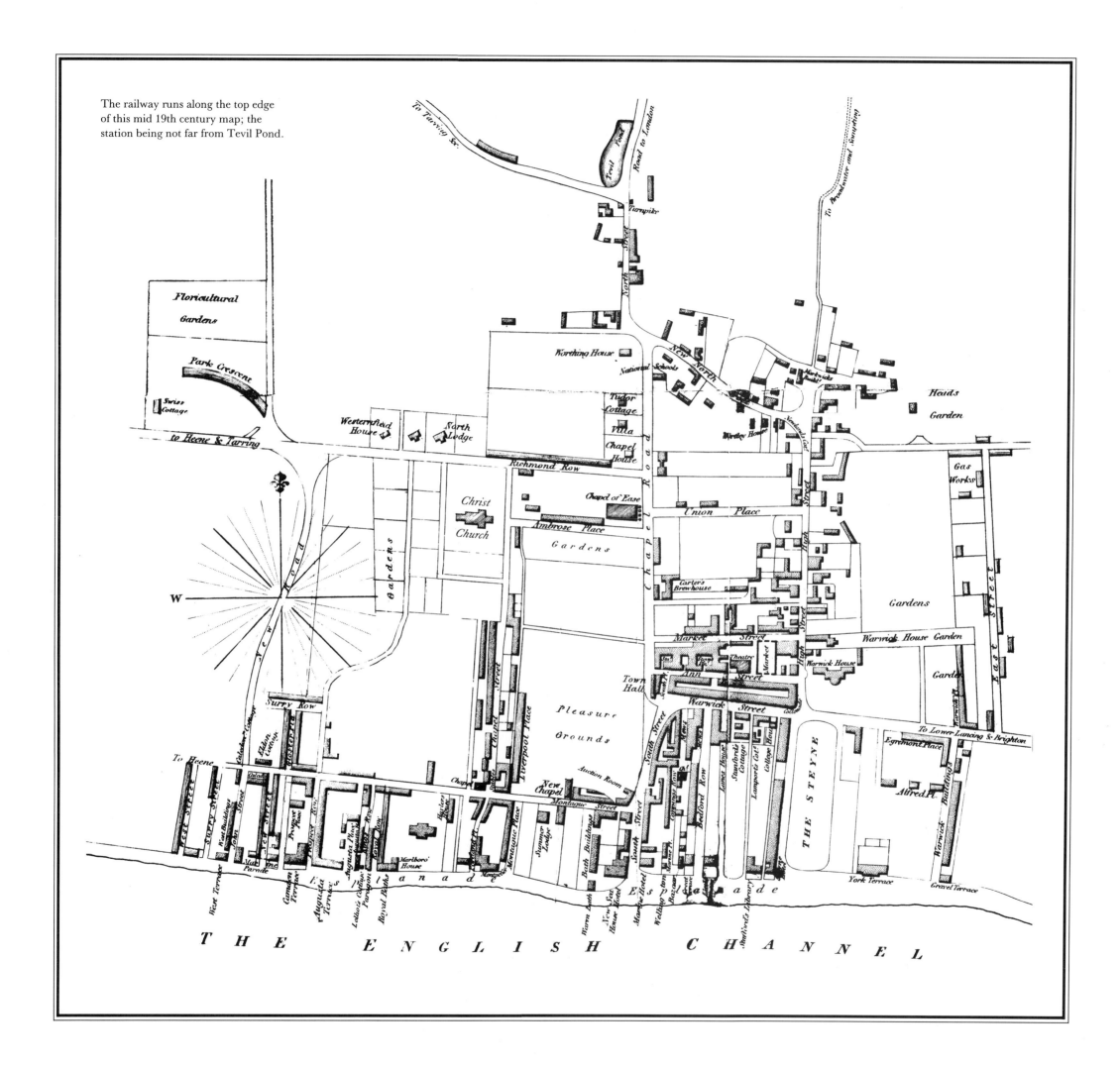

The railway runs along the top edge
of this mid 19th century map; the
station being not far from Tevil Pond.

THE ENGLISH CHANNEL

A view of part of Worthing from the sea. On the far left is the *Marine Hotel* with the adjacent *Wellington Inn,* and on the far right is York Terrace (later the Warnes Hotel) next to the Steyne Garden

The meeting heard that in response to a public appeal, the libraries in the town had already raised £100.

With reference to the best means of raising subscriptions, Rev. Davidson thought it desirable that a committee should be formed, and that they should arrange house-to-house collections throughout the entire parish. He concluded that an appeal should be advertised to the public-at-large, the form of which should be determined by the committee; and that subscriptions should be collected by the following London bankers:- Sir John Lubbock & Co's, Mansion House Street; at Messrs. Strahan & Paul's, 217 Strand; and at the London & County Bank, Lombard Street.

The bankers appointed in Sussex were: Messrs. Hall Borrell & Co. ,Brighton; Messrs. Comper & Co. , Chichester; Messrs. Henty & Co. , Worthing; and the London & County in Worthing. Subscriptions could also of course continue to be deposited with the two libraries in the town.

A bird's eye view from the top of the *Sea House Hotel.* The main thoroughfare is South Street, leading to the Town Hall, where the public meeting was held. Here the road narrows into Chapel Road, leading to the Chapel of Ease. Left of the chapel is Ambrose Place and then Christ Church

The meeting decided that a committee be formed of the Rector of Broadwater, Rev. P. Wood; the magistrates; the Guardian Mr. E. Braley of North Street; the Overseers Mr. G. Heather and Mr. W. Penfold of Chapel Street and Bedford Row respectively; the Churchwardens Mr. C. Ballard and Mr. G. Cortis of Broadwater and High Street respectively; and such other gentlemen as the meeting might propose.

As a result the committee also included Mr. W. Whitter of Chapel Road, Captain Hargood R. N. of Liverpool Terrace, Rev. J. Bailey of Broadwater, Rev. J. Harvard of Lawn Place, Dr. Furnival of Caledonian Place, Col. Wallace of Camden Terrace, Mr. Patching of High Street, Miss Carter of Carters library and Mr. J. Phillips a bookseller of South Street.

The meeting continued with Mr. Thomas Hillman, sub-agent for Lloyds, reading a letter which he had received from the secretary in reply to an application he had made, wherein they informed him that they had directed £25 to be placed at the disposal of that meeting. This was warmly applauded and Mr George Corney of Littlehampton, the agent, said he would hand the amount over to the committee as soon as appointed.

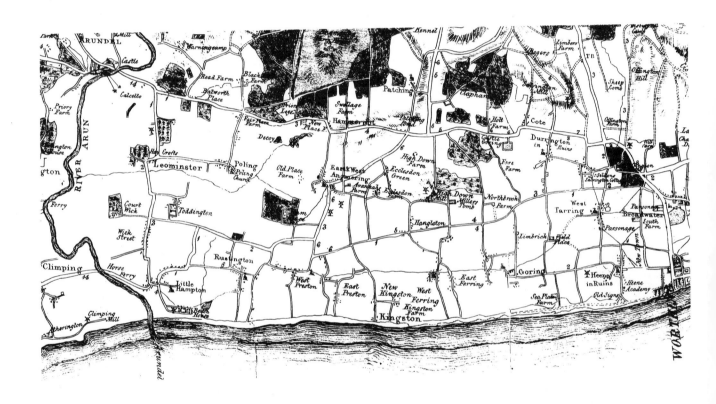

Worthing's western environs

When Mr. G. Bernand of the Stock Exchange, residing at the Marine, Worthing, in an interesting speech, said he had been requested by the gentlemen of the Stock Exchange to place at the disposal of the committee £150, he received tremendous applause.

Mr. R. E. G. Johnson, manager of the London & County Bank, on behalf of the bank, presented £5; Mr. Paul submitted £5 from Messrs. Strann & Paul, bankers, London; and Messrs. Henty & Co. , bankers, produced £3.

The Rev. W. Davison presented £5 raised by the Loyal Victoria Lodge of the Order of Odd Fellows, which had been collected at a special meeting called expressly for the purpose on Tuesday evening. Another donation, from the Law Clerks' Insurance Office, was produced by a Mr. Whatford.

Other subscriptions from private sources, including the clergy, gentry and trade up to the close of the meeting amounted to almost £430.

Captain Forbes R. N. from Lancing, told the meeting that some time ago there had been a vessel off

Shoreham in a similar situation to the barque off Worthing on Monday; a boat with six pilots had gone off to its assistance, but unfortunately the boat was overloaded and struck at sea, and all the men were lost. Since that occurrence a lifeboat had been provided for the port, and no similar accident had occurred there since.

He proposed that as another *Lalla Rookh* disaster could happen at Worthing at any time, a lifeboat should be provided for Worthing by subscription. He believed it would not cost more than £50 or £60 and the proposal was seconded by Rev. Davison, who said that a public appeal in this direction should be a distinctly separate one from the present matter of compensating the bereaved. As soon as that was fully settled, he hoped an appeal for a lifeboat fund would be set about in good earnest. The motion was carried.

Other speakers included, Mr. W. H. Dennett of Bedford Row, Rev. C. Farebrother of Marlborough Terrace, Mr. Simeon, Mr. S. Smith of Charmandean, Mr. Roberts of Warwick Street, Mr. T. S. Brandreth J. P. of the Steyne, Mr. M. Culhane also of the Steyne, Dr. Turnville, Mr. Sydney Beck, Mr. Shelley, Chas. Tinling of Summers Lodge and Mr. J. T. Whatford. After Mr. W. Burnie of Park Crescent proposed a vote of thanks to the chairman, the committee remained behind to make the necessary arrangements for the general appeal and appointed Messrs. Henty & Co. , Worthing bankers, as treasurers.

It was decided to place advertisements in newspapers throughout the country for the relief fund, and the final task of the meeting was to formulate and despatch these.

On the following Saturday evening, Mrs. Harriot Marchant a fishmonger living in Montague Street, who had for some years been living with Jim Edwards, one of the unfortunate men, suddenly died. It appeared that Edwards, who had for some time lived apart from his wife and children, had accumulated with his common-law wife some personal property consisting of boats, nets, furniture, etc, and that they had each executed separate wills several years earlier, giving to the survivor all the property that they possessed.

When Mrs. Marchant was informed of the death of her common-law husband, her grief was so intense that she was heard constantly expressing the poignant sorrow which she felt, insisting that she could not survive it and that her heart would break.

Some of Edwards' boats had been in joint names with his wife, who lived in Worthing with her children. Not being aware that a will had been made, the widow set about taking possession of certain things belonging to her deceased husband.

Unbeknown to Mrs. Edwards, Mrs. Marchant, through her solicitor, had given instructions for any person found removing any of her partner's effects to be arrested, and the widow, the woman who had been made the victim of such accumulated and long suffering, was the first on whom this stroke fell.

As a result, Mrs. Edwards was requested by Superintendent Beswick, with a kindness which always accompanied his firmness to suffering people, to go with him to the magistrates' clerk's office, where the hapless widow for the first time heard of her husband's will in favour of Mrs. Marchant, to the utter exclusion of herself and offspring.

The magistrates' clerk informed Mrs. Edwards that she must not meddle with any of her late husband's property, and she was allowed to leave.

Mrs. Marchant herself was so badly affected that she needed regular visits from a doctor for a week, and though she was suffering much mental agony, she kept about and was up as usual on Saturday. That evening, one of the crew of the lugger, who had succeeded in boarding the *Lalla Rookh* called to see her and told her what the captain had said, "That the cries of James Edwards for help whilst hanging to the waterlogged boat, were truly awful."

This statement greatly excited and affected her already perturbed state of mind. At about half past nine, when several friends were with her, she sank back in the chair exclaiming, "Oh, Fanny, Fanny," (Tom Blann's fiance Fanny Belville who was present), and died.

During her life the 39 year old woman had been exceedingly charitable and kind to the poor, and ever ready to relieve distress. She had been born in Brighton, maiden name Tattersail, and was taken there for internment.

On the Sunday afternoon the remains of Steve Edwards were conveyed to Broadwater for internment. The funeral procession left the house at half past one: his widow and children travelled in a fly next to the hearse; then came a solemn procession in pairs, his brothers, sister and other relatives forming a long train; followed by Steve's friends.

Every Worthing fisherman, to a man, was in the cortege.

Hundreds lined the road on either side of the procession, and many joined along the route. On reaching the churchyard, the solemn cortege was met at the north gate by Rev. Bailey.

The disconsolate, broken-hearted widow, borne on the arms of her late husband's two brothers, followed the corpse into the church.

Her weeping fatherless children and the long train of mourners followed; but by now so many people had joined the procession that there was difficulty in accommodating them all in Broadwater Church. Nearly a quarter of an hour passed while the large number of people from the cortege were packing in and finding seats before the minister could begin the service.

Broadwater Church, 1 mile north of Worthing, in 1850

When the congregation had settled down, the vicar read the service with so much feeling and emotion that many were deeply affected.

After the impassioned service, the coffin was taken to its resting place and lowered into the grave, in the presence of 700 to 800 people. The anguish of the widow and the sobs of the children brought tears from many a stout heart, enlisting the sympathies of the bereaved.

Most of the mourners then returned home, but many remained for an afternoon service. The church was again filled, and Rev. Bailey preached an impressive sermon from the 20th chapter of the last book of Samuel, part of the third verse, 'As thy soul liveth there is but a step between me and death.'

That evening in the Wesleyan Chapel in Bedford Row (now the sports bar of the Thieves Kitchen pub), Rev. John Harvard gave a sermon designed to soften the late calamity, from the 13th chapter of Luke, the 2nd and 3rd verses: "And Jesus answering said unto them, 'suppose ye that these Galileans were sinners above all the Galileans, because they suffered such things? I tell you nay, but except ye repent ye shall all likewise perish." The minister clearly explained the meaning of his sermon to the unusually large congregation which included many fisherfolk, and his understanding was greatly appreciated.

At the same time, in the Chapel-Street Chapel, the Rev. John Mac Raf Moir M. A. preached a sermon to relieve suffering from the late awful event, from the 19th chapter of Luke, 41st and 42nd verses: "And when he was come near, he beheld the city and wept over it, saying if then hadst known, even thou, at least in this thy day, the things which belong unto thy peace! But now they are hid from thine eyes." The subject was ably expounded and discussed; its application deeply affecting the congregation.

It soon became apparent that the Slaughter family had suffered an extraordinary string of tragedies: the drowned Harry Slaughter's father of the same name, who had been an old man-o-war's man, also met his end in a drowning accident; three brothers were drowned; a fourth perished at sea being frozen to death; and his sister was burned to death in a terrible fire accident.

At an early hour on the Tuesday week after the melancholy disaster several boats were cruising about the spot, expecting that being the ninth day the bodies would float. They continued the search for another three days but without success.

Subscriptions for the relief of widows and children of the unfortunate fishermen, amounted to £1,357 19s. 11´d. by the night of Friday 6 December. Donations were coming from all quarters far and near, and the prediction of G. R. Paul Esq. was fast receiving its fulfilment; though at the time many considered him too sanguine and even smiled at his statement at the public meeting, that a sum of £2000 or £3000 would be realised. By 13 December the sum was actually nearer the latter amount.

Meanwhile, strident efforts were being made, particularly by Captain Forbes R. N., to raise subscriptions for a lifeboat to cover our own immediate coast.

During the third week of December, five of the drowned men were picked up along the coast between Worthing and Newhaven. Harry Bacon, Bill Wicks, and Jim Edwards were buried at Broadwater on the Thursday afternoon, when another impressive service was performed by Rev. Bailey. My great great great grandfather, John Belville, was buried there the following afternoon. I found the following inscription on his memorial stone:

'Sacred to the memory of John Louis Belville, one of the 11 unfortunate fishermen who lost their lives by the oversetting of a boat in an attempt to render assistance to the distressed crew of the barque *Lalla Rookh* off Worthing during a storm on the 25th November 1850. Aged 49 years. '

He was buried at the same time as Jim Newman senior. Newman's great grandaughter, Mrs. E. Stevens, told me that her grandmother remembered the day of the disaster, and how her hair turned white as a result of the shock of losing so many of her family in a single tragedy. Jim's watch chain was still attached when his body was washed ashore, and that chain has been handed down through his descendants. Mrs. Stevens, who is now 86 years of age, and whose mother's middle name was Newman, asked me to take Jim's chain and look after it in memory of her antecedents.

By now the public were responding zealously to the lifeboat appeal - subscriptions were progressing satisfactorily - and with perseverance the lifeboat committee felt that its desirable objective, that of providing a lifeboat for our own immediate coast, could be accomplished.

My perception of Christmas 1850, which was only four weeks after the cruel disaster, is one of sombre sobriety, with a marked absence of jollity and merrymaking in the fishing community. To any visitor at that time, it must have seemed as though a dark and dismal cloud had descended and enveloped Worthing.

Soon after Christmas the body of Bill Hoskins was found washed ashore, the eighth of the 11 unfortunate fishermen to be recovered. The burial took place at Broadwater on Thursday 2 January 1851 after a full funeral service.

A committee of enquiry had been set up, namely: Rev. C. Farebrother, G. R. Paul and Morgan Culhane Esquires, to ascertain the debts of the drowned men. They reported at the beginning of January that the total debts of the late fishermen, who had left no effects, amounted to approximately £298 5s. 5d. ; excluding the debts of Jim Newman senior, which were paid by Mrs. Newman out of the effects left by her late husband. Mrs. James Edwards had no debts; and nothing had been left owing by the three young men - James Newman Junior, Bill Wicks and Harry Slaughter.

For two to three hours on Monday afternoon 6 January, the committee appointed to manage the disaster fund met behind closed doors. Even Sydney Beck, who had recently been appointed honorary Worthing agent of The Shipwrecked Fishermen and Mariners Royal Benevolent Society, was refused entry to the confidential session. He had collected £70 for the cause himself.

Compensation for services rendered to the *Lalla Rookh* by 23 Worthing watermen, was paid out on Monday 13 January. Messrs. R. Isemonger & Son of Littlehampton had been chosen as arbitrators, but because they had been unable to agree, an umpire was appointed who awarded the sum of £539 6s. 6d. to be paid by the owners, which included £54 costs of the arbitration. Other costs and expenses were borne by the salvors, which eventually reduced the sum, each of the 23 fishermen receiving £12 0s. 4d.

The lugger took one share making 24 altogether. Messrs. Isemonger, Corney and T. Hillman (the Worthing agent) met the parties at *The Wellington Inn* where the settlement took place.

The Worthing fishermens relief fund committee sat again on Tuesday 11 February, attended by several widows and relatives of the deceased. A decision was reached to award £10 to each widow and £5 for each child. These sums were paid over to those mothers present. In turn, part of these settlements was immediately handed to creditors of the deceased who were present. The claims were discharged after payment of 10s. in the pound on outstanding debts.

The mackerel season in February turned out to be a bumper one. I think that it must have been a good omen after the violent weather of the previous November and the trauma of the catastrophe, not only in terms of bereavement but also financially. One of the Worthing boats, the one belonging to John Miles, brought in two large catches on two consecutive days: the lugger brought in more than 2000 mackerel on a Wednesday, and the next day this was actually doubled to an amazing 4000. The fish were in demand and readily realised 20s per 100.

Earnings of Worthing fishermen, normally spasmodic, were greatly enhanced during that excellent season which provided many bountiful mackerel catches.

Worthing seafront looking west from the bottom of South Street

During the last week of March, the relief committee at length decided on purchasing annuities of £15 per annum for each widow who had been receiving 10s. weekly. They also decided to divide the surplus between the parents of the young men, Slaughter and Wicks, and the children of the drowned men: about £32 to each child and £32 to the surviving mother or father of the two young men.

There was excitement in the town on Saturday 19 April when some foreign mail arrived off our coast. About midnight, a pilot boat, the *Spartan*, brought ashore eight bags, 14 boxes and eight passengers from the barque, *Lady Valliant*, being the mail despatches from Mauritius (from where the vessel was), from Adelaide, S. Australia, and from the Cape of Good Hope. The packages were deposited at the Worthing post office until Monday morning when they were forwarded to London by the first mail.

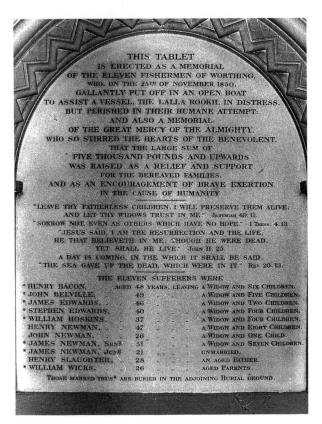

The stone tablet inside Broadwater Church in memory of the 11 victims of the *Lalla Rookh* disaster

Money had been raised by a Brighton committee for the relief of dependants from the Worthing disaster. On Saturday 2 August this fund was disposed of at the boys school in that town: £5 to each son and daughter over 21 and £10 to each son and daughter between 16 and 21 years of age. Mrs. Edwards who had no children under 16 received £10; and the parents of the three single men were allotted £10. The remainder was invested for those children under 16: the mothers to receive the interest according to their number of children.

The nationwide appeal for the widows and orphans had been nobly responded to, resulting in a total of more than £5,000 being raised.

This bizarre catastrophe had galvanised the people of Worthing into raising money, not only for the victims dependants, but also afterwards towards establishing their own lifeboat station, and thus heralded the beginning of organised saving of lives off the town.

All that remains to commemorate the tragedy, apart from a stone tablet in Broadwater Church, are the words of this 19th century lay:

In November, eighteen fifty,
When the winds were fierce and shifty,
   And the seas swept with a grinding roar,
      On Worthing's stony beach,
Scudding swiftly on before 'em
Drove the Lalla Rookh for Shoreham,
   Barque ill-fated, heavy freighted,
      For a port she ne'er would reach!

Broke the morning wild and gusty,
And the boatmen, sage and trusty,
   Shook their heads and gave you warning
      Not to put to sea that day.
"There's some dirty weather brewin',
There'll be ugly business doin'!"
   "Will that barque fetch up to Shoreham?"
      "Shouldn't like, sir, yet, to say.

"For the wind, sir, looks like shiftin',
And to leeward she'll be driftin',
   And - justlook, sir - it has caught her
      Dead athwart her starboard bow.
No - it warn't, sir, quite judicious,
With the weather lookin' vicious,
   To hug the land so closely -
      It's an awkward case, sir, now!"

Darker grew the sky each minute,
And a storm, with fury in it,
   From the south-east, hoarsely growling,
      Burst upon the labouring ship.
Lightening rent the clouds asunder -
Hoarser, hoarser growled the thunder,
   And the savage, hissing breakers,
      Seeded to hold her in a grip.

Nearer, nearer came she landwards -
Ever nearer, nearer, sandwards,
   Where the foam and fleck were showing
      Where good ship might find a grave.
And the surf leaped up around her,
And on rock and sandbank ground her,
   And the watchers cried,"It's over
      If we haven't strength to save. "

Then stood forth a good and true man
Of the fisher folk, James Newman,

11

And he cried,"I can't stand idle
    While those shrieking fellows die.
It's quite possible to save 'em -
Perils are there? well, let's brave 'em,
    They're our brother men, mates, aren't they?
        Harkye, I, for one, shall try!"

Then his two sons and his brother
Said each, "I will, for another,"-
    And James Edwards and six more at once
        Stood forth and made a crew.
Then they ran a boat out quickly,
Through the rollers, coming thickly,
    And the foam dashed from the oar-blades,
        Now on high, now lost to view.

On they lifted, fiercely straining,
And the goal were nearly gaining,
    When a monster sea burst on them
        With a rush and sullen roar.
With a desperate strength they drove her,
But the good boat toppled over,
    And of all that brave eleven,
        Living soul ne'er reached the shore.

Ye who love our folk seafaring,
And their kind hearts and their daring,
    Bend your steps some summer evening
        'Mid Broadwater's roadside graves.
There on tombstone, plain and hoary,
You can read this simple story,
    And lament these gallant victims
        To the fury of the waves.

Footnotes Ch. 1

[1] George Wingfield - was extremely poor and lived in one of the West Worthing Coastguard cottages with his wife and children.
[2] Bill Marshall - his great great grandson Derrick Marshall Churcher, a retired Royal Naval seaman lives in Worthing.
[3] Harry Wingfield - his great great grandson Mr. West lives in Worthing.
[4] Harry Newman - his terraced home in Gloucester Place was demolished to make way for a multi-storey car park in the 1970's.
[5] Steve Edwards - Edgar Edwards, a present day descendant and Worthing resident, who enjoyed fishing in his younger day, told me that his family have lived and worked in Worthing for over 200 years.

Ch. 2

Boatman Blann's Last Voyage. 1852-8

By Christmas 1851, Worthing still had no lifeboat due to insufficient funds, despite all the hard work by the lifeboat committee. This was partly due to the heavy expense involved. The cost of stationing a lifeboat here was going to be far in excess of the original prediction and a subscription list which had been opened at Miss Carter's library, produced only about £54 during the eight months up to the middle of January 1852.

To further the cause, Captain Hargood R. N., a local magistrate and lifeboat committee member, personally canvassed Worthing residents and consequently raised another £14. Following his endeavours, further donations were collected at Miss Carter's, which brought the total to £71, of which, apparently, only £31 had been subscribed by Worthing citizens.

By this time, the committee had obtained plans of several lifeboats, and had been communicating with the National Shipwreck Institution.

Not only had the committee become aware of the fact that the £71 raised would only cover half of the cost of building a suitable lifeboat, but that the provision of a carriage would be necessary, to transport the boat across the sands at low water, or along the coast road as necessity demanded. Additional funds were therefore needed for the construction of a carriage, and also for a boathouse.

Notwithstanding the absence of ready cash, the committee ordered a self-righting lifeboat to be built by Harveys of Littlehampton.

A few months later, on Saturday 3 April, the following article appeared in the Sussex Agricultural Express:- 'We are gratified to be able to announce that a lifeboat, possessing the power of self-righting and freeing herself of water, with other suitable qualities, is now in the course of construction at Littlehampton for this place, and it is expected that by the month of June the Worthing lifeboat establishment will be completed; and we have also much pleasure in stating that the National Shipwreck Institution has most liberally contributed the handsome sum of £50 towards the expense, but the funds are still insufficient for the completion of the entire arrangements, and we sincerely hope that the indefatigable exertions of the gentleman who has been mainly instrumental in accomplishing this great desideratum for our coast, will be seconded by a cheerful and liberal contribution of the money which is yet wanting to complete this laudible undertaking.'

June came and passed and Worthing still had no lifeboat.

Ten months later, in April 1853, a further sad loss was experienced by the Bacon family, who had previously suffered as a result of the drowning of Harry Bacon in the great disaster of 1850. My research revealed that one George Bacon was accidentally drowned while fishing in the English Channel off Plymouth, in April 1853. He was one of the crew of the *Lord Nelson* mackerel boat from Worthing, under the charge of Henry Harwood, the master.

By contrast, a couple of weeks later there was joyful merrymaking when my great great granduncle Ed (Edwin Blann), aged 22, married his fiance, Ellen Venn, on Tuesday 3 May. Twenty one year old Ellen was 'given away' by her father Edward, a labourer, at a simple marriage ceremony at Broadwater Church.

Seven weeks after the marriage, Ed, his younger brother Tom, and other Worthing fishermen not at sea at the time watched an amazing spectacle.

It was Saturday 25 June 1853, and the trial of Worthing's first ever purpose-built lifeboat was being carried out by Lieutenant Robert Willcox R. N., with a cheerful volunteer crew drawn from the Worthing Coastguard and from H. M. cruiser *Camelion*.

The trial was keenly observed by Admiral Forbes, chairman of the Worthing Lifeboat Committee, Captain Hargood R. N., Captain Winthrop R. N. and Captain Griffiths. The lifeboat, designed by Mr. Peake, was 27 feet long, seven feet across the beam and took 10 oars. Its capabilities and power, tested to the full by boisterous weather, were watched intently by hundreds of eager spectators.

After launching the craft through the surf to the edge of the breakers, its crew endeavoured to capsize her, firstly by all standing on the starboard broadside and attempting to turn her bodily over. That failed and Capt Willcox then directed the men to rush alternately from one gunwhale to the other, but the stability of the boat was so good that they still failed to capsize her.

Subsequently, they sailed out to sea in a strong SSW breeze, lowered the sheet and then tried her rowing capabilities. Tom watched excitedly as the buoyant craft was put through its paces.

The results of the trial were most satisfactory. In a letter, dated 27 June, to the chairman of the lifeboat committee, Lieutenant Willcox wrote: 'Under all circumstances I can fairly pronounce her to be in every way adapted for the service for which she was designed, as well as for the station (Worthing) to which she is appointed.'

The £71 already subscribed at Worthing and the £50 generously donated by the National Shipwreck Institution covered Harvey's bill of £120 for building the lifeboat. But there was concern as to how the Committee were going to raise the extra money required for the carriage and the boathouse.

I discovered the following extract from a report in a contemporary newspaper: 'We should hope that the gentlemen to whose indefatigable exertions Worthing owes great obligation for placing on our coast a lifeboat, boathouse, carriage & c, will receive the hearty co-operation of the affluent and kind-hearted in placing a sufficient sum at their disposal to defray the cost already incurred, and to enable them to fully complete this noble and laudable undertaking, an undertaking which in its results is calculated to afford blessings to our fellows, which cannot be calculated by any monetary equivalent, and can only be remotely approached by imagining the horror and anguish of spirit borne by 11 brave men who recently perished off our shore in sight of their distracted relatives, and that too for the want of a lifeboat.'

The necessary funds were evidently forthcoming because, before the end of 1853, construction of a stone lifeboat house was complete. It measured 30 feet long by 20 feet wide, with an eight foot high door that was $10\frac{1}{2}$ feet in width. The Worthing lifeboat station was now established with its volunteer crew drawn from local fishermen, including Tom and Ed Blann.

Worthing's first lifeboat house, built of stone with a slate roof, situated at the west end of the town on the beach next to the coastguards' flagmast and among fishing luggers and bathing machines. The building on the left is the coastguard station which was replaced by the Coastguards House which still stands today

Fishermens earnings were sparse and sometimes amounted to as little as only three shillings in three weeks. So they were very optimistic following the landing of a rather large catch, as reported in the South Coast Journal on 15 October 1853: 'About 20,000 herrings were brought ashore on Monday, taken the previous night by our fishermen, for whose sake as well as for the good of the town, we trust this may prove the earnest of a good season.' However, this was not to be, the West Sussex Advertiser reported a few weeks later that the good luck of the fishermen was intermittent as no large quantity of herrings had been caught since.

After Christmas, coastguardsmen were recalled from all the stations along the south coast for active service in the Crimean War, to form the nucleus of new crews in the Baltic Fleet. On Monday 13 February 1854 seven men from the coastguard, having been drafted to Portsmouth, left Worthing, under the command of Lieut. Willcox, on the Parliamentary train, giving three cheers at each railway station on the way. As soon as they had embarked on the ship, the commanding officer returned to Worthing.

On Tuesday 4 July, at about 4 p.m., a fisherman by the name of Charles Slaughter, better known by the nickname 'Pompy', nearly lost his life by an act of impudence. Slaughter, a relation of the late Harry Slaughter drowned in the *Lalla Rookh* disaster, sailed from the beach alone in a small boat.

When he was out in the Channel beyond the luggers, a sudden gust of wind took the full set of sails and capsized the boat, throwing him into the water.

On seeing the accident, some fishermen from one of the luggers put out their boat and went to his rescue, arriving just in time: he had sunk twice already. They took 'Pompey' ashore where they lectured him on how stupid and thoughtless he had been.

A report on this potentially disastrous incident, in the West Sussex Gazette, ended thus: 'We warn the visitors to Worthing never to venture into a boat without first satisfying themselves that it is to be manned with at least two efficient hands.'

Towards the end of that year my great great grandfather, Tom Blann, married his fiance Fanny Belville, daughter of John Belville, drowned attempting to rescue the *Lalla Rookh*. Both 21 years of age, they married on 4 December at Broadwater, the main church which traditionally served Worthing, witnessed by her brother James and Charlotte Newman, a fisherman's daughter.

Just after Christmas Rear Admiral Henry Forbes, the very first Chairman of the Worthing Lifeboat Committee, died at his home in Lancing on 13 January aged 67 years. He was a highly respected senior magistrate on the Worthing bench whose integrity, uprightness and generosity had secured the esteem of all with whom he associated.

During a gale on Friday night 26 October 1855, a small boat was discovered by the police at 11.50 p.m. being tossed high in the sea. The police turned on their light as a signal for the boat to approach. Manwhile, Sydney Beck of the *Wellington Inn,* John Carter and W. Overington provided ropes and other equipment in preparation for the boat's approach. Forty minutes later the boat, which had lost its rudder, managed to reach the shore. It belonged to the schooner *Catherine* of Selby, which was bound for London from Guernsey laden with 175 tons of stone. Having left Guernsey on the previous evening, she had encountered a heavy gale and had started leaking. Most of the crew were at the pumps for 24 hours but they were fighting a losing battle.

At 5 p.m. on the Friday, when the rate of water intake exceeded the expulsion rate, the order was given to abandon ship; the jolly boat was lowered and the crew jumped into it immediately without collecting their belongings. They had scarcely left the ship before she went down, 12 miles from land and about four miles from the Ower's light.

Adrift for seven hours before beaching at Worthing 17 miles away, the six crew suffering from the affects of cold and exhaustion were fed and put up for the night by Mr. Beck at his inn.

On the morning of Wednesday 7 November 1855, a multiple tragedy occurred, which badly effected the fishing community. Five Worthing fishermen and a lad from Salvington were lost when a lugger, the *Ocean Queen,* was in collision with another ship 20 miles off Ramsgate. Having already taken in nets containing about 10,000 herrings, the crew had been hauling in the last four or five of their nets, when an iron steam boat ran into her obliquely, completely staving-in the side.

The fishing lugger, owned jointly by Mr. W. Potter with Messrs. Hide & Patching sank almost immediately with £18 in cash, part of the boat's earnings from a previous haul, on board.

The mast, which had previously been lowered, floated, and the nets clung on to it. Seven of the eight crew tried desperately to cling on.

Richard Wells, who had been on watch, succeeded in catching a rope thrown from the still-moving steamer, and was drawn partly submerged behind the vessel for 100 yards. The steamer reversed engines as soon as possible, while a half-drowned Wells was hauled aboard. She went back, and with considerable difficulty they managed to get William Heather, the master of the lugger, on board in an almost exhausted state.

None of the other five fishermen were saved: Alf and George Heather who were both single and brothers of the master, Ben Wheeler who supported a widowed sister and family, Bill Ball who was a young batchelor, and Bill Belton[1] who was married with a large family.

The steamer, *The Stadt of Dort*, landed the two survivors at the first port they came to, from whence they were dispatched to London. The two fortunate fishermen reached Worthing the following Sunday.

Although Ramsgate had a lifeboat which was described in a national survey that year as being 'complete and most efficient', the tragedy happened too quickly to have launched it. In the same survey the Worthing lifeboat also received the same commendation.

A committee of 17 Worthing dignitaries was set up for the expressed purpose of raising funds for the two survivors and for the dependants of the victims. Subscriptions were collected by Worthing banks and libraries in the familiar manner.

Worthing's association with the sea was expounded by a local vicar, Rev. W. Bean on Sunday evening 2 December 1855. He preached a sermon, specifically for sailors and fishermen on their return from the dangers of their calling, filling the Independant Chapel in the town to capacity.

The luggers that fished away had a good season in the autumn of 1856. A short statement of the accounts from one of them, the *Prosperous*, showed that total earnings were £405 10s 9d and expenses £90 4s 4d. The balance of £315 5s 8d was divided into 11 shares: six for the boat and nets; and the remaining five for the crew, amounting to £28 13s 3d for each man.

But by contrast the failure, of the boats that stayed behind to fish in home waters, was so bad that no boat's crew shared more than £3 per man for the entire season; and as a result relied on charity which was usually dispensed to poorer fishermen during the winter months.

The weather had been particularly violent during that October with the sea breaking over the beach and esplanade, washing away large sections of both, and flooding several house basements. The water flowed up South Street as far as the Nelson Hotel (on the south side of the Nelson Passage, now converted to a shop), like a river with several boats rowing about. To the east of the town, the Lancing road was washed away and the Sea Mills bridge (near the present day Brooklands boating lake) was destroyed.

South Street showing the shops, among which is the *Nelson Hotel*. Opposite are fields

The following year, some Worthing luggers together with some from Hastings, were again very successful when fishing off Scarborough. They caught some large drafts of herrings which reportedly realised an average of £600 - £700 per boat.

Tom and Fanny Blann were blessed with the arrival of a baby son on 10 April 1858, part of a future generation of lifeboatmen, and christened him Henry John, after his grandfather, at Broadwater Church.

Tom's brother Ed (Edwin) took out boating parties for pleasure trips at times when fishing was slack. On Thursday 26 August his services were required, by a Mr. Torr, for a cruise. Mr. Torr, who had rented Augusta House[2] for a short period to give his family a holiday from London, went down to the beach and selected the *Mary Eliza* for his family to sail in. His intention was for them to enjoy a pleasure cruise on the two-masted boat, owned by Thomas George Wood and skippered by boatman Ed Blann, while he and his wife went to see the Littlehampton Regatta with his sister Mrs. Smith, who had joined them on holiday.

Mr. & Mrs. Torr gave instructions to the servants to look after the children safely: their four children, his sisters six children, and four year old Clementine Jackson - a friend of the family. The Torrs then left for the Littlehampton races in a carriage driven by a Mr. Wright.

By 2 p.m. the two crew, 27 year old Ed Blann and Jacob Tester, 19, had prepared the boat and the happy band of children were lifted into the craft. On that beautifully fine day the 11 holidaying children were being supervised by six domestic servants from Augusta House, including Ed's wife Ellen Blann, my great great grand auntie, who were joined by the coachman's wife, Louisa Wright, with her child.

The total of adults, children and crew amounted to 21 persons in all: not an unusually large party for Ed and Jacob. In fact, on a previous occasion they had taken out 28 adults in the boat. The weight of this human cargo posed no danger because as the recently-built craft, although registered as three tons capacity, was quite capable of carrying up to eight tons.

The boat was launched from opposite Augusta house, where it was normally beached and, initially, Ed sailed eastward to enable his passengers to view the seafront. With the sails set, the merry party glided over the glittering sea which was as calm as a mill pond. Ed then turned about and sailed towards Goring as Ellen started to sing to the excited youngsters.

About two miles from Worthing, they reduced the sail and joined another boat called the *Fairy*, keeping a distance of about 200 yards between the two boats.

While Ed was steering the boat he began singing to amuse his young freight while Ellen took a break. Jacob was foreward, tending the sheet while they were tacking. The boat was partly under sail: a 2nd size jib, a foresail and mizzen; and there were two reefs in the mainsail.

Suddenly, within a mile of the beach, an unexpected gust of wind filled the sails with an almighty power, as if the devil himself abruptly vented his rage on the unsuspecting *Mary Eliza*.

The stern of the boat dipped into the sea instantly, water flooded in and she sank almost immediately!

As one of the survivors later commented, "The boat went down from under us as if a whirlwind had screwed her down stern first."

Ed, was an excellent swimmer, and several panicking children clutched onto him for dear life.

Jacob, apparently, was on the windward side and when the boat went down, his legs were caught by the ropes running from the mast to the bulwarks. This enabled him to secure a foothold on the mast, and support himself using the ropes on either side. Jacob managed to balance in that precarious position for about 15 minutes, whilst clutching Emma Smith aged six under one arm. Another child, five year old George Torr, was on his shoulder with one hand grasping Jacob's hair and the other gripping his guernsey.

Tester, in this terrible state, called desperately to the crew of the *Fairy* which seemed so distant, "Sailor, come here sailor, come here." His anxious plea could only just be heard above the screams of the female servants, Matilda Lacey, Emma Sharp and Ellen Redding, who were clinging to the front of him; while the coachman's wife Louisa Wright, with her babe in arms, hung onto him from behind.

He pleaded with Mrs. Wright to release her grip because the pressure on his guernsey exerted by her weight was almost strangling him.

Fearing for her own life, she refused and he subsequently began to lose consciousness through lack of air, as they began to sink deeper.

He was almost completely submerged and close to death by the time the *Fairy*, with its two crewmen rowing furiously, managed to reach him. The three children were taken aboard first and then the three servants followed by Louisa Wright.

Finally, the totally exhausted teenager was hauled aboard and the *Fairy* sailed back to Worthing with all eight survivors on the brink of death.

Hundreds of people gathered on the beach making anxious enquiries about the victims as they were rushed to the Royal Baths. Here they were successfully resuscitated by several doctors, who had been fetched for the emergency.

The Royal Baths (demolished in 1940), to where the victims were rushed

Other boats immediately put out to sea in the direction of the catastrophe to find the remaining crew and passengers but, when they reached the spot, they saw through the clear water that something was horrifically wrong.

All of them lay drowned on the sea bed, still clinging to each other!

The grasping, fearful youngsters had pulled Ed Blann down to his death. According to his watch, which had stopped at 3.25 p.m. when it filled with water, the accident happened only one hour into the fatal voyage It must have been a most distressing sight. Thirteen people, who had only a short time previously been part of a happy group enjoying the warmth of the Worthing climate, drowned under distressing circumstances.

Part of Worthing from the sea - Augusta Place to Portland Place. The tall building on the left housed the Royal Baths

The 13 unfortunate people were:- five of the six Smith children: Martha, nine years; Thomas, five; George Henry, three; Clara Ann, one; Richard Torr Smith, seven. Three of the Torr family: Elizabeth, seven years; Ada, three years; Florence, eight months. Clementine Jackson, an only child. Three of the domestic servants: Ann Henness, Harriet Humphrey and Ellen Blann. And in this sad episode the master, Edwin Blann, went down with the boat.

A message was dispatched to Littlehampton for Mr. & Mrs. Torr to return immediately. Mr. Smith and the Jacksons were instantly telegraphed in London but were not told of the extent of the personal loss. When Mr. Jackson travelled down by the last train, he was met at Brighton station where the calamitous news was broken to him, whereupon he was grief stricken at the loss of his only child.

The bodies, having been recovered, were carefully laid out on the floor of the Royal Baths - dressed in white and decently composed. Four of the innocent little children had their hair neatly combed and were washed. The bodies of the adults lay next to them, with the effects of the sea quite obvious on their countenances.

An inquest was held the next day at the *Spaniard Inn*, Chapel Street[3], before R. Blagden esq. and a highly respectable jury: Messrs. W. Tribe (foreman), W. Patching, W. Potter, P. French, W. C. Blaker, H. J. Berry, J. Fowler, C. Ede, G. S. Wyatt, E. Snewin, W. Walter and W. Verrall.

Jacob told the inquest about the suddeness of the squall: "Nothing was to be seen on the water, it could not have come on the water. It seemed to come down right from above. I have never before heard of it in these parts, it is sometimes at the Equator."

Pete Edwards[4], one of the two men crew of the *Fairy*, told the inquest, "I felt the effects of the squall. It took our boat and sent her in the water. It struck our head sails and she went down and up again directly." Pete added that Ed Blann was an experienced sailor, and that Tester had three years experience in a fore and aft boat.

Lieutenant Harvey Nicholl of the Coastguard told the inquest that he had sent his chief boatman to assist, and that they had returned with four of the drowned victims.

After the inquest, the bodies of nine of the little children were returned to London. The disfigured body of Richard Torr Smith was not found until 8 a.m. on Monday by a Mr. Blaker while taking a walk. It had been cast up by the sea on the beach at the first groyne east of Warwick Buildings, some three miles east, downstream from the fatal incident. Face and body were swollen, open eyes staring, and blood oozed out of the ears as the body was carried to the *Egremont Hotel*, on the corner at the north end of Warwick Road. It was identified almost immediately and removed under the coroner's authority for burial with the others.

The funeral of Ed and Ellen Blann and Harriet Humphrey took place at Broadwater on the Sunday evening, in the presence of a very large congregation which extended into the church grounds. The Blanns' coffins were carried by fishermen and Ellen's pall was borne by their wives, followed by a procession of almost 150 people. My great great grand uncle and Auntie were buried in one grave, side by side; and Harriet was placed in her own grave at their feet.

Jacob Tester later received £2 3s.6d. from a public appeal, for his heroic services in saving life. On acquiring news of the award in December, a Mr. Arthur T. Hewitt of London wrote to the Daily News, 'I cannot but think that Tester should have been more amply rewarded, and as I beleive many would cheerfully contribute to this object I am willing to accept subscriptions.'

Ed and Ellen left behind two orphans wholly unprovided for, Hannah aged five and Alice, two. Ed's brother Tom was only a poor fisherman and friends of the parents were also hard-up and unable to support them, so a Mr. & Mrs. Harris very kindly raised a public appeal on the infants' behalf.

The tragic death of Edwin Blann was notably felt by the community because not only was he one of the crew of the very first Worthing lifeboat, but he had also been one of the crew that successfully rescued the *Lalla Rookh* in 1850.

Footnotes Ch. 2

[1] Bill Belton - his descendant Danny Belton is a present-day full-time fisherman whose pitch is on the beach opposite the Dome Cinema.

[2] Augusta House – later became the *Stanhoe Hotel* and was demolished in 1948. A multi-storey car park was built on the site in the 1960's.

[3] *Spaniard Inn*, Chapel Street - Now the site of Boots shopping store; and the street has been renamed Portland Road.

[4] Pete Edwards - one of the crew of the lugger that went to rescue the *Lalla Rookh* eight years previously.

Ch. 3

A 'Pirate' Boat 1858-63

The Worthing lifeboat service, which was not part of the RNLI, relied upon local contributions for its funding and up until the last quarter of 1858, Rear Admiral Hargood had collected £260 5s. entirely by his own efforts. To continue the momentum he then decided to ask fellow citizens to subscribe annually towards the lifeboat establishment. Even though the Worthing station was not under the auspices of the Royal National Lifeboat Institution, it did receive advice from them.

At the end of October 1858 Richard Lewis, secretary of the R.N.L.I., circulated a letter from headquarters to all lifeboat establishments including Worthing. There had been some accidents around the British coast caused by incorrect handling of boats when running ashore in heavy seas; and the circular was intended not only for lifeboat coxwains but for boatmen generally.

'Although the proper management of a boat when running before a broken sea to the shore is well understood at many parts of our coast, yet as mismanagement or carelessness under such circumstances is still the cause of many boats being upset by broaching-to, the committee of the R.N.L.I. think it important to call the attention of all their lifeboats' crews to the cause of such accidents, and to the proper mode of preventing them, as indisputedly proved by experience.'

'The cause of a boat's broaching-to is the propelling of her rapidly before the sea, whether by sails or oars, instead of checking her speed and allowing each successive sea to pass her on its approach.'

'There is therefore extreme danger at all times in running a boat with speed before a heavy broken sea in shoal water. Excepting where the beach is steep, the safer management of a rowing boat in a really heavy sea is to back her, stern forward, to the shore, keeping her bow pointed to the seas and propelling her slightly against each sea until it has passed her or is under her stern.'

'If a boat is rowed to the shore with her stern to seaward, her oars should then be regularly backed, so as to stop her way on the approach of each wave; and way should not again be given until the wave has passed to her bow, and her position thereby be retained on the outer or safe side of the wave.'

'This treatment runs exactly counter to the natural desire to get quickly over the apprehended danger; but it is the only safe mode by which a boat can be taken to the shore before a heavy broken surf.' - Richard Lewis, secretary.

On a more light-hearted note, although I'm sure it wasn't thought so at the time, an ironic situation came about on 6 February 1859: the Worthing lifeboat could not go out to a ship in distress because the boathouse key could not be found.

The reality of some of the dangers that deep seamen were exposed to was all too often illustrated. Steve Belville, son of my great great great grandfather John Belville[1], was rescued in the Black sea from the wreck of the grain ship *Herald* of Shoreham, on 13 December 1859.

Six weeks later on Friday 27 January 1860, in home waters, a vessel called the *Number Four* was seen to be in difficulties. The Worthing lifeboat was launched but when they reached the craft they found the Goring and Kingston Coastguard galley boats already there. As the lifeboat was clearly not needed Coxwain James Hutchenson ordered his ten crew to return. They were: George Woods, George Wells, Richard Wells, Henry Wingfield, Tom Bridges, Will Street, Rob Upton, Will Freeman, Charlie Groves and John Belton.

Another ship, the brig *Guana Lina* stranded off Worthing on Tuesday 27 March between high and low tides. The captain of the vessel, carrying coal from Sunderland, had thought it was high tide, but when the brig ran aground he checked his watch with another and discovered that it was slow. But fortunately the damage to the brig was minimal and the crew managed to get the vessel away on the next high tide, the following day.

A hurricane swept the town on Saturday 2 June 1860, the likes of which had scarcely ever been known, especially at this time of year. The wind had been gradually rising during the day, and towards evening it increased to a terrific gale.

With extraordinary violence chimney pots were blown away, and posts and railings knocked down. Two fine elm trees in the grounds of Warwick House were uprooted and an old tree in Steyne Gardens was leaning dangerously above the public road. Large limbs of trees were cropped off and their foliage scattered everywhere.

Warwick House, illustrated here on the right at the southern end of High Street

By the sea shore the force of the atmospheric currents was, perhaps, more apparent: spray from the waves was carried high up in the air; and the falling rain came like hail against faces exposed to it. A small boat was lifted off the ground, twirled round once or twice in the air, struck a lampost and split in two.

Anxious people watched fishing boats which were anchored some distance out. The tide rose fast and the gale seemed to increase in fury. If their moorings held there was little danger, but if any broke away they could be dashed to pieces.

Several of the luggers could hold no more and dragged their anchors. Others broke their cables under the strain of the violent sea.

One of the larger luggers, *The Lord Nelson*, owned by Mrs. Beck, was driven aground to the east of the town where, with great difficulty her crew managed to get ashore before the crashing waves smashed the boat to pieces. Two other luggers were driven even further to the east and ran aground nearly opposite the *Half-Brick Inn*. One was only slightly damaged, but the other, the *Eliza* skippered by fisherman Belton, was smashed into a thousand pieces by the crashing breakers.

At approximately 7.30 p.m. a vessel in dire distress was spotted out at sea but driving fast to land. The Worthing lifeboat was launched to go to her assistance but unfortunately struck a groyne and staved her bottom. Notwithstanding this the brave crew carried on and had nearly reached the wrecked craft, which by then had driven aground off Lancing, when they were obliged to run the lifeboat in shore because she was half full of water. The sea was particularly ferocious on this occasion and the gallant fellows who risked their lives manning the lifeboat deserved praise for their skill and courage.

The crew of this wrecked ship, T*he Plough* from Whitby bound for Arundel with a cargo of stone, were afraid, it seemed, to venture in such a violent sea in a small boat, even though they were close to the beach. Eventually three men and a boy were seen to lower themselves in the jolly and negotiate their way through the mountainous sea.

Suddenly a huge wave dashed the captain, J. Peacock, into the unappeased sea. The poor man, still grasping an oar managed to keep himself afloat for some time, but the tide was running fearfully strong and his strength was failing him.

One of the bystanders who had gathered on the beach when they saw the wreck, a man by the name of Yates, tied a rope around his waist, rushed into the water and swam to the drowning man. He succeeded in saving him before being carried back by the surge. They carried the unconscious captain to the *Horseshoes Inn* where he recovered.

With every sail ripped from *The Plough* the tormentuous waves broke completely over her and before the night was out she was smashed to smithereens. Masts, planks, ropes, nets and barrels were strewn everywhere.

It transpired that 13 of the fishing boats had been driven ashore. Two of them, from Brighton, were severely damaged. Frenzied excitement prevailed on Worthing beach for the next day: fishermen were recovering their nets and equipment from the wrecks, while elsewhere along the shore small groups of people were hauling their boats higher up on the beach, lest the storm should continue on the next tide. Carts were being loaded with the flotsam and pulled away as fast as possible.

A large coal brig, the *Mary's* of Portsmouth, had been wrecked some distance to the west of Worthing and her cargo lost. The crew, by good fortune, were saved, but one man was severely injured when a wheel fell on him. He was carried to the watch-house at Goring and a local doctor sent for, who treated the suffering man's injuries to the best of his ability.

Coal from the wreck washed ashore in large quantities. Poor people in the local community rushed to the beach on the Sunday and collected as much as they could in makeshift carts and buckets.

A subscription list was opened in Worthing to reward the lifeboatmen who had braved the hurricane: coxwain George (Johnny) Tyler, second coxwain George Hutchinson, Walker Burden, William Goble, Chas. Slaughter, Richard Wells, John Belton, Harry Freeland, William Freeman, Chas Giles and John Riddles.

Another collection was organised for the crews of the luggers, *Lord Nelson* and *Eliza*, who lost almost everything they possessed in the storm.

My research revealed an interesting anecdote. One George Ball was charged the following week with carrying away a tub of butter, one blanket, three brooms, a scrubbing brush and a candle box belonging to the brig *Mary's*, of Portsmouth, which was wrecked at Goring. The goods were found in the prisoner's house.

There was always more than one complete crew available for the lifeboat, as those that were deep sea fishermen could be away from home for months at a time. This first generation of Worthing lifeboatmen was already procreating. A prospective 2nd generation lifeboatman was born on 25 March 1861. He was Tom and Fanny Blann's second son, William, and was christened at Broadwater Church.

During the Autumn of this same year, a fatal accident occurred while the lugger *Marquis* of Anglesea was leaving Shoreham for herring grounds. The sail was caught by a sudden gust of wind, swung across the deck and knocked one of the crew overboard rendering him insensible.

Steve Parsons unfortunately drowned and was washed ashore a week later. Ironically, he had been one of the crew of the lugger that successfully reached the *Lalla Rookh* in 1850. Steve, a Worthing fisherman, had reared a large family and left behind nine offspring.

Another fatality occurred to a Worthing seaman at Shoreham Harbour during the first week of November 1861 on the vessel *George & Henry* of Arundel bound for Worthing with a cargo of 33 tons of stone from Littlehampton. The two crew had taken William Goble aboard off Worthing at 9.30 a.m. to assist with unloading the freight onto an open ferry boat. About half an hour later a ferocious storm had blown up, and as they could not run into the beach they had sailed for Shoreham Harbour, reaching the head of the harbour arm at about 2 p.m. and had struggled to manoeuvre the boat in.

The boisterous sea had been so turbulent that the craft had driven out with the tide, and they had to beat to windward, sailing the vessel for hours, until at 9.30 p.m. they had again attempted to enter the harbour mouth.

Suddenly, the ferocity of the sea wrenched the rudder. The tiller, in the hands of Captain Henry Grace who was steering, broke and struck Goble in the face.

The flowing tide, frantically aided by howling wind from the south west, drove ashore the ship. It struck the beach astern at approximately 10 p.m. and immediately all three men hove the boat up.

Just then, enormous waves swamped the ship and filled it with water.

All three on board went forward in fear of their lives. The Captain and the mate, Thomas Hebbard, hung onto the forestay while Goble clung to the windlass.

The Captain was then able to jump onto the anchor and into the water to get ashore while the mate dropped from the bowsprit into the water and was washed onto the beach. They both called to Goble, who was laying quite still on the vessel now quite close to the beach.

Gobles cries for help could be heard as the Coastguard, John Hodges, ran down to the beach with rescue gear. They threw lines onto the deck of the ship but Goble could not reach them.

There was no means of getting to him and the sea was running very high. At that moment the craft broke in two and the mast fell down.

They heard Goble holla as the vessel was dashed to pieces by the powerful and wicked breakers, but they never saw him again.

His body was later found washed-up on the beach at Aldrington, was identified by his brother Charles, a wood sawyer who lived at Field Row, Worthing, and was the subject of an inquest held at Aldrington on Thursday 7 November.

Another vessel, this time a small sloop, was seen off Worthing, apparently in difficulties in a heavy sea, between 7 p.m. and 8 p.m. on 29 November 1861, a dark, rough night. As it was burning lights on board an attempt was made to get the lifeboat out to her, but an unreasonably long time was spent in getting the boat ready.

Meanwhile not only was there danger to life and limb, there was fear for the safety of a new creation still under construction, Worthing Pier. There was no light on it, and the sloop very nearly ran against the Pier head.

A couple of coastguardsmen ran out on its decking and burned a blue light which probably saved the little craft from destruction. The sloop, with a cargo of oil cake belonging to Mr. A. Cortis, got clear away, and the lifeboat, which had only just been launched after it took an hour to prepare her, was not now needed.

But the sloop did run aground later the same night, further up the coast, off Littlehampton. The following day she was refloated and taken by a man named Burtenshaw into Shoreham Harbour.

Worthing Pier in its first form

The Worthing Pier, which was a simple jetty with a landing stage at the sea end, was completed and officially opened on 12 April 1862, enabling residents and visitors to enjoy the pleasure of strolling out over the water without the usual risks of shipwreck or sea sickness. A Piermaster was appointed - 52 year old Henry Hayden[2], a Worthing Coastguardsman - to be in charge of the pier.

The newly completed pier proved very useful to the lifeboat crew for testing some new fangled safety gear. Cork lifebelts made on the Captain Ward principle, had been obtained for the Worthing crew by Admiral Hargood and subsequent experimenting on Wednesday 30 April proved a novel sight for the 600-

strong crowd that gathered. The lifeboat was launched just before noon from the boathouse at the Coastguard Station, with each of the 12 experienced crew wearing one of these easily, but securely, fastened lifebelts. The crew rowed it past the town to the east and then brought it slowly up towards the pier and anchored off the pier head.

The West Sussex Gazette of 8 May reported, 'Several of the men jumped overboard and disported like playful porpoises on the surface of the water, one or two of them making unsuccessful attempts to keep themselves under it. Two of the men, Nicholls and Marshall, then swam to the steps of the pier, and all dripping and shivering, walked up to the fashionable company of spectators above, who thus had an excellent opportunity to inspect the cork armour they wore.'

The belts were similar in appearance to cricketers' leg pads, consisting of long slips of cork fastened together in a flexible manner. After a short rest the two crewmen stood on the guard rails of the pier and jumped into the cold water below, wearing all their heavy clothes, except their boots. Despite making a great splash and commotion in the fall they scarcely sank below the surface, proving the wonderful buoyancy of this new invention. The belts, in addition to their buoyancy, provided protection from physical injury and insulation from the cold.

On Tuesday 2 October 1862 when the lifeboat was launched for a practice session, a great many spectators assembled on the pier. Some of the crew again wore these new lifebelts and jumped overboard to test them. Several swam to the pier and walked up the steps by the landing stage. One of them jumped from the top into the water and immediately rose again like a cork.

On this occasion, many of the crew, who were not the strong and stalwart men that might have been selected for such a responsible duty, appeared to manage the boat with difficulty. Although it seemed very heavy and sluggish, it was a most serviceable craft and her capabilities might have been judged more fairly perhaps in a boisterous sea.

Many of the lifeboatmen relied upon sea fishing as their main source of income. At the beginning of January 1863, fourteen fishing boats left Worthing, with 100 fishermen on board, for the waters off Portsmouth. The harbour there afforded great facilities for the speedy landing and disposal of the fish during the mackerel season, as well as providing a haven in bad weather.

However, the continuing rough and unsettled weather was very much against them. Many caught nothing at all, but two boats landed 600 to 700 fish at one time, which sold for 58s. per 100.

The fishermen, half of them married with children, were a very deserving and hard-working class. A few good catches of mackerel or herrings would have brought many a meal where it was not unfrequently wanted. Not only were their families dependant on their catches: the street-hawkers, ferrymen and packers had an interest in the exertions of the fishermen; as well as fishmongers and 'speculators on the fish exchange'.

Meanwhile one morning back at home, a foreign barque was seen off Worthing, apparently sailing aimlessly. Many people gathered and gazed in wonder for several hours. Eventually a man named Parsons, a fisherman who was not in the flotilla of luggers off Portsmouth, went out to her in a boat and somehow, despite the language barrier, managed to ascertain that they wanted a pilot. Parsons, who was one of the brave fishermen involved in the *Lalla Rookh* rescue in 1850, then successfully piloted the foreign ship to her destination at Newhaven.

A few weeks later, on 8 February 1863, a Sunday afternoon when our beach was usually quiet, a rather noisy commotion was taking place. A quantity of fish had been brought in: one boat had 900 which was the result of three nights catches. The first caught were sold for 43s. per 100, the others for 41s. and 36s. per 100.

On the Monday and Tuesday further boats came in with more catches: a Brighton boat had 1500 to 1600 fish which were sold for 24s. per 100. Supply was outstripping demand and other lots of fish were sold even more cheaply.

The fishermen who had dual roles, doubling their dangerous lifestyle by being lifeboatmen, would again be required to help an ailing vessel on Thursday 12 March.

A sloop had been seen at three o'clock in the afternoon, about a mile from the Worthing shore, labouring under considerable difficulties and being driven in fast towards land by a strong gale. The lifeboat was promptly launched and went to the assistance of the *Iron Duke* from London. On reaching her, some of the lifeboat crew boarded her and found that her bowsprit was gone, rendering the craft extremely difficult to manage. But, using their skills, the lifeboat crew bravely struggled to control the disabled sloop which was laden with guano.

Assistance was offered by the Shoreham tug which went out from the harbour. Alongside the sloop, the tugboat captain learnt from the lifeboatmen that they could manage, and the tug returned to Shoreham.

But when conditions worsened in the afternoon she again steamed out. This time their help was welcomed and on the suggestion of the tug pilot, the crew of the lifeboat were transferred to the deck of the steam tug and the lifeboat taken in tow.

Without warning the powerful, swelling sea forced the two boats apart with such gusto that the towline broke and the lifeboat drifted away into the darkness.

The lifeboatmen returned to Worthing without her, but she was found the next day, somewhere near Hove, luckily with only slight damage which cost 30 shillings to repair.

Meanwhile, the sloop, which had been bound for Milford, was driven by the storm onto the piles outside Shoreham Harbour, subsequently released by the steam tug and towed safely into the harbour.

Immediately after the *Iron Duke* affair there were pressures to get the Worthing boat affiliated to the R.N.L.I. On 17 March, only four days after the rescue attempt, the Member of Parliament for Worthing and Shoreham, Mr. Cave, attended the annual meeting of the R.N.L.I. where he gave a speech. He said there were two fine boats in his constituency: at Shoreham and Worthing, the latter of which had just distinguished herself by the rescue of a disabled vessel - yet neither of them belonged to the Institution.

The West Sussex Gazette reported: 'Mr. Cave M.P. hoped the noble chairman, Lord Lovaine, would not consider them piratical craft. His own opinion was that private enterprise and public organisation might go hand in hand in such matters. He saw that 358 lives had been rescued during the year; and when they considered the rank of life of most of these men, and that they were in most instances bread winners to their families, they would never see that even in an economical point of view it was most desirable to support such means of saving life, as almost every hardy sailor so rescued meant a family kept out of the workhouse. He was sorry, however, to see that for every life saved during the past year there had been nearly two lost, which proved the necessity of increased exertion in this good cause.'

The frequent wrecking of boats led to an increased turnover in the supply of new craft. By the 1860's there was evidence of boatbuilding in Worthing itself. At the beginning of May 1861 a schooner, built in New Street by Chas. Bridger, was launched over the beach opposite New Street.

Worthing's Christ Church in Chapel Street (now Portland Road)

For sailors at home and abroad, the Seamen's Mission provided religious instruction. To further their cause an appeal was made on Sunday 8 February 1863 in aid of the Mission when an earnest discourse was preached at Worthing's Christ Church by Rev. R.B. Boyer, B.A. after which a collection of £20 was made. Another collection at that church brought in £8 8s.0½d.; while £5 17s.0d. was collected at Broadwater Church on behalf of the society.

Only six weeks after the Worthing M.P. had made a public statement abhorring loss of life at sea, another terrible event occurred off the town. On Saturday 2 May 1863, the crew of the lugger *Harkaway*, invigorated by four months of highly successful deep-sea fishing, were confidently fishing four miles off the coast. At one in the morning, Bill Jeffree, who was forward with Henry Collier[3], had his cap snatched off his head by the foresail. He grabbed to reclaim it just as the lugger lurched to leeward and overboard he went.

He reappeared on the surface aft, and immediately Henry threw a foreyard over to him. It landed less than five yards from him; he swam after it but couldn't catch hold of the rope.

He kept trying to grab hold of the line while managing to keep his head above water for several minutes. But the strong wind was blowing the boat along quite fast: about nine miles an hour. Henry couldn't swim and none of the others were prepared to risk their lives by jumping in to help. It must have been very difficult for Bill to swim fully clothed, with a tan frock over his guernsey and heavy boots on his feet.

Tom Butcher, one of the crew, saw his head drop under while his body floated continually like a cork.

As the crew would have been unable to stay or turn the lugger to go back for Bill in time to save him, Henry stood forward and waved his hat to attract the attention of a Hastings boat not too far away, but it was quite ten minutes before its' crew realised what was happening.

They immediately made towards the *Harkaway* and picked up the exhausted 38 year old man who by now had been in the water for 25 minutes and was 100 yards aft of the Worthing lugger.

When they got him aboard, attempts were made to revive him but, alas, he was quite dead.

An inquest on Bill Jeffree was held on the Monday afternoon at the *Anchor Inn*, High Street (now called the *Jack Horner*) by Richard Blagden esq. Here it was made known that Bill's quiet unassuming manner had won the esteem of all who knew him. This batchelor had been the mainstay and comfort of his ageing mother. The two other crew, Pete Edwards[4] and Jim Wells, gave evidence at the hearing, which was more of a formality than an inquiry.

An inquest was held at the *Anchor Inn* (the building on the left) at the corner of High Street and Anchor Lane (now Lyndhurst Road)

A contemporary newspaper commented on the Jeffree incident: 'Happily we are not often required to notice such melancholy occurrences, illustrative though they are of the continual danger to which the seafaring classes are exposed.'

<u>Footnotes Ch. 3</u>

[1] John Belville - drowned rendering assistance to the *Lalla Rookh* in 1850.
[2] Henry Hayden - his great grandson Philip Hayden still lives in Worthing.
[3] Henry Collier - a relation of John Collier who went to assist the *Lalla Rookh* in 1850. Henry Collier's great grandaughter is now living near Littlehampton.
[4] Pete Edwards - one of the crew of the *Fairy* who went to assist my great great granduncle Edwin Blann who drowned in a boating accident in 1858.

Ch. 4

Labours & Lifestyles 1863-5

The mackerel season in the spring of 1863 was very productive for not only Worthing fishermen but others along the south coast. On Sunday 3 May, more than 13,000 mackerel were brought in during the morning and sold on Worthing beach. Some were kept for consumption in the town but the vast majority were packed up and sent off to London. The prices they fetched ranged from 18s. per 100 to 24s. per 100. The latter was realised by a Hastings boat which landed 2,500 fish. After selling their catches the crews purchased provisions and returned to their 20 luggers anchored off the town and sailed out to sea that afternoon. During the following few days they returned, many of them bringing ashore considerable quantites of fish.

Our fishermen often journeyed into unthinkably dangerous waters, and a serious loss was sustained by some of them during a gale on Tuesday night 26 May 1863. A lugger owned by Mr. Wood was 20 miles from Worthing towards the Isle of Wight when the nets and ropes entangled in the masts of a sunken wreck. The fishermen, Legatt, Lindup and my great great grandfather Tom Blann managed to recover some of them when the tide slackened. But the cost of the 30 to 40 lost nets was about £100. Consequently this was a bitter financial blow to these fishermen, particularly as it was the beginning of the season.

For those fishing off Worthing the fine weather in May didn't suit, and the resulting catches were very poor. Fine fish, such as those brought in at the beginning of the season, preferred to remain in cool waters of the sea during the warm and still weather, rather than risk the unpleasantness of becoming dried and pickled.

A cloudless sky and unruffled sea, however, were not without their advantages: they combined to put the fish in good humour, in fact, to make them quite playful. They frequently came up to the surface in large shoals, and as high tide approached, very close to the shore. The presence of these fish was indicated by a long dark band on the green waters, which, as the sun shone down upon it, reflected a line of prisms from the backs of the mackerel. Many thousands of the fish amused themselves, glittering in the sunlight like a belt of moving silver.

Sometimes, men on the beach would drag a boat down to the water, row towards the fish, and endeavour to enclose them in a circular net, dragging the ends of it towards the shore. In this way many fish were netted quite close to land, and the operation was watched with considerable interest by loungers on the beach and promenaders on the pier. Mackerel, however, were very wary fish, and their hunters often returned empty-handed. But a Brighton fisherman, who caught most of his fish near Shoreham, made over £160 in one week using a sieve net; and one or two Worthing boats caught a lot of fish in this way, also off Shoreham. But larger fishing luggers were having a bad time, catching few fish.

During this fine weather a shark got entangled in the nets from one of our fishing boats off the Isle of Wight. It struggled in vain to escape until, having exhausted itself, the fishermen hauled it onto the deck.

They took it back to Worthing where it was exhibited on the beach in an impromt tent with a couple of old tarpaulins supported by reversed oars. A large board placed outside had the following inscription chalked on it: 'A Live Shark to be seen'.

At the solicitation of a very polite fisherman spectators were induced to invest a penny to see the 'Monster of the deep', which weighed about 600 pounds. It was nine feet long and four feet in breadth; and its opened jaws contained three rows of most formidable teeth. After a day or two, fishermen dragged its decomposing body down the sands to the low water mark, and the returning tide carried it away.

The good weather changed dramatically in the evening of 10 June, when a raging storm battered some of our little fishing boats.

A ferry boat, which was enchored a short distance from the shore, was driven to the beach as high as her line would permit; and after the waves continually dashed over her, she sank!

A conscientous fisherman waded through the surf with the water nearly up to his neck and managed to cut the rope. The boat then washed ashore where it was dragged up by onlookers out of the reach of the insatiable waves.

The turbulent waves threatened to swamp another small boat, further out to sea, as the tide receded. The owner, being concerned because £15 worth of nets were on board, induced five or six men to venture out in a large ferry boat to rescue her. As they rowed out every wave dashed completely over them, and despite wearing oilskins they were saturated. The tide ran so strongly that it bore them right past the small boat; and for a long time they failed to make any progress, battling against the strong wind and the powerful tide.

At last they succeeded in getting within oar's length of the tiny craft. One of them made a grab for the vessel with a boat hook, while another, a young man named Jacob Tester[1], leapt into the sinking boat. Lest it should capsize and throw him into the sea, he divested himself of some of his more cumbersome clothing, before cutting the anchor rope.

He skilfully sculled the craft through the breakers and, as soon as he had beached the boat, the much-relieved owner thrust a 'stiff glass of grog' into his hand.

Inclement weather was acepted by fishermen as an occupational hazard which they had to endure, but the size of depleted fish stocks was worrying them. There was concern that sea fishing did not generally produce as much as in previous years, caused by catching certain fish out of season, according to an article published at the time.

'Who, for instance, will wonder that the supply of mackerel should fall short when we destroy the breeding fish by millions when heavy in roe?' There were regular months for catching salmon and fresh-water fish, yet sea fish were taken at all times and seasons; and in the case of mackerel and herrings, the breeding fish were preserved for the market because the consumers liked full-roed fish. The writer continued: 'I have watched the working of the trawl net for many years, and it appears to me preposterous to charge that apparatus with destroying spawn-beds, amongst which it cannot possibly be used, whilst the same time its detractors are encouraging the destruction of fish in full roe, containing each from 300,000 to 500,000 ova. There is an old and homely saying that it is well to "put the saddle on the right horse", and, as a fisherman myself of long experience, I do not feel disposed to allow the trawl to be condemned without a word in its favour.'

The trawl, apparently, did no harm by disturbing the spawn beds, but did destroy losts of young fish such as sole and plaice, only a few inches in length.

The article's author asked: 'What then is the remedy for our failing fisheries? Clearly to regulate the size of the mesh by law; to inflict a penalty on those taking fish under a certain size, and, above all not to permit the wholesale capture of spawning fish. Our rivers would soon become barren were there no regulations for their preservation; and it is by no means surprising that notwithstanding the supposed enexhaustibility of our seas, the want of proper rules and regulations should be beginning to tell on the supply of fish.'

Between 200 and 300 tons of fish were sold daily at Billingsgate Market which amounted to nearly £4,000,000 worth of fish a year. A conservative estimate of the amount of brood-fish would have been 50 to 60 tons sold daily in that one market alone. Each mackerel or herring contained 300,000 to 500,000 ova, soles about 100,000, and codfish about half a million!

The fisherman concluded: 'The remedy for this wholesale destruction of an element of future food, is surely the prohibition to take any class of fish during its own peculiar breeding season, and the only cure for the existing evil is to extend to our sea-fish that protection which is afforded at spawning time to the fish in our fresh waters.'

To assist fishermen and their families in times of severe crisis, there were three excellent societies for the benefit and welfare of the seafaring community: the Seamen's Home; the Mission Afloat; and the Shipwrecked Fishermen and Mariners' Society which was instituted some 30 years earlier.

This message to Worthing fishermen was printed in a local paper in December 1863:

'The late disastrous gales have brought the Shipwrecked Fishermen and Mariners' Society prominently before the public; and the amount of good it has effected cannot be overrated at such calamitous periods as we have recently experienced. Still it might be made the means of doing very much more even than it has hitherto. The relief if affords might have been participated by many a poor family now left destitute upon the world. We wish we could persuade the fishermen of Worthing - everyone of them - to join this excellent society. Out of 40 or 50 men, only two are amongst its members. It is quite sad to see such an indifference to the welfare of kith and kin'.

'The fact is, there is not half so much disposition to help one's self, as there is to depend on the help of others. Worthing is known to be a most charitable place, and if any ill befalls a poor fellow his case is at once taken up by benevolent persons. Now, to some extent, this is an evil. It fosters improvident habits, and destroys honest manly independence. It should be a personal matter with every men to look after his own; for there is truth in the old saying that God helps those who help themselves. It is a man's duty to think of his wife and children - to consider what would become of them if anything should happen to him. It is true the times are hard; yes, we know they are, very hard indeed. But the poorest might pay all the Society asks from him; it is but 3s, a year, ticket and medal included. This is ha'penny a week - and you must be poor indeed if you cannot afford to give as small a sum as that.'

A total of 11,000 seamen had been relieved by the Shipwrecked Mariners Society in 1862; some had reeived as much as £20, some even more. During the first week of December 1863, as many as 62 wrecks were recorded.

The article continued: 'The poor fellow whose body was picked up on Worthing beach the other day, had suspended round his neck a medal of this society. There was nothing else on him to tell who he was or from whence he came. And yet this medal led to the discovery of his name and his home. His wife will receive some pounds from the society; and she will, moreover, have the satisfaction of knowing that his remains are no longer in the keeping of the waves, but are laid in the more quiet resting place of the earth's still grave. Every fisherman's wife ought to persuade her husband to belong to such a noble institution as the Mariners' Society, and the husband ought to require little or no persuasion to induce him at once to accede to her wishes. Commander Nickoll - the honorary agent of the society - will gladly receive the name of any seaman who thus shows his independence and thoughtfulness by joining the Shipwrecked Mariners' Society.'

If more local fishermen had succumbed to these pressures to suscribe to a fund for alleviating personal distress and loss, I believe that the family budget would have been overstretched at times. For example, when the Worthing fishing boats returned from Yarmouth and the North Foreland at the beginning of December 1863, the results they brought with them of the past season were by no means encouraging. Fish were plentiful enough, but the prices were low beyond any comparison with recent seasons.

In some cases herrings were sold for manure, and whole barge-loads at a time were sent up country for that purpose. The weather had been very much against the men, and some had suffered considerably by losing their nets in recent gales. They spoke of their late voyage as a most dangerous and disagreeable one.

Indeed, many of them stressed that they couldn't remember such a long period of continual rough weather as they had just experienced. Day after day the drums had been hoisted, warning fishermen not to venture out to sea because of imminent gales. But for those who did pluck up enough courage to face the fearsome elements in pursuit of their livelihoods there was disaster!

No less than eight luggers were lost in the dreadful storms. But, thankfully, each and every one of the crews was rescued by their mates, in those boats which had withstood the ferocity of the elements, and they all returned home safely.

They brought back tales of their experiences in which navigation had been dangerously hampered by wreckage floating in every direction. Partly submerged masts and spars were hazardous and severely damaged their nets.

Some spoke of drowned cattle frequently floating past, which must have been an awesome sight; and one boat picked up half cwt. box of needles and other flotsam.

Some boats, which had left the town in September, had scarely paid the expenses of the voyage. But Mrs. Searle's boat, which had been the most fortunate of any, made about £400 during the season.

Fishermen aboard the lugger *Consolation:* Tom Belton and his three sons - David James and Tom - with Fred Dean, who were all associated with the lifeboat when they weren't away at sea

By the time they had repaired their nets and maintained the boats if was Christmastime. Directly after the festive season, the mackerel season began, but before embarking on their deep sea voyage many of our seamen attended a service at Worthing's Christ Church on Saturday 28 December.

The vicar, Rev. P.B. Power addressed himself exclusively to them, observing, 'Time is slipping fast away; another year is almost past. The tide of life is swiftly ebbing, and if you do not make haste you might be stranded on the shore of a fearful eternity. There is a season for your fishing, which if you neglect, your chance is gone. There is also a season of opportunity, which if neglected, would be gone forever. You are now about to enter on your mackerel voyage. I hope you will be successful and bring home money; but I also more earnestly desire you might come home with what is far better than earthly riches - the peace of our Heavenly Father.'

While fishermen were away for the mackerel season, a Captain Buller sought to establish a reading room for the exclusive use of our watermen.

A local paper of the time described it thus: 'A room which they can always frequent, and where they will invariably find a genial welcome, without the possibility of being "picked-up", as many an unsuspecting seafarer too often is. A fishermen's room such as this we hope to have here long at Worthing; for we fancy it will inculcate lessons of thrift and prudence, and tend to raise Jack's notions a little higher than the smoke issueing out of his "long clay".

'It will also, when the men are assembled together, enable gentlemen like those who addressed the fishermen's meeting a week or two ago, to converse with the seamen under more favourable circumstances; and a word spoken in season how good it is. The fisherman can here smoke a pipe with his chums, talk over the last voyage with his friends, and enjoy himself with old companions in a rational and sober manner. The room will be comfortably furnished, and contain a carefully selected library. There will be thus all the best attractions of the beershop, in the shape of society, & c, but none of the evils of intemperance.'

'If Captain Buller succeeds in his philanthropic exertions to better the condition of the fishing population, he will deserve the thanks of the whole community. We know such good results cannot be attained without considerable cost, but we feel sure the people of Worthing will assist him in his undertaking, if he should ask them to do so.'

When the luggers left on their seasonal journey to distant seas, Worthing fisherman, Bob Upton, had to remain behind to appear at the West Sussex Epiphany Sessions at the biginning of January. He was charged with stealing a quantity of herrings valued at 6s. and a box valued 3d., the property of Edward Booker, at Broadwater on the 21st November last.

The Court heard that Booker, a Worthing fish hawker, had left the fish in some stables which he had locked up before leaving for Littlehampton.

On his return the following morning he had found the lock lying on the ground broken.

It transpired that Upton had helped to clean out the stables with a fellow called Charlie Groves, who was regularly employed for this purpose. When they had finished, Charlie locked up and put the key in its usual place under a piece of slate.

Later the same day, Upton and Charlies brother Jim, a hawker, were seen selling herrings similar to those that had been stolen; and one of them sold the box which was also identified.

When 26 year old Upton and his co-defendant Jim Groves, aged 29, were questioned, they each implicated the other by declaring that when they both met on the Saturday evening the other had the fish in his possession.

It was never revealed how the two divided the spoils of the sale but there was obviously no argument about that. The jury found the prisoners, who both had a previous conviction, guilty, and sentenced each of them to eight months hard labour.

On Tuesday 12 January 1864, an usually high tide brought the sea over the promenade and flooded various grass plots as well as the Esplanade. Fortunately the wind was not strong, otherwise many residents would have had an unwelcome intrusion of water into their basements.

When the tide receded, the top of the beach was covered with lively insects, locally called jumpers, hopping about among the shingle in countless thousands. Near the pier a large oak beam was found, washed ashore from a ship's deck.

Almost three weeks later, on 31 January and 1 February, casks and broken ship's timbers were washed up by the sea on Worthing beach. The name *Triune* was found painted on one of the larger pieces of wood, apparently from a vessel wrecked off the Bognor coast during January.

On Friday 15 January 1864, three days after the extraordinarily high tide, there was an unusually noisy bustle on the beach. Five Worthing fishing boats, whose crews had attended a special church service to wish them success before embarkation, had returned that morning with enormous catches of mackerel.

But because of their poor quality they fetched only 15s. per 100. Mr. Edward's boat brought in a catch of more than 12,000 which realised £90. Mark Benn's boat landed about 7,000 mackerel, the same size as Mr. Cook's boat; while Mr. G. Wood's boat counted close on 6000 fish. Mr. Beck's boat, the least successful, produced only 2,000.

So vast was this heap of fish that it kept the fishermen and their helpers busy until dusk. Men and women packed the fish into 'pads', baskets filled with approximately 60 mackerel, and sent them to the railway station, where most of them were despatched to London.

Nearly 700 pads were sent away from Worthing that night which, reckoned at 7s.6d. each, represented a total sum of £262.

Three days later, Messrs. Cook and Streeter's boat *Will Watch* landed a further 1500 mackerel, which were sold at a higher price, one guinea per 100.

Although the proceeds from these recent successful hauls benefitted the fishing community, this was generally a time of much distress and poverty among fisherfolk. In an attempt to pursuade fishermen to set aside some money for hard times, Captain S. Buller invited a number of them to a meeting at the Workmen's Room in Montague Street, on Saturday 23 January 1864. Mr. King, the seamen's missionary, was to have been present at the religious meeting, but when he unavoidably failed his engagement , the Captain himself had to address the men.

After his speech, a rule in connection with the Seamen's Penny Bank was adopted, whereby each member should, on the death of a member, suscribe one shilling for the relief of his widow.

During the course of the meeting, one fisherman humbly knelt down and earnestly thanked Almighty God for the abundant catch of fish he had so graciously given him and his comrades, He seemed to feel that their recent providential draught of fish, coming in the midst of much distress and poverty, was an answer to their prayers.

A report on the meeting, printed in a local paper of the time, ended thus: 'We hope that their thoughts may be henceforth more directed to Him who promises to give "good things to them that ask him" (Matt xii 11). We hope a heart change has really begun among the fishermen, and that the work of reformation will speed and spread among them.'

Members of the Penny Bank were to be treated to an excursion to East Grinstead, organised by Captain Buller. Details of the arrangements were given at an assembly of fishermen and coastguardsmen, from Worthing and Goring, at the Workmen's Reading Room on Wednesday 17 August at 1.30 p.m. After issuing all the relevant instructions, the Captain offered prayers in gratitude to Almighty God for the past successful mackerel season, before closing the meeting.

A group of watermen and their wives, totalling 120 persons in all, met for the treat at Worthing railway station by 6.30 a.m on the following Friday. After they had boarded the train, it went to Brighton to collect more fishermen, before completing its journey up country to East Grinstead.

When the trippers alighted they made their way to the local church, where the Rev. E. Clay, from Brighton, preached a sermon. After the service they proceeded to a beautiful cricket ground, which had plenty of covered space in case of inclement weather, where a generous dinner was supplied at midday. It was provided for all those who remembered to take the yellow tickets which had been distributed by Captain Buller at Wednesday's meeting.

During the afternoon numerous games were organised for these fishermen before it was time to sit down to tea. After the refreshment, prayers of thanksgiving for their enjoyable outing were offered up, before returning to East Grinstead railway station for the homeward journey.

During the month of February 1864, the general public were invited to suscribe to the Shipwrecked Mariners Society. Donations to this philanthropic institution were collected at Mr. Henty's Bank, the libraries, and at Mr. S. Eardley's Waterloo House.

On Sunday 14 February, the Rev. T. A. Walrond, secretary of the Mission to Seamen, devoted his services at Worthing's Christ Church to the charity. His text for the sermon in the morning service was taken from 15th of Luke, 7th verse "I say unto you that likewise joy shall be in heaven over sinner that repenteth."

At the evening service his preaching was founded on the words, "Salvation belongeth unto the Lord: thy blessing is upon thy people, " taken from 3rd Ps.8th verse.

A report on the sermons in a provincial newspaper contained the following paragraph. 'In advocating the claims of the sailor the rev. gentleman dwelt upon the peculiar trials and difficulties that beset the mariner's path, which he pleaded in extenuation of the "riotous living" and recklessness of a spiritually-neglected class of men. They were far from being the hardened set that some would make tham out. There were many fine traits of character to be found among the seamen, and the operations of the Society had been abundantly blessed in developing them still more.'

The mission, on a national basis, employed 13 chaplains and 12 scripture readers to cover their overstretched network with tasks including visiting fishing boats, merchantmen, Royal Navy ships and foreign vessels. But the vicar felt that this number of agents was but a drop in the ocean compared with the wide range of opportunities at home and abroad where the Society might exercise its influence. He said "If the Society could afford to employ twice the number, it could find as many important stations tomorrow where they might be occupied. Not the least good effected by the Mission is the protection it affords homeward-bound seamen from the demoralising influences of low lodging houses."

The preacher, who was a devoted missionary among our Worthing seamen, collected a total of £17 17s.7d. during the two services.

The following year the annual collections made at Worthing's Christ Church, on Sunday 26 March, for the Missions to Seamen[2] amounted to almost the same figure, £17 14.2½d whereas Broadwater Parish Church and the Chapel of Ease collected £1 11s.0d, and £2 7s.10½d, respectively. But it was thought that the unfavourably bad weather conditions that day may have prevented some people from attending church. And so collections were made again on the Sunday after, when the boxes at Worthing's Christ Church produced £1 6s.1d and a second collection at Broadwater Church realised £3 4s. 6d.

A north west view of Broadwater Church

Captain Buller never rested on his laurels. After having established a reading room for the fishermen of Worthing, and having set up the Penny Bank to assist their interests, he continued to strive for Worthing's fishing community.

Because of his benevolent and energetic aspirations the Worthing Fishermen's Mutual Insurance Association was established in 1865, to provide a fund for insuring local fishermen's boats and nets. Capt. Spencer Buller was appointed president and treasurer by a committee of management which included John Miles, E. Edwards, Jacob Tester[1] James Osbourne, Wm. Beck[3], Mark Benn, James Searle, and the honorary secretary Mr. Nathaniel King, who was also lay missionary to the Missions to Seamen. The committee agreed that £100 was needed to meet the initial requirements of the society. About £55 was collected by Capt. Buller before a public appeal was launched on 24 August 1865 in an attempt to raise the balance of £45.

The captain's efforts were sympathetically rewarded with enormous support from the well-to-do classes; and within two months the fund quite amazingly totalled £160, far in excess of what was needed to get the association started. Sir Percy Burrell and Steven Cave both suscribed towards the captain's new scheme for benefitting our seafaring people; and Mrs. Thwaites, with her apparently usual liberality, sent a cheque for £85.

In addition the fishermen members themselves contributed to the fund on a scale laid down in the rules. There was no shortage of members as deep sea fishing was the principle industry of Worthing at this time; there being a considerable fleet of luggers based here.

A Worthing sailor, Richard Fuller, was killed in very distant waters on the other side of the world, during the New Zealand war. On 29 April 1864, Fuller, a seaman with H.M.S. *Esk,* was mortally wounded in an engagement against the Maories.

On Thursday 11 February 1864, a large steamer lost her direction in very foggy conditions and ran quite close to the Worthing shore. At high tide, when a stiff breeze was making the sea rough, the lifeboat was prepared in readiness to go off to the ship.

The steamer's pilot suddenly spotted the coast through the haze and veered out again into deeper water. This move most certainly saved her from grounding and fortunately the services of the lifeboat crew were not required.

A local fishing boat belonging to Mr. Davis was involved in an accident on Sunday 1 May 1864. During the night the boat ran upon an anchor, splintering part of the underneath of the craft, and sank.

Next morning her owner was astonished to see only the very top of the mast remaining above water; when the tide had ebbed Mr. Davis searched for the mainsail and other gear, but they had evidently been washed away.

Information about a ship foundering at sea came into the possession of a fisherman, by the name of Greenyer, on 18 May, when he picked up a bottle on Worthing beach. He opened it and took out a piece of paper upon which was written the following.

'Latitude 19.30, longitude 2 W. Whoever picks up this bottle is requested to send the enclosed to the Board of Trade. Ship Victoria - no provisions left - ship making water very fast. Circular hurricane blowing in all directions. Wind up and down the mast.'

I assume that, as the finding was reported in a newspaper, the Board of Trade were informed of the ship in distress. But I did not find any continuation of the tale in ensuing editions of the newspaper.

Whilst fishing in local waters, Worthing fisherman caught considerable quantities of mackerel during May 1864. Every morning the beach was busy with activity amongst buyers and sellers. Prices varied according to the extent of each haul, but generally fluctuated between 20s. and 25s. per 100.

In the following month of June, mackerel continued to be in abundance and prices fell drastically. Fish became so cheap that occassionally they were hawked about the streets for as little as 12 mackerel for one shilling; a price equivalent pro rata to 8s.4d.per 100.

On Saturday 23 July 1864, when the crew of a lugger were hauling in their nets, they were amazed to find an extremely heavy fish. It was a shark eight feet long, similar to the one inadvertently caught by Worthing fishermen in 1863.

They returned to Worthing the next day, and a character known as Pompey exhibited the somewhat large and unusual specimen on the beach. He erected an old sail around it and charged people an entry fee to view it. Again, I understand it's enormous mouth was wedged open with a piece of wood to show off the three rows of fierce-looking teeth.

By Tuesday the stench coming from the slowly decomposing shark was unbearably worse than Worthing's odourous seaweed. Pompey enlisted the aid of three men to put it back in the sea, whereupon it floated away.

Some good catches of fish were brought in at Worthing during February 1865 and, despite the very fine weather, also during the summer using seine nets (large vertical fishing nets).

At about 7 a.m. one morning that summer, a dozen shoals of mackerel were observed from the pier going in a westerly direction. The sea was as smooth as a mill-pond; and the shoals, or 'skeles' as fishermen called them, surfaced and disappeared again, glistening in the bright sunlight.

This very pretty sight attracted a lot of attention from strollers on the promenade, as did the usual splashing noise from their peculiarly lively movements which rippled the surface of the water.

An old fisherman of the time said that in some of the skeles there were 15 - 20,000 mackerel.

On one occassion several boats went off in the hope of securing some of the shimmering tribe, and a long seine net was cast and drawn around a tempting skele, about half a mile from the beach. But in the haste and excitement of the moment, many thousands of fine fish escaped through the mouth of the net, and rumour had it that not even one mackerel was left to reward the exertions of the boatmen.

The R.N.L.I. authoritatively took over the Worthing lifeboat station on 23 January 1865, and the first meeting of the Worthing branch committee, comprising Admiral Hargood, Capt. Davis, Dr. Collet, J.H. O'Bernie Esq., W. Harris Esq. and W.H. Dennett as honorary secretary, was held at the house of Rear Admiral Hargood. His son, who was also on the committee was elected chairman the following year.

On Tuesday 7 March 1865 The Worthing lifeboat, which had recently been handed over to the R.N.L.I. with all the fittings, was tested by Capt. Ward who was sent down from London to try her capabilities and seaworthiness. After the crew launched the boat, they rowed about for some time before a capsize test. A large number of spectators on the pier gazed upon the proceedings with curious interest. The crew got out of the vessel, a 'take' was passed underneath it's hull and hauled from the pier head. By this means she was slewed over; but instead of righting herself, she remained bottom upwards in the water until she was manually righted again. Although she had been designed and built as a self-righter, after 12 years of active service she was no longer up to standard.

A decision was taken to build a new lifeboat for the Worthing station; but it was to be many months before it could be delivered and prepared for service.

Meanwhile, on Sunday morning 29 October 1865 a southerly gale raced with teriffic violence. Through the haze of the heavy squalls that had started early that day, a vessel named *Billy Boy* was spotted at about 11 o'clock in the morning, about a mile away and abreast of Tarring Lane, flying a distress flag.

Three horses belonging to Messr. Thorn & Co. were harnessed to the lifeboat carriage and, with valued assistance from residents of West Worthing, the old lifeboat was drawn rapidly over the sands and along to that part of the beach nearest the vessel.

But the old carriage couldn't stand the pace and the spring of the hind axle-tree gave out and the bottom of the lifeboat was considerably damaged when it hit the beach about one mile along.

Towards noon, when the weather worsened, Coxwain Parkes decided to have a go at rescuing the crew of the ailing craft, despite the damage to his lifeboat!

The ten crew under Coxwain Parkes successfully rowed the leaking craft through the breakers. But it took in so much water that eventually the Coxwain had to order his men to turn the boat about and return to the shore.

Towards late afternoon the wind moderated, and the sun breaking through the clouds revealed the *Billy Boy* still rocking heavily. Her distress signal had been lowered and so no further rescue attempt was considered necessary.

This was the last service for the old lifeboat prior to her retirement from saving lives at sea. She was removed from the station just after Christmas 1865.

Footnotes Ch. 4

[1] Jacob Tester - the hero from the *Mary Eliza* disaster in 1858.
[2] Missions to Seamen still has offices locally - at Littlehampton.
[3] William Beck - a relation of Sydney Beck who owned the ferry boat which capsized going to assist the *Lalla Rookh* in 1850.

Ch. 5

The Initiation And Fullfilment Of The *Jane*. 1866-8

A new Worthing lifeboat, built by Messrs. Forrest of Limehouse, was harbour-tested in London where her self-righting and other qualities proved to be completely satisfactory. It was granted a free conveyance by the London, Brighton and Coast Railway Company, as was a new transporting and launching carriage, constructed by Mr. J. Robinson of Kentish Town.

Capt. Ward R. N., Inspector of lifeboats to the R. N. L. I., travelled down on the train with the new boat and carriage, on Tuesday 23 January 1866. He was met at Worthing railway station by a deputation of the Worthing Branch R. N. L. I.

Eight horses were hitched up to the carriage and the new 32 feet long lifeboat was drawn ceremoniously through the town in a procession of local dignitaries, led by the 11th Sussex Rifle Volunteer Corps and their band. The magistrates and clergy were next in line, followed by members of Worthing Local Board of Health. Members of the Worthing Branch R. N. L. I., followed by two fishermen carrying a banner, and Capt. Ward proudly marched in front of the lifeboat itself, which measured seven feet six inches across the beam.

Local coastguardsmen followed behind the new lifeboat in this patriotic parade for showing this new acquisition to the town, while the National and other schools brought up the rear and completed the procession.

They marched along Warwick Street, pictured here, to the Town Hall which is out of view at the far end of the road

The emotional and joyful carnival atmosphere created by this proud body of disciplined men marching to the beat of military drums attracted many boys as they paraded down Chapel Road from the station, along Ambrose Place, left down Chapel Street (now Portland Road), along Montague Street, left into West Buildings, and then left again along Marine Parade to the Steyne. They marched in time with the band along Warwick Street to the (old) Town Hall, and finally down South Street towards the Pier.

It was a glorious day as the sun shone on all the pretty banners and flags in the Lifeboat procession watched by Worthingites lining the route, gathered to witness this momentous occasion. In fact the whole town seemed more alive than ever before.

On arrival in front of the pier, the Sussex Rifle Volunteers, under the command of Col. Serg. Cortis, halted between the *Marine Hotel* on their left and the *Royal Sea House Hotel* on their right, and presented arms as the lifeboat passed by.

The Parade marched finally down South Street towards the pier. Its toll-house is just visible between the buildings

The horses were unharnessed from the carriage, and some cheerful volunteers pulled the boat over the beach to the water's edge on the west side of the pier. Here the soldiers were then stationed around the stern of the boat in a semi-circle, inside of which was a select party of ladies and gentlemen of the lifeboat committee.

As Capt. Ward climbed up on the boat, silence befell the crowd, and he began a short speech in which he explained how a very generous lady had presented a large sum of money to the R. N. L. I. to provide a new lifeboat for Worthing. He expressed his confidence in the local committee, the crew, and in the boat itself, before officially handing over the lady's noble gift to the residents of Worthing.

Capt. Warren was called upon to reply, and in a few suitable words he acknowledged the bounty of the unknown lady who delighted to do good and who blushed that it should be known. He also expressed his belief that the crew should at all times do their duty by risking their own lives to save others.

The Rector offered up a special prayer in blessing the lifeboat, 'that in God's good providence it would be the means of rescuing many of our fellow creatures from the dangers of a deep water grave.' He humbly implored the protection of heaven over the crew, that they might have physical strength and wisdom in times of emergency and, finally, he thanked God that he had instilled into the heart of the benefactoress the desire to present the boat which was badly needed here.

As Admiral Hargood's wife approached to name the boat, the crowd cheered. Taking the bottle, which was suspended by a ribbon at the stern of the boat, she announced in a clear voice, "I name this boat the *Jane.* May God bless her," and dashed the bottle against the side of the rudder.

The crew, accompanied by Capt. Ward, then took up their positions in the lifeboat, and when the command was given, the coastguardsmen ran the carriage into the sea, and the boat was launched. It dashed gallantly into the sea, amidst the cheers of the spectators, the firing of cannon, the 'feu de joie' of the volunteers, and the distant strains of 'Rule Britannia' by the rifle band on the pier.

A coach arriving at the *Marine Hotel*

The lifeboatmen, under Coxwain A.Dean and my great great grandfather 2nd coxwain Tom Blann[1], exercised the craft and made an unsuccessful attempt to capsize her. There was, of course, never any question about her self-righting or self-relief of water qualities, and the crew were delighted with the ease with which they rowed her through the water. The double bank of 10 oarsmen were: J. Marley, Wm. Wood, W. Greenyer, R. Wells, G. Wells, T. Davis, G. Goble[2], F. Honess, Bill Marshall[3], and T. Tester[4].

During the month of February, a Worthing gentleman received some contrary information which stated that the ordering of a new lifeboat for Worthing had been dependant on sufficient funds being raised from certain charity concerts. A small handbill sent to Robert E. Nichol Esq. from London was accompanied by the remark, 'See what we do for Worthing in London'. The handbill read, 'Sir Hugh Middleton. Lifeboat Fund. Deacon's Music Hall, opposite Sadler's Wells. The committee of the above fund on laying before the public the list of talented artists who have generously tendered their valuable assistance for the evenings of Tuesday and Wednesday, November 28th and 29th, beg most respectfully to state that should these concerts realise the still required sum, the boat will at once be proceeded with and placed by the R. N. L. I. at Worthing.'

Then followed a list of names including: Mr. J. H. Stead, the celebrated 'Cure'; 'Little Roberts' of the Christy Minstrels; Mr Harry Liston 'The Star Comique'; the Elvill Family, 'England's Premier Gymnasts', and a host of other equally celebrated characters. Besides these, two bands were said to be engaged, namely, Dunn & Hewitt's, and that of the 'G' division of the Metropolitan Police.

While Mr. Nichols did not doubt the authenticity of the statement, he was puzzled because it had been publicised that the existence of the *Jane* was attributed to the munificence of an individual.

This perplexity was taken up by Wm. Hugh Dennett, honorary secretary of the Worthing Branch R. N. L. I., who made enquiries of head office in London. The national secretary confirmed: 'It is quite true that the desire and purpose of the Sir Hugh Middleton Lifeboat Fund was to obtain a sufficient sum of money to provide a lifeboat establishment at Worthing, and from the generous efforts of the managers of that fund, a sum of £187 10s. had been raised in November. Meanwhile, a lady placed in the hands of the R.N.L.I. a sum of £582, and her magnificent gift was at once placed to defray the expense of the Worthing lifeboat establishment. The amount realised by the the Sir Hugh Middleton Lifeboat Fund was then placed to the general credit of the R.N.L.I.'

Therefore, the announcement at the time of the launch, that the *Jane* was paid for by a lady, was correct.

The *Jane* was larger than its predecessor: measuring 32 feet in length and seven feet six inches across the beam. As the existing 30 feet long boathouse was too short to accommodate the new lifeboat, the Committee of Management decided that a larger one would have to be built. On 16 November that year, the R.N.L.I. bought a piece of land in Crescent Road from a developer, Robert William Chinnock, for £68. It measured 16 feet along the boundary with Crescent Road and had a depth of 50 feet. On this site, which was near the present-day Salvation Army Citadel, a new boathouse was constructed; the cost of £242 12s.0d. being philanthropically donated by the same lady who anonymously paid for the new boat. This commodious and substantial boathouse, built to accommodate the larger boat on its carriage as well as stores, was designed by C.H.Cooke Esq. of London, the honorary architect to the R.N.L.I.

The local branch under the guidance of honorary secretary W.H.Dennett Esq. was successful in obtaining regular contributions for the future support of the station, which required an annual budget of around £50 to keep the lifeboat constantly ready for any emergency.

By now the R.N.L.I. had 153 lifeboat establishments under its charge, 19 of which were stationed on the coasts of Sussex, Hampshire, Kent and the Isle of Wight. But for the indefatigable exertions of this great and important Institution many brave seamen would have had their last requiem sung by the ruthless waves. During 1865 the R.N.L.I. saved 532 lives around the British coastline, and a further 182 lives were saved by fishing boats and other craft, for which services the Institution granted monetary rewards.

The total number of lives saved since the Society's formation was 14,992, either by its lifeboats or by special operations for which it granted rewards. For those services 82 Gold Medals and 751 Silver Medals had been awarded, and £21,111 had been paid out in cash rewards. Apart from the rewards it had granted, the R.N.L.I., since its formation, had spent a total of £128,860 on setting up all the lifeboat stations.

In furthering the cause of the R.N.L.I., Sussex newspapers listed these places for making donations: all London and country bankers; the honorary secretaries of the various branches on the coasts of Sussex, Hampshire, the Isle of Wight and Kent; and finally Richard Lewis Esq., the Institution's secretary at John Street, Adelphi, London, W.C.

The lifeboatmen's other role was that of professional watermen, and their stock in trade was fish. The market prices for this important food oscillated greatly: in January 1867 a fishing boat, the *Reform*, brought ashore 1700 mackerel at Worthing, which fetched as much as 58s. per 100 on the beach; whereas, in the 1868 season, a boat belonging to Chris Cook caught 2200 mackerel, but only realised 16s. per 100.

Appalling weather resulted in atrocious conditions for lifeboatmen and fishermen. The crew of a Worthing fishing boat belonging to Edward Edwards narrowly escaped disaster on Saturday 6 January 1866 when a terrific gale arose. Some of our boats had sailed out to catch the first mackerel of the season when they were dangerously buffetted about by a sudden squall.

Making a run for the shelter of Shoreham Harbour, a huge wave swamped the boat. For a moment it seemed as if she would go down but, fortunately, with the aid of the crew leaning over the port gunwhale, she soon righted.

All of our boats subsequently gained the safe haven of the harbour without sustaining any loss or damage in the gale, which was the worst experienced by our fishermen for quite some years. In fact, it registered 32 lbs per square foot on a nemometer at Liverpool, a height seldom reached.

Terrible weather prevailed for the rest of the month of January, 1866 causing distress and consternation throughout Worthing's fishing fraternity. The resulting trepidation motivated a local newspaper to carry the following report on 8 February 1866.

'We are very sorry to hear that the families of many of our fishermen and boatmen are in circumstances of the extremest poverty, owing doubtless to many causes, but chiefly, we believe, to the continued boisterous weather which is most unfavourable to their calling. Many of the men have not earned anything at all since Christmas. We know of no class who are more deserving of public sympathy than the seafaring population, and we regret exceedingly that they should now have to undergo privations which are terribly hard to bear.'

On seeing this publication, a reader wrote to the editor claiming that, if they could not fish, fishermen could repair roads to earn money, and branded them lazy.

The fishing community were outraged and this letter of reply was published the following week.

'Your correspondent has been found fault with for directing attention to the poverty existing among the seafaring population, and accused of diverting the streams of charity into an unworthy channel. We have been told that the fishermen are not so poor as we made them out to be, and that if they were not such idle fellows, they might get plenty of work "on the roads."

The paper noted, 'Our censor is wilfully ignorant or grossly misinformed about the true state of things.

The distress among the seamen's families in this town is an unmistakeable fact, and we are truly glad that since we wrote the few lines upon this subject in this paper last week, the sufferings of many poor women and children have been alleviated. We may tell our sympathising, critical friend that his "flint-cracking" plan is a ridiculous suggestion, for he ought to know that our fishermen spend most of their time at Shoreham and other ports waiting for a favourable tide to put out to sea, and thus their "idleness", of which he complains, is a compulsory thing. If we had really been guilty of misleading the public upon this matter, it is rather singular that a precisely similar appeal to ours should be made this week by the Rev. F. Clay on behalf of the Brighton fishermen, and that that appeal should be backed by the Mayor of that town.'

The enduring bad weather culminated in a terrific gale on Sunday 11 February, prohibiting our fishermen still further from indulging in their livelihoods. The strong winds which wreaked havoc by displacing chimney pots and breaking windows did, however, provide bricklayers and glaziers with plenty of extra employment.

Bricks crashed down in the streets while slates and tiles whirled in the air but, despite this frightening situation, some youngsters ventured outdoors. Girls were seen on the seafront, to quote a colloquial expression, 'scudding before the gale'.

Lamps on the pier were damaged. Its toll-house oscillated to an alarming extent just as a zinc roof from one of the pier shelters blew clean off and landed 100 yards away with a resounding splash in the sea.

At West Worthing a great deal of glass was broken. Many fine trees in the neighbourhood couldn't resist the high velocity of the gale and bowed their lofty heads right down to touch the ground. A large elm at the north end of Steyne Gardens fell across the road, taking with it part of the railings and stonework of the enclosure.

At 4.15 p.m. a vessel was reported stranding four miles to the west of Worthing. Within 15 minutes the lifeboat crew had been summoned and the *Jane* prepared. The lifeboat on its carriage, accompanied by the Committee Chairman, Mr. H. Hargood, was pulled along the road towards Kingston by six horses.

The distressed vessel, which proved to be the brig *Cyprian Queen*, carrying cotton seed from Alexandria, had laid anchors when a S.S.W. gale blew up on its way to Littlehampton. But the strong wind was so powerful that it had parted from its anchors and was driving ashore between Ferring and Kingston.

The carriage was backed into the cruel sea at Kingston and seven strong helpers dragged the boat off its rests and into the vicious waters as the waves broke over them. As soon as the bow hit the water, forward oarsmen pulled furiously to ease the strain of the volunteer helpers. At 9.30 p.m., one hour after high tide, the lifeboat was successfully launched with 13 crew aboard: Alfred Dean - coxwain, Tom Blann - 2nd coxwain, Tom Davis, Bill Wood, John Marley, John Tester[5], Tom Bridger, H. Bashford[6], T. Bacon[7], C. Marshall[8], Harry Harwood and Bill Greenyer.

The lifeboat performed exceedingly well and 15 minutes later they reached the *Cyprian Queen* and anchored on the windward side of it. The lifeboat crew showed an oil lamp and shouted to attract attention but received no response from the brig.

By this time the gale had begun to subside and Coxwain Dean assumed that the brig's crew now felt more in control. The sea was stealing rapidly on the ebb tide when Coxwain Dean ordered his crew to weigh anchor and sail back to Worthing, where it beached at 11.15 p.m.

Meanwhile, the carriage was still on its way back from Kingston on a slow journey hampered by bad visibility on a rough night. When it eventually arrived at Worthing, it was backed down the stones on the beach to reclaim the *Jane*. The seven helpers assisted the crewmen to winch the lifeboat onto its carriage and then the six horses pulled the carriage up the sharply rising gradient of stones.

It was 4.15 in the morning before the boat was housed after the long and arduous rescue attempt.

I believe that the stamina possessed by these men was far greater than that which is the norm nowadays.

The crew had been at work for a period of 12 hours: for which they were paid £1 each. The horses had been hired for 8s.8d. each and the men who assisted in launching and hauling-up the boat were given 2s.6d. each. The total direct cost to the R.N.L.I. of £17 18s.0d. for this futile rescue attempt was corroborated by the honorary secretary of the Worthing Branch, William Hugh Dennett.

Despite a neap tide the sea was awfully wild on Sunday and the high wind drove the brig aground about four miles west of Worthing, where the crew had to unload by hand and cart ashore more than 30 tons of cargo before they were able to float her off three days later on the Wednesday.

When the weather improved, fishermen were able to pursue their calling with varying degrees of success. By the end of the month some boats had done exceedingly well while others had caught nothing: a lugger belonging to a Mr. White of Hastings caught 25,000 mackerel in one session; two Eastbourne boats unloaded 12,000 fish each in Shoreham; Mr. Cook's *Emily and Alice* took 3,000 fish in one catch; but only very small quantities were landed on Worthing beach.

On Saturday 17 February the price was 43s. per 100 for some mackerel catches, but the majority, being of poorer quality than in previous seasons, were sold for prices between 22s. and 25s. per 100.

The following month, on Saturday 24 March, a strong S.S.W. wind was effecting a broken sea, when a schooner, the *Julie & Marie* was spotted off the town in a dangerous position flying a distress signal.

The lifeboat crew were immediately summoned and the *Jane* was launched at 3.30 p.m. on the high tide, with the aid of 12 volunteer helpers.

When the rescuers were within 500 yards of the 59 ton vessel, an unexpected signal appeared from the pier head and the schooner hauled off and made sail to complete its journey to Shoreham carrying oil cake from Nantes.

The schooner's five crew under the master, Gachet, made good headway, so lifeboat Coxwain Dean ordered his crew to return to shore.

The *Jane* performed well and beached at 5 p.m. With the assistance of 12 men she was hauled up the beach and returned to the boathouse. The helpers received 2s.1d. per man, while each crewman was paid 10s. The crew under Coxwain Alfred Dean were: Fred Honess; Bill Wood; C.Groves; John Tester; George Tyler; John Bacon; H.Hammond; J.Benn; H.Collier[9]; J.Wingfield[10] and W.Beck[11]. Apart from the last three they had all crewed the lifeboat on previous rescue services.

So ended another abortive rescue mission which cost the R.N.L.I. a total of £7 5s.0d. in direct costs. The brave fishermen who crewed the lifeboat risked life and limb, and all to no avail.

Around the coastline of the British Isles there were a total of 122 cases in 1866, where a lifeboat was launched or else the crew had just assembled, in reply to signals of distress which eventually did not require their services. Nevertheless, 15 vessels were saved by R.N.L.I. operations and 381 lives saved in this year; while rewards were granted for the saving of 495 lives by fishing and other boats. Throughout 1866 the Institution expended £29,667 on its 172 lifeboat stations around the United Kingdom, making a total of £160,400 spent since the inauguration of the R.N.L.I.

After an uneventful summer, a very large crowd of on-lookers who had been drawn to the beach by the intermittent firing of a small cannon, were amused by an unexpected incident.

It was a regular lifeboat practise and the crew had been summoned by setting off of the maroon. The boat was launched in excellent style and the crew performed their duties well. The tide was running very strong and there was a stiff breeze.

When the boat was returning, still under sail, she came in too fast and, in trying to avoid running on a groyne, a wave caught her broadside and threw out all the crew into the breakers, to the entertainment of hundreds of laughing spectators.

One year later, a crowd turned out to watch a watermen's boat race, held on Saturday evening 13 July 1867, between Tom Davis[12] and Bob Upton[13] in the *Water Lily*, and William Greenyer[14] and Tom Clarke in the *True Blue*.

The sea was rolling heavily, and the little boats danced over the waves in a lively fashion as the watermen rowed along the course, from the pier to West Worthing and back.

When they reached the spot boat off West Worthing, the *Water Lily* had a slight lead, but in turning she lost an oar and with it her chance of winning. Her crew returned to the pier, again challenged their rivals, and the race was rowed a second time, when the *True Blue* which was the favourite among the spectators on the beach, was beaten by about three lengths.

Three nights later, on Tuesday 16 July, a violent gale accompanied by slashing rain raged along the coast. Our small fleet of fishing boats anchored off the Worthing beach strained fearfully at their anchor cables, watched with excitement and consternation by seamen and onlookers from the shore.

As the tide rose it became apparent that some of the smaller craft were dragging their anchors. One of them, the *Crystal Spring*, a pleasure boat moored to the west of the pier, was rapidly carried along by huge waves and it was feared she would strike the pier; but she just cleared the end of the structure and went ashore opposite Beach House, where a crowd of men and boys - who seemed to enjoy the rough mood of the elements - cheerfully hauled her up the beach.

Two other fishing boats drifted and were driven in further eastwards; but plenty of assistance being at hand, they were both drawn up from the sea, and sustained little damage.

The following year, at daybreak on Monday 13 January 1868, a strange thing was seen off of Worthing to the east of the pier. A large black object appeared from the depths among the distant breakers of low tide looking like some weird oceanic monster.

As the tide flowed, it was again submerged. But at the next low tide it surfaced even nearer to the beach;

and was finally washed-in opposite York Terrace.

A large crowd assembled there to watch with avid interest as the waves dashed menacingly over the huge helpless creature, when it soon became clear that it was the upturned hull of a vessel.

The sea also washed up a mast, a spar, and other pieces of timber, which were collected by some of the more venturesome onlookers and piled in a heap on the parade.

When the water once more receded, coastguardsmen, and others in authority, began to inspect the wreck. On a shelf in the cabin, amongst saturated parcels of coffee and tobacco, they found some papers which showed that the derelict ship *The Restless*, registered number 45,129, had been laden with grain.

How strangely significant her name was.

Deep gouges were found in rock beds on the beach, showing where the 115 ton hull had been violently dashed along towards the pier which, fortunately, it missed, otherwise it would have inflicted serious damage.

A boatman by the name of Dean[15], who had been the first to go off to the hulk, claimed salvage in the usual manner; and a few days later she was sold for firewood.

Early one Friday morning at the end of February 1868, a brigantine spotted off Worthing was in such a state that it appeared that she would imminently sink.

The Coastguard galley and a boat manned by Worthing fishermen went out to her.

By the time they reached her, six miles out, she was so heavy with water her gunwhales were almost submerged and they could not read her name.

On boarding the French vessel and finding no sign of any crew, they lowered her sails to make the craft less vulnerable to the weather.

But when the rescuers were returning to shore in their own boats, the brig rapidly sank upon what was known as the Kingmer Rock.

When they reached the shore the courageous philantropists were informed that the brig's crew had been taken off that morning, by the vessel that ran into her, and landed at Portsmouth Harbour.

The wreck of the French brig remained on the rock for some time, and her masts, which were the only part of her not submerged, could just be seen from Worthing with a naked eye. But steps should have been taken to remove the ship from this position in busy waters, where she was a danger to other craft.

Five weeks later, at the beginning of April, a Shoreham trawling boat capsized some miles off Worthing during a squall. The two fishermen crew were spotted, clinging to the upturned hull, by some Worthing fishermen who took them aboard and returned them safely to the Worthing beach.

A strong south westerly gale visited the Worthing coast on Saturday 18 April 1868, increasing in force through the night and the following morning.

Two boats wisely made for the safety of Shoreham Harbour; but seven or eight other fishing boats remained anchored off Worthing and late on Sunday afternoon their position caused some anxiety to the few onlookers who had dared to venture outdoors in such rough weather. But, as they considered that the boats would be able to 'sweat it through' no attempt was made to bring them ashore.

However, the violence of the gale brought some of their owners to the beach between 2 a.m. and 3 a.m. on Monday. It was then low tide, and the wind due south blowing 'great guns'.

The *Crystal Spring*, belonging to Messrs. Osbourne and Dean, had filled with water and Mr. Dean succeeded in cutting her cable, in order that she might drive ashore.

But shortly afterwards she capsized, her masts broke free and she broke up!

The *Marquis*, a large lugger belonging to a Mr.Searle, which had begun to drag anchor earlier in the night, came up on the beach opposite West Buildings at about midnight, with her sides stove in.

Mr. Churcher's boat, the *Pride & Envy*, bore the rough attacks of wind and wave for some time, but it ultimately sank and was driven ashore opposite Grenville Terrace; her boastful name sadly at variance with her broken beams and shattered sides.

A boat owned by a Mr. Deadman was damaged to the extent of many pounds.

Only one out of the little fleet - a vessel with strong ground tackle belonging to Mr. Beck - did 'sweat it through'. After the storm a large quantity of broken timber was washed ashore on Monday and subsequently heaped in piles on the parade.

At daybreak on Tuesday, a vessel was seen off East Worthing supposedly on her beam ends with the crew hanging on to her sides. Lieut. Sullivan R.N. of the Worthing Coastguard fired the maroon to summon the lifeboat crew. Those available who were not away fishing were: coxwain Dean, 2nd coxwain John Marley, John Tester, J. Poland, H. Freeland, William (Bill) Freeland, R. Ayling, Bill Marshall, Luke Wells, T. Bridger and W. Davis.

Only two horses could be obtained quickly; so with the aid of 16 helpers the *Jane* was trundled up West Buildings and left along the coast road, to be launched from the beach opposite the *Marine Hotel,* using the Pier as a breakwater from the mountainous waves.

It was 6 a.m., two hours into flood tide. Despite the harshness of the strong west south westerly wind, the 11 crew, who had all had previous experience of crewing the Lifeboat in an emergency, reached the wreck in just ¾ hour.

But there was no sign of any crew, and the name of the vessel could not be found.

The lifeboatmen, returned to shore by 7.30 a.m. and were later paid 10s. each for their services; and the helpers received 2s. each. The horses having been hired at 3s. each, the total direct costs for this service were £7 18s.0d.

The wreck later proved to be part of the hull of the French brigantine which had sunk after a collision off Worthing some eight weeks earlier.

Through the driving rain propelled by a W.S.W. gale, at 10.30 a.m. on Sunday 27 December 1868, a 170 ton brigantine was observed in the heavy sea dangerously close to the Worthing coast.

Its flag was at half mast, a sign of distress!

Immediately, a Coastguard Officer ordered the lifeboat to be launched. Within 15 minutes, under the gaze of a number of people who had congregated on the pier and the Parade to witness the excitement, Coxwain Dean and his crew were afloat.

The wind was blowing with tremendous force and the sea was white with foaming waves, but it took them just 45 minutes to reach the brig *Hilena.*

When Coxwain Dean boarded the brig, its master, Macdonald, told him that he and his six crew were totally ignorant of their navigational position and, but for the lifeboat, would have eventually run the craft ashore. Apparently, they had no knowledge of this part of the coast and had flown a distress signal to gain the assistance of a pilot.

Four lifeboat crew were put aboard and safely piloted the brig with its cargo of grain to Shoreham Harbour. The brigantine *Hilena*[16], of St Johns, Newfoundland and owned by Messrs. Peake Bros. & Co. became the first vessel to be saved under the auspices of the R.N.L.I. at Worthing.

The lifeboat itself returned to Worthing at about 12 noon to the cheers of the crowd, which by then, had grown much larger. The crew were: R. Ayling, J. Poland, G. Goble, T. Bridger, Bill Marshall, W. Greenyer, F. Honess, G. Davis, J. Tester, J. Bacon, L. Wells and W. Wells; all of whom had previous experience of emergency lifeboat services.

This was the first highly successful rescue by the crew of the *Jane* and they chalked-up six lives rescued on their 'scoreboard' at the lifeboat station.

Footnotes Ch. 5

[1] Tom Blann - a hero of the *Lalla Rookh* disaster in 1850.

[2] G. Goble - a relation of William (Bill) Goble tragically killed at sea during a storm in 1861.

[3] William (Bill) Marshall - great grandfather to Derrick Marshall Churcher who is living in Worthing.

[4] T. Tester - a relation of Jacob Tester the hero from the *Mary Eliza* tragedy in 1858.

[5] John Tester - a relation of Jacob Tester the hero from the *Mary Eliza* tragedy in 1858.

[6] H. Bashford - a forefather of some of the present day Worthing Bashfords.

[7] T. Bacon - a relation of Henry (Harry) Bacon drowned in the *Lalla Rookh* disaster of 1850.

[8] C. Marshall - a relation of brave William (Bill) Marshall who boarded and assisted the *Lalla Rookh* in 1850.

[9] H. Collier - a relation of John Collier - one of the successful rescuers of the *Lalla Rookh* in 1850

[10] J. Wingfield - a relation of George Wingfield - another successful rescuer of the *Lalla Rookh.*

[11] W. Beck - a committee member of the Fishermen's Insurance Association.

[12] Tom Davis - a fisherman, whose boat sank in a storm in 1864; and crewman of the *Jane.*

[13] Bob Upton - a fisherman convicted of stealing herrings in 1864.

[14] Bill Greenyer - crewman of the *Jane.*

[15] Dean - coxwain of the *Jane.*

[16] *Hilena* is the name in the service record book of the *Jane*, while the name *Hispania* is marked on the 'scoreboard' taken from outside the lifeboat station and now at Worthing Museum.

A Catalogue Of Lives Lost. 1869-75

Fund-raising by the Worthing Branch R.N.L.I. took many forms, and citizens of the town were keen to help in their differing ways. For example, a charity concert in aid of the Worthing lifeboat fund was presented at the Montague Hall on Wednesday evening 6 January 1869. A group of young men, styling themselves the Worthing Amateur Christy Minstrels, played an overture to a capacity audience of fashionable citizens. The extensive programme included a rendition of 'Papioca' imparted by Bones, who was also quite sensational in 'Picayune Butler'.

Mr Tolinson sang 'Phillis, dear Phillis' followed by the old salt Pompey[1], who favoured the company with 'Hunkey Dorum' and 'The Ten Little Niggers'.

After Mr. Macdonald had sung 'Maggie May', Bones, who was the life of the troupe, caused raucous laughter with his comical presentation of 'Ada with the golden hair'. Johnson sang 'Poor old Joe', and the programme terminated with 'Off to Brighton' by Pompey.

The result of this very successful evening was £14 15s.6d. which, after paying all expenses was donated to the Worthing Branch R.N.L.I.

The wonderful scene across Brighton Bay on a clear day had always been appreciated by local folk, and never more so than on a winter's morning in 1869. Soon after daybreak on Tuesday 26 January, exceptionally grand weather produced a magnificent view from the beach. Early strollers on the beach must have been delighted to witness the beautiful appearance of the eastern skyline as the sun grandly rose as it were out of the sea. The cliffs at Brighton stood out with surprising brightness, and the windows of the houses there glittered like silver. A brilliant roseate hue suffused the heavens, a scene not easily forgotten. But this was a far cry from the dangers that lurked out at sea.

Gloucester Place: small terraced homes to seafarers and fishermen, most of whom raised large families

A Worthing sailor had been drowned in an accident further along the horizon, off Beachy Head, on Friday 1 January 1869. It was Charles Churcher's[2] first voyage as mate of the *Dart* of Shoreham, a vessel chartered by the Worthing coalmerchant Mr. Warner. Churcher, of Gloucester Place, who had been a steady and respectable man, left a wife and five children under the age of ten in circumstances of utter destitution. Several of Mrs. Churcher's friends kindly looked after her, and a fund set up for the poor widow reached £25 within four weeks.

A young man, Henry Nicholl, was more fortunate than Churcher. He narrowly escaped drowning in another incident at the beginning of May. He had been about to bring-to a lugger which had just arrived off Worthing from Brighton. As the fishing vessel went alongside a small boat, Nicholl attempted to jump from the lugger into the tiny craft.

But he misjudged and his chest struck the gunwhale knocking him backwards into the sea.

Providentially, Nicholl was an excellent swimmer, for despite wearing heavy sea boots and other cumbersome clothing, he managed to keep himself afloat. He was in the water for some 20 minutes while being carried by the strong current to the lugger, where he was hauled on board.

Dr. Worthington, who happened to be amongst others on the promenade watching the events, immediately put off in a boat to the young man's assistance.

Nicholl, luckily, soon recovered from his ordeal and was off on another fishing trip the next day.

Certain large fish that were foreign to this section of the English Channel occasionally made their presence felt. One unfortunate fish, rarely seen in these parts, came to an untimely end on Wednesday morning 16 June 1869. It was accidentally caught in fishing nets, from Mr. Belton's[3] lugger *Good Hope* about 12 miles from Worthing. It turned out to be a thresher fish, remarkable for its long tail, from whence it derived its name. At 11 feet long it was probably the whale's most formidable opponent, apart from the swordfish. The nets were badly damaged while extricating the piscatorial wonder; and when the craft returned to Worthing, the thresher was displayed for public interest on the beach.

Sea defences on Worthing beach were seriously damaged in a succession of heavy gales in the early months of 1869. And it was only the existence of the groynes which saved the town from an inundation. The breastwork was breached in several places, piles and planks snapped like lathe-wood, and the marl backing thrown into the road.

Acres of land to the east of the town were flooded. At the H*alf Brick Inn* the sea encroached to such an extent as to render the Lancing road quite impassable for some months. A block of coastguard cottages, and a pair of private dwellings known as the Navarino Houses, all of which were in an enclosure near the public house, were battered by the invading waves and destroyed.

The beach that once sloped to the sands offering a gradual resistance to the force of the waves was washed away at East Worthing. With the gale continuing, at the next high tide the billows dashed against a clay embankment - the only protection left - and threw aloft immense masses of water which completely enveloped the houses opposite. Clouds of spray were blown a hundred yards inshore, and, as the moon shone brightly, they appeared indescribably beautiful.

The *Half Brick* withstood the battering of the waves for considerably longer than many expected. "He'll surely come down this tide," it was said, yet there it stood for a further three days, until finally, it yielded to the repeated, forceful attacks of its powerful, superior adversary.

Further along towards Lancing the sea made some very alarming inroads, it even penetrated the road and flooded many acres of marsh land[4] at Sea Mills Bridge. Lancing Common was also submerged.

The raging sea forced its way over the promenade near Worthing pier, which remained undamaged, and ran up beyond the post office in South Street. Men were employed to keep the drains clear, and the water ran back with the ebb of the tide causing very little damage.

The encroachment of the sea was nothing new in Worthing: exactly 50 years earlier the town was inundated with salt water; and a few years later in 1824 there was a more serious incursion, when Sea Mills Bridge was destroyed, and people had to use boats to reach Sompting and Broadwater.

Within the lifetime of many inhabitants three distinct blocks of Worthing Coastguard houses had been destroyed by the impinging sea. One of the stations used to stand about opposite Selden Terrace at East Worthing, much further south than the ones just destroyed, and had been built upon what was called 'The hare beaten bank.'

From 1819 to 1869 at least 29 acres of land on the south of the Lancing road between Worthing and the tollgate disappeared into the sea. Formerly there was an extensive common in front of the town, but by 1869 it had been completely covered by sand. Worthing seemed more vulnerable to erosion by the sea than other coastal towns, possibly because the town was on a projecting part of the coast, known by mariners as 'Worthing Point.'

The road by the pier flooded, watched by spectators from the grounds of the *Royal Sea House Hotel*

More gales ravaged the coast in September 1869 when, once again, the sea intruded to the east of the town. A shed temporarily occupied as a beer house, immediately behind the site where the Half Brick formerly stood, was washed away. The landlord's favourite old hen used to roost on one of the rafters in this shed, and he fully expected that the poor bird had gone with the shed. But to his astonishment, when the tide had ebbed at daybreak, he saw her busily pecking about amongst the ruins, as if nothing had happened.

Beyond throwing up a quantity of shingle over the Parade, these latest very boisterous south westerly gales caused no appreciable damage to the sea defences in front of the town itself.

But a Mr. Clarke lost one of his rowing boats: swept away by the swirling current. To recompense him for this misfortune, a subscription list was organised amongst visitors as well as residents.

A larger vessel was reported to be in distress at 10 a.m. on Sunday 19 September 1869[5]. The wind was still blowing strong from the S.W. and a heavy sea running when it was seen about four miles off Worthing. The local committee ordered the lifeboat to be launched at 10.15 a.m. and the maroon was fired.

The crew rushed to the lifeboat station to man the boat and the *Jane* was launched into the foaming breakers of high water just 15 minutes later.

It took them one hour to reach the craft which they found to be a small fishing smack, the *Active* of Selsey with no one on board, having evidently parted from her anchor during the night; Coxwain Dean put three of his crew aboard the smack, who then brought her to Worthing where they ran her ashore on the beach.

The *Jane*, on her way back to shore, picked up a small boat, keel uppermost, with *Brave Chillon*[5] Boulogne marked on her stern, and landed her back at Worthing, at 12.25 p.m.

When the lifeboat crew discovered that the smack *Active* belonged to a poor man, James Wilshire of

Selsey, himself one of the crew of that town's lifeboat, they unanimously agreed to relinquish any salvage claim, having recognised that the ship and cargo together were probably valued at £20. The lifeboatmen did of course receive their usual R.N.L.I. payment of 10s. each.

This crew, Coxwain A. Dean, William (Bill) Wood, J. Poland, Fred Honess, T. Davis, T. Harris, William (Bill) Beck[6], L. Wells, C. Ayling, J. Rouse, J. Clarke[7], T. Bridger, and G. West, were so proud that the day's events warranted a double entry on the 'scoreboard': not only the saving of the smack *Active* of Selsey; but also the *Brave Chillon* of Boulogne - saved boat[5].

Fishermen, who supplemented their income by serving on the lifeboat, were extremely pleased with a successful herring season in October 1869, which was slightly earlier than usual. The extraordinarily large and plentiful catches were a Godsend to the poorer fishing classes, selling herrings in the streets at the price of one shilling for 40 fish, and providing many a family with food and money at a time when other work was scarce.

One of those men who enacted the dual roles of fisherman and lifeboatman, Fred Honess of Worthing, was tragically drowned during a fishing expedition off Ramsgate on Monday evening 1 November 1869. He was one of the crew of the Worthing boat *The Reform* which had taken 17,000 herrings into Ramsgate that day. As the boat had left harbour, after unloading its catch, Fred was knocked overboard as he was shifting a sail. His further misfortune was that he had been carried away by the fast flowing current and sank before a boat could have reached him.

The public were generous in responding to an appeal which was made on behalf of his widow, who was in poor health, and four young children. Within a week the subscription list in Mr. Paines library at 12 Warwick Street read thus: Friend £1, Admiral Hargood £1, Mrs. Living £1, Mrs. Graham £1, H. Hargood Esq. 10s., H. Smart Esq. 10s., Mrs. Dennett 10s., Miss Dennett 10s., Miss Borrodaile 10s.6d., C. Groome Esq. 10s.6d., Rev. W. S. Lewis 10s., Mrs. Tribe 10s., Rev. J. G. Gresson 10s., Capt. Warren 10s., Rev. F. Wickham 10s., Admiral Lyons 10s., Miss Byrom 10s., T. S. Brandreth Esq. 10s., Dr. Goldsmith 10s., Rev. J. R. Dawes 5s., Mrs. Dawes 5s., G. J. Mills Esq. 5s., Mrs. Mills 5s., Mrs. W. J. Harris 5s., W. Patching Esq. 5s., Mrs. Robinson 5s., F. N. 5s., Mr. C. C. Cook 5s., plus a number of smaller donations. A noble gentleman, who wished to remain anonymous, stated that he would add 5% to the final total of the fund, to encourage people to support the bereaved family.

When the fishing luggers returned from the east coast at Christmastime, their crews, who had collected a sum of £7 2s. amongst themselves on behalf of their late colleague's family, gave the magnificent donation to a Mr. Burtenshaw, who was accepting subscriptions for the widow Honess' fund. Their liberality was indeed a credit to them and was considered by fellow citizens to be most charitable.

On a murky March evening, Wednesday 23rd, one of the Worthing Coastguards was alerted by noises from the sea, when he was pursueing his beat along the seafront. He detected the sound of voices at sea, and, listening more attentively he heard the splashing of oars. Looking in the direction of the sound he could see nothing, as there was a thick fog.

He knew the sea was running too high for any boat to effect a safe landing on the beach, and so the coastguardsman, with great presence of mind, did not draw his pistol or make any sign for the boat to come ashore, but instead instantly ran along the Parade to summon assistance.

He met two other coastguardsmen, and all three hastened to the end of the pier, where there was always a navigation light burning at night, and shouted for the crew of the invisible boat to pull towards them.

Within a few minutes the boat reached the landing steps with 17 men in her, one of them lying down, so weak that he was unable to move a limb without assistance. He was carried to safety up the steps, and the others managed to scramble up before the small craft was rendered unseaworthy by being dashed against the pier.

It was now about 11 p.m. and, apparently, the bedraggled fellows had been at sea some seven or eight hours in this open boat on an extremely cold, wet and unpleasant night.

It evolved that they were sailors from the the Spanish barque the *Benvenue*, which had struck the Owers rocks off Selsey Bill, about 18 miles from Worthing. The ship had been hurriedly abandoned. Unable to save anything at all the crew had only the soaking wet clothes they wore, some of them wearing very little.

The coastguardsmen immediately set about finding lodgings for them, while several residents supplied them with complete kits of clothing. Refreshments were supplied by adjacent hotels. For some time the coastguards were unsuccessful in finding a place of shelter for the bedraggled crew: most of the public houses being unable to accomodate such a large party at that late hour. But the landlord of the *King's Arms*, himself a master mariner who in his time had roughed-it, and therefore well able to sympathise with a brother tar in distress, on being told of their plight, at once cheerfully admitted them. Moreover, he provided everything that his house could afford, indeed everything that was needed for his half-famished, dripping and shivering visitors. Every possible kindness and attention was given to the sick man who had been conveyed in the arms of his messmates: he was wrapped in blankets before the fire and hot water applied to his feet.

At the suggestion of Mr. Richmond, manager of the gas works, the men stripped off most of their saturated garments, which were then taken to the gas works to be dried in front of the furnaces.

Under the exhilerating influence of the cheerful hospitality of the house, the crew like all other sailors did not talk much about the dangers and discomforts they had just experienced; but instead spun many a yarn, sang songs and generally passed the time in jovial spirits. One lively lad from Lancashire caused roars of laughter by cutting capers round a hat placed on the floor in the centre of the large room, where his companions and other visitors had gathered out of curiosity. In that room were Dutchmen, Germans, and several coloured men besides the English sailors, all sitting round the tables, most wrapped in blankets.

The next morning, at about 10 o'clock, the crew set out for the Waile Street Sailors' Home in London, accompanied to the station by Capt. Davis, the Worthing officer of the Shipwrecked Mariners' Society, who provided them with money for the journey. Mr Flynn, chief officer of the Worthing Coastguard Station, praised Capt. Payne, the landlord of the *Kings Arms*, for his unquestionable hospitality to these unfortunate shipwrecked sailors.

The first mate, before leaving, revealed that the 414 ton *Benvenue* had met with very severe weather and contrary winds, which had delayed her for three weeks, and then they had run short of provisions. The day before the disaster, the ship, laden with a valuable general cargo, consisting mainly of spices, tobacco, sugar and block tin, had returned from Penang in China past the Eddystone lighthouse. An easy passage from the Start Point had been anticipated, but on Wednesday the weather had been so thick that the captain, George Brown, had been unable to establish the position of his ship, which at that time was travelling at the rate of seven knots.

They had consequently been obliged to take soundings, but at 3.40 p.m. when they had been about to heave the lead, the ship struck a rock and tore open a hole in her hull.

As the powerful waves had thrust the boat heavily against the rock she rapidly sank. The captain immediately ordered his crew, of 16 men including the chief and second mate, to abandon ship, and a boat was hastily lowered into the swirling froth.

But before any of the crew could get into her she was swept away.

Fortunately, they had one other boat, albeit a smaller one, which they lowered and jumped into instantly before this, their final lifeline could be snatched away by the uncontrollably violent sea. There was a sick man on board who was entirely helpless, and in removing him one of the crew accidentally fell into the sea, but being a strong swimmer he managed to regain the boat.

They rowed until they approached terra firma, but were afraid to land lest the large waves should dash them to pieces against unseen obstacles in the darkness. When their signals for assistance received no reply from Bognor or Littlehampton, they pulled along the shoreline, intending to wait until daylight, when suddenly they were hailed by the Worthing coastguard from the pier.

As you now know, they landed safely and tasted Worthing hospitality, before journeying to London.

Only a few days after the landing of the shipwrecked crew, there was further excitement on Worthing beach. A revenue cutter chased after a smack, about 1/2 mile offshore, watched with intense interest by a crowd that had gathered on the Parade.

The smack continually manoeuvred to escape her pursuer, until the cutter fired a couple of shots, and then it hove-to. The revenue men, on boarding the craft, were seen to handle the crew in a rather rough style; before the cutter escorted the smack, which had been evidently suspected of smuggling, away in a westerly direction.

A waterman rescued a youth in 1871. A number of people on the beach, during Tuesday afternoon 27 June, witnessed a young man's narow escape from drowning. He was sailing in a canoe when a sudden gust of wind grabbed his sail and instantly overturned the craft, throwing him into the sea.

Luckily, it happened within a short distance of the shore, and three boats immediately put off to rescue the youth named Hambrough, who was seen clinging to the upturned canoe. He was picked up and taken ashore by a boatmen named Marshall[8].

Since fishermen worked under horrific conditions, the liquor bottle provided their only means of escape, and many became habitual boozers.

Fisherman George Davis[9], a hardened carouser, was charged on 10 October 1871 with being drunk and disorderly in the streets. The case was proved by P. C. Dennis Faith, who had seen the prisoner in South Street the previous day, rolling from one side of the pavement to the other. After he had bumped into a lady and knocked down a child, he had been arrested; but, while resisting being taken into custody, he had hurled vernacular abuse at the witnesses.

The constable had summoned assistance and the accused had to be literally carried struggling into the police station. Three previous convictions for similar offences led to Davis being sentenced to 14 days imprisonment with hard labour, and a further 14 days if 10s. 6d., the costs of bringing the case, were not paid.

The fisherman most frequently 'before the beak' on charges connected with excessive drinking, at this time, must have been William (Bill) Freeman[10]. He was an incorrigible drunkard convicted of drunkeness a total of 31 times.

On the last occassion he had gone to the police station on Tuesday 10 October 1871 and demanded to see a prisoner being held there. Because he had been intoxicated his request had been refused, whereupon he had begun swearing at Superintendant Henderson, using the most disgraceful language. The officer had walked away from the situation and into South Place, but Freeman had followed him, maintaining his barrage of verbal abuse.

Two constables, returning from their beat, had gone to the superintendant's assistance, whereupon the accused had been arrested and taken into custody at the police station, where he had continued his offensive oral onslaught for several hours.

Charged with drunkeness and using obscene language in the street, Freeman faced a custodial sentence. On account of his previous convictions the magistrate, Capt. Warren, sentenced Freeman to 14 days imprisonment, and to be kept in prison for a further 14 days if he defaulted on 10s. 6d. costs. This was a large sum for a fisherman to pay; and especially if he was unable to sail out during bad weather and earn money, he would be better off financially by serving extra time and receiving free food. As Bill was being removed from the court he expressed his determination to 'take the lot'.

Another continually drunk and troublesome figure, fisherman Charlie Belton[11], appeared before the magistrate, Capt C. C. Chetwynd, on Friday 1 December 1871, charged with using obscene language in the streets.

It appears that the prisoner had been very insolent to a gentleman by the name of Wallace, who had reported Charlie, and the police had subsequently apprehended him.

In his defence, Charlie said that he had had too much to drink. But the magistrate felt that this excuse was an aggravation rather than a mitigation of the offence, and fined him 5s. plus costs.

Another member of the tough Belton family got into trouble with the police in 1872. On Monday 25 March, George Belton was up before the magistrates charged with assaulting P. C. Puttick whilst in the execution of his duty.

The previous afternoon, the complainant had been endeavouring to take Belton home, when he was under the influence of drink; for most of the way George had co-operated. Then he had suddenly stopped, refusing to go any further, becoming violent and had kicked the constable in the head and arm. Other policemen had been called, and it had taken four of them to force the struggling prisoner to the police station.

George's excuse to the court was that he had been annoyed in the first place by boys in the street "pulling him about", and explained "that being the worse for liquor I didn't know no more what I was about than an unborn child." The magistrates, E. Henty Esq. and Capt. Chetwynd, sentenced Belton to one month's imprisonment with hard labour.

Not all families of Worthing fishermen were notorious. At a meeting of the trustees of Humphreys' Almshouses held at the Town Hall on Monday 19 February 1872, George Edwards[12] aged 60 and his 67 year old wife were selected from a list of candidates to occupy a vacancy that had occurred.

They thus obtained a handsome reward for their long lives of industry, honesty, sobriety and general good conduct. An opening only ever came about on the death of a surviving spouse, and George felt honoured and secure to have been chosen for this sought after charitable residence.

In addition to having a comfortable house, rent and taxes free, each married couple received an allowance of 5s. per week, continued to the survivor. The almshouses, erected and endowed to perpetuate the pious memory of Harry Humphreys by his sorrowing parents in 1858, were for six aged poor men and their wives who were members of the Church of England.

Most of Worthing's deep sea fishermen were having a good time of it in September 1872. One of our boats off Ramsgate took in a bumper catch of 27,000 mackerel which realised 7s. per 100.

Humphreys Almshouses which faced the south side of Christ Church. These Buildings were demolished in 1970 and new almshouses erected which are still in use today

The menacing dangers of the sea were only too apparent. On Friday evening, 19 July 1872, when two lads went out rowing, unexpectedly high waves turned their boat right over. Fortunately their cries for help were heard by a young waterman on the beach, by the name of Davis[13], who immediately put off in a boat and brought them safely ashore.

Two months later, two young fishermen were not so lucky. On Thursday evening 26 September three of our prawn trawling boats put to sea. At about 2.30 during the night, about one mile out off Lancing, Anthony Beck[14] exchanged small talk across the water with Chandler junior[15] and young Ayling who were crewing another craft.

Shortly afterwards, a sudden squall sprang up and compelled the boats to run for the shore. Two of the vessels made it, but the third, crewed by the two lads, was taken by the powerful wind, capsized, and was last seen at daylight floating bottom upwards.

The bodies of the two ill-fated young men were picked up at Brighton on the Saturday evening, and carried to the town hall to await the coroner's inquest on the following Tuesday, when the facts of the case were given. The jury returned a verdict of 'found drowned.'

The remains of the two young fishermen, who were both considered to be of excellent character, were interred at Broadwater Cemetery on Thursday 3 October, together in one grave, where Chandler's father later erected a handsome stone monument over them.

Further stormy weather prevailed during December 1872. On the first day of the month the tide overflowed some parts of the Parade, leaving behind drifts of shingle, and fortunately leaving the groynes undamaged. This same day the sea made considerable inroads on the coast towards Lancing, flooding many acres of land.

A teriffic gale on the following Sunday blew down several telegraph poles between Worthing and Brighton, but, luckily, little other damage resulted from the storm.

Just before Christmas, a great deal of wreckage washed ashore on Worthing beach from an unknown ship.

The next notable ferocious storm was not until 22 October 1873 when, in a worsening gale, two fishermen tried to run *The Pride and Envy* ashore. Watched by scores of anxious fishermen eager to help, she was unable to land at the desired point on the beach, and was carried some distance eastward, where she struck a groyne and was stove in two places.

The two fishermen were in great danger of being sucked from their boat and swallowed by the swirling currents in the boisterous sea.

Fortuitously, the craft remained intact and the succeeding waves drove her up the beach, where a group of watchful fishermen, waiting with ropes and equipment, hauled-up the seriously damaged boat. On this occassion the two crew of *The Pride and Envy* had a very lucky escape.

Just over six weeks later, seven fishermen eluded death when their lugger was run down, five miles from the South Foreland.

It was a clear Monday night, 8 December 1873, when the *Consolation* of Shoreham started out from Ramsgate after a most successful fishing season thus far. The moon was shining brightly, when the three men watch saw a steamer about one mile distant; imagining the lugger to be a pilot boat, the steamer put up two rockets before steaming towards her. Even though the lugger was burning bright side lights, the steamer just kept coming, bearing down on the powerless boat like a puffing dragon. It struck the fishing boat on the port bow and went right through her.

She sank immediately!

The crew, of seven Worthing men and a boy, struggled in the rough water, some caught hold of oars, others clutched barrels and nets. By the time the steamship, the *Vallander* of Antwerp had stopped and lowered a boat, it took $\frac{1}{2}$ an hour for its crew to row back to the scene of the accident. They successfully rescued all seven men, but the boy, Richard Hacker, was missing presumed drowned.

When the rescue boat returned to its mother ship, the survivors were taken aboard and dried out. The next day they were transferred to a pilot cutter and landed at Dover shortly after 4 p.m., where they stayed the night at the Sailors' Home.

The boatless crew, James Belton[16] – captain, David Belton[16], Stephen Baker, Thomas Grover, William Morris, William Banford, and George Davis[17] returned to Worthing the following evening.

Adding to the distress and suffering of young Hacker's mother, her husband met with a serious accident on the very day that the sad news of her son's death reached Worthing. Hacker fell from a roof and injured his spine, which not surprisingly left him in a critical condition for two days. As his condition improved it became obvious that he would be unable to work for many months; and his wife could never work anyway since she was a permanent invalid.

How was this seriously disabled man to support his wife and five young children? He did not belong to a 'sick club' because the one he had been a member of for many years had disbanded, and he was too old to join another.

On account of the family being left totally unprovided for, the benevolent citizens of Worthing were once again called upon to dip into their pockets. A subscription list was opened at the office of a newspaper correspondent, Mr. Paine 12 Warwick Street; and C. Roberts Esq. kindly consented to act as treasurer to the fund.

By Christmas, generous amounts of money had been received, besides four stamps from a poor person in Portslade and 12 from an unknown friend at Portsmouth. A small parcel of tea and sugar had been sent anonymously from Brighton. These donations helped to dispel the misery surrounding the Hackers at Christmastime and the ensueing winter months.

Another fisherman suffered a shocking death, only two months after Hacker drowned, but this time it was by the deceased's own hand. William (Bill) Marshall[18], who lived in a small cottage in a passage leading out from Ann Street, had fallen behind with his rent to the extent of £2. His landlord was due to sue him in the County Court on Monday 9 February 1874 for his rent arrears, but due to his absence from the court the case did not proceed. Bill's sisters, concerned that he had not been seen recently, asked his neighbour, Butler, to break into Bill's humble abode.

At 8 p.m. he entered and found Bill hanging by the neck above the staircase. Butler, a labourer, cut the rope and took him down, but he was quite dead.

An inquest was held by F. J. Malim Esq., on the following evening at the Warwick brewery. Evidence was given by Butler who said that he last saw him alive on the previous Friday, when Marshall, who had been tipsy at the time, told him he had been County Courted for his rent, but supposed that they wouldn't hang him for it. Sadly his wife had died about Christmastime and Bill, being unable to cope without her, had taken to drinking ever since. His wife's death had been a great shock to him, and his mind had become impaired.

Fifty year old Marshall, although trained as a butcher, preferred the outdoor life as a fisherman but hadn't earnt any money recently. James Baker, a bootmaker of South Street, whose wife was a sister of the deceased, said that he had chiefly supported him; and there were some bacon, sugar and tea, which he had given him, found in the house. Mr Baker had last seen him alive on the previous Saturday morning and wanted to speak to him, but was avoided by the deceased.

Ironically, Bill had made arrangements to take other lodgings, and had already packed his belongings ready to move. The jury returned a verdict that 'Deceased destroyed his life while in a state of temporary insanity'. Apparently, to add to the irony, Bill's uncle and aunt had also both committed suicide.

A well-known Worthing fisherman, Mr. Belton, effected an extraordinary sight for Whit-Monday excursionists on 25 May 1874. He had been out on the water early in the morning and had managed to surround a large school of mackerel with his seine net. There were so many fish, well in excess of 10,000, that he dare not attempt to haul them into the boat in the normal fashion lest the net should burst. So he decided to leave them there until the tide had receeded sufficiently to enable him to stand in shallow water and remove them from the net by hand.

As the tide went out, the fish were seen in countless numbers, splashing and leaping in the sparkling water. Several hundred people, many of them down from London for the day, were soon attracted to the scene. Lots of them waded into the sea with the water up to their knees, carrying nets, baskets, and all kinds of contrivances; but in their eagerness to share a portion of the spoil, they inadvertently lifted the bottom of the net.

Thousands of mackerel escaped; but one man alone managed to capture more than 100 with his bare hands; another divested himself of a bright blue necktie, with which he 'threaded' several dozen beautiful live mackerel. It really was an amazing scene. Many women had the coolness to walk inside the net and, with their small handbags, ladle-up half a dozen fish at a time.

Mr Belton, the rightful owner of the catch, remonstrated without effect. Indeed, he was far too busily occupied with taking the mackerel from the net, to see the full extent of the depradations going on around him. The 1,100 fish, which he salvaged from what had been an enormous catch; although remarkably good mackerel fetched only 7s. per hundred. Supply had outstripped demand.

The potential dangers that frequently confronted deep sea fishermen cannot be stressed too strongly. On 6 February 1875, a Worthing fisherman drowned in an unfortunate accident. The fishing smack *Sir Robert Peel,* owned by William beck[19], was returning to Shoreham Harbour from St. Valery in France.

At 10 p.m. the skipper, Mr. Allan, suddenly became aware of a vessel bearing down on his smack and immediately ordered his crew to take evasive action by sailing windward.

In the near-panic that followed, Allan stumbled on a coil of rope, tripped and went over the gunwhale into the sea.

He struggled in the darkness to keep himself afloat while awaiting assistance. But the smack was travelling at a speed of at least six knots, and it took a while before she could be brought-to and a small boat lowered. During this lapse of time, his pitiful cries for help had only been heard in the distance twice.

The crew sent out to rescue their captain found no trace of him. He had sunk.

Allan, a quiet and respectable man as well as a competent seamen, had been employed by Mr. Beck for more than 20 years. His poor widow was left to support seven children, three of them quite young, but with no financial means of doing so. Members of the public sympathised with her situation and sent donations to relieve her bereaved family.

Footnotes Ch. 6

[1]Pompey - an infamous local character who exhibited a shark on the beach in 1864.

[2]Charles Churcher - A relation of Alex Churcher who was involved with the *Lalla Rookh* rescue in 1850.

[3]Mr Belton - A forefather of Danny Belton who is the only descendant of a 19th century Worthing fishing family still fishing full-time. His 'box' is on the beach opposite the Dome Cinema.

[4]Marshland - now Brooklands boating lake.

[5]19 Sept 1869 - This is the correct date for the ensueing event, is the date recorded in the original lifeboat service record book and is corroborated by a newspaper report published in 23 September 1869. The date, 29 September, shown on the surviving lifeboat 'scoreboard' in Worthing museum is unfortunately incorrect. *Brave Chillon* of Boulogne – saved boat. This rescue is marked differently on the original 'scoreboard':– barque *Chillon* of boulogne, saved vessel and boat.

[6]Bill Beck - one of the Beck family whose ferry boat capsized drowning 11 fishermen in 1850.

[7]J. Clarke - who lost a rowing boat in the recent storm.

[8]Marshall - A crew member of the *Jane.*

[9]George Davis - from a family of fishermen and lifeboatmen.

[10]William Freeman - a crewman of the *Jane.*

[11]Charles Belton - A forefather of Walter (Wally) Charles Belton who is the brother of Danny, a full-time fisherman. Both brothers live in Worthing.

[12]George Edwards - a relation of the Edwards family involved in the *Lalla Rookh* disaster of 1850.

[13]Davis - from a family of fishermen and lifeboatmen.

[14]Anthony Beck - a relation of William Beck.

[15]Chandler junior - son of the landlord of the *Buckingham Arms*, Montague Street (now The Body Shop on the corner of Buckingham Road).

[16]James and David Belton - of the well known Worthing Belton family.

[17]George Davis - Worthing lifeboatman.

[18]William Marshall - No known relation to a crewman of the same surname on the *Jane* at the time of its ceremonial launching.

[19]William Beck - his father before him was a boat owner.

Ch. 7

A New Berth 1875-7

The lifeboat house in Crescent Road was a little way off the seafront and somewhat inconvenient for maritime rescue work. Eventually the Committee of Management instructed that a new one be built opposite the sea. The new lifeboat house, with a panoramic view of the sea from its lookout turret, was the pride of Worthing lifeboatmen.

On Monday 22 February 1875, it was formally opened amid a carnival atmosphere with a procession through the town. Shortly before 11 a.m. the *Jane* was taken out of its old house in Crescent Road and drawn on its carriage by four horses to the beach, and launched on the east side of the pier.

A lifeboat exercise took place, while the band of the Scots Greys, positioned on the colourful flag-adorned pier, played to enthralled spectators. A huge crowd of excited residents watched as the crew rowed heartily as far as West Worthing and back again, before demonstrating their skills, such as accurately throwing lines. After the display the Worthing lifeboatmen ran the craft onto the beach opposite the *Steyne Hotel*, where it was once more mounted onto its carriage.

The *Steyne Hotel* (now the Chatsworth Hotel) and the pier in the background

The crew, in their red caps and cork lifejackets, took up their places in the lifeboat, while a procession was formed headed by the band of the Scots Greys who re-assembled after leaving the pier.

The Union Jack was hoisted, coastguardsmen fell-in behind the *Jane* and the band moved off in slow time playing Rule Britannia.

Patriotic fervour encompassed the excitedly cheerful crowd of Worthingites as they followed the procession into Bedford Row, left into Warwick Street and left again down South Street to arrive opposite the pier where they turned right to proceed westward along Marine Parade.

On arrival, opposite the handsome and substantial new lifeboat house at 107 Marine Parade, near the west coastguard station which was delightfully dressed with flags for the day, the band stood in formation to the side of the road, while the boat was run through the opening (about 14ft 6ins wide and 13ft high,created by folding back the doors into her new quarters) to the inspiring strains of their excellent music. This enviable and prestigious new home for the lifeboat with its split flint facia adorned with a welsh slate roof and a proud look-out turret, delighted many observers. The building measured 17ft 6ins in breadth and was 40ft long.

During the day, entertainment organised by Messrs. Palmer & Son on behalf of the local R.N.L.I. committee and staged at Montague Hall, swelled the institution's funds. The regimental band gave two performances, both to capacity audiences. The well-chosen selection of music was thoroughly appreci-ated, for Worthing had seldom seen two such successful performances as these given by the Scots Greys. Other recreational delights included sword feats provided by military instructors, exercises, single-stick encounters and melees, which all evoked enthusiastic applause.

The dashing soldiers merited the cordial vote of thanks given by the Worthing branch R.N.L.I. committee for their voluntary services, at a dinner provided for them at the *Marine Hotel.*

The site for the new boathouse, which had been owned by a member of the Worthing branch R.N.L.I., had been purchased by head quarters for the sum of £240. The new building, designed by Charles Hide and constructed by Mr. E. C. Patching's firm at a cost of £370, was ideally suited for its intended purpose. Now that the lifeboat house was facing the sea and close to the coastguard station, communications would be more efficient.

At a meeting of the general committee of the R.N..L.I., held on 4 March 1875 at its head office in John Street, Adelphi,London, the president of the R.N.L.I., his Grace the Duke of Northumberland, resolved that the old lifeboat house and site at Crescent Road, Worthing be sold to Mr Charles Hide for £150. The actual indenture document for this sale was signed four weeks later on 1 April.

The year 1875 passed without any serious maritime incident. But the sea made alarming encroachments of the Lancing road at the end of December 1875, and continued to make inroads, when rough weather coincided with high tides, for some years to come.

The Parade in Worthing was frequently being strewn with pebbles on these occasions; and in an attempt to ease the clearing-up operations, a locally-invented horse-drawn plough was brought into operation on the morning of Monday 27 March 1876. However, the opinions of those who saw it working were not altogether favourable and little more was ever heard of it.

Twelve months had passed since Mr. Allan had drowned accidentally at sea. During this period, I was pleased to discover there was no serious seafaring mishaps involving Worthing seamen, neither off the town itself nor elsewhere. During this welcome lull, in February 1876, the Mariners' Friend Society were able to set up a branch at Worthing, to serve the Sussex coast.

The aims of this society, which was founded in 1848 and reorganised in 1866, was the promotion of religious, intellectual and social elevation of all classes of seafaring people of every nation. Moves towards these objectives were: preaching the gospel not only on land but also at sea; and the distribution of pamphlets and bibles to ships' libraries. The Society, which was non-sectarian, employed four chaplains and six missionaries. Five branches throughout Great Britain supported free Sunday schools, reading rooms, and a Band of Hope.

To assist the fledgeling branch, six large parcels of religious publications, some as heavy as 60 lbs, were sent to its office at 2, East Street, Worthing, by various societies in London, Eastbourne and Scotland. Altogether, many thousands of religious books and tracts were sent to the office. Among them were 50 copies of the new testament, purchased from Mr. Loveday's Bookshop in South Street by local supporters of the society.

Worthing fishermen were thankful to the Almighty for enabling them to catch large quantities of good quality prawns and fine mackerel during April and May 1876. The first catch of the season, about 2500 mackerel, was brought ashore from Mr. Newman's boat and auctioned on the beach for 19s. per 100. An Eastbourne boat brought in 1200 mackerel.

A little anomaly arose in August, concerning a salmon and an eel. A 17 lb salmon was caught in a pool on the sands, where it had been trapped by the receding tide. It was nearly dead when caught, and was supposed to have been bitten by a large conger eel, which was found in the pool at the same time.

During the herring season, in November 1876, our longshore fishermen were very pleased with their huge catches. In fact one small boat caught such an enormous amount of fish that its gunwhales were almost submerging and, to avoid sinking, its crew ran her ashore at Lancing. The herrings were later retailed at the very low price of 40 for a shilling.

Retired fisherman Henry Blann, my great great great grandfather, was chosen from a selection of candidates to enter Humphreys' Almshouse. In April 1876 he was appointed gatekeeper, earning 5s. per quarter on top of his normal weekly allowance. He relinquished the post in September 1877 and remained in the almshouse, secure in its charitable status. As well as being a fisherman, Henry had been a lighterman. In his younger day he had crossed the English Channel and back regularly on smuggling trips, until the Customs and Excise men caught him.

They had sawed his boat in two, to teach him a lesson.

Being full of the tenacious Blann spirit he had not deterred and had taken to smuggling again.

But when he was caught a second time customs officers set fire to his boats and burnt all of his fishing gear on the beach, as a more severe punishment.

Without the tools of his trade he eventually became a pauper, and it remains a mystery to me how he came to be selected as a man of good record by the Almshouse committee.

Henry's wife, Mary, had died in 1871 at 18 Richmond Place, the home of one of her sons, Jesse Blann, a mariner.

Henry came from a line of fishermen. His father, my great great great great grandfather Edmund Blann, as well as being a fisherman, had at one time been the landlord of the *Nelson Hotel* in South Street[1]. Edmund had let his back room on 13 June 1803 for half a guinea to a group of gentlemen, who formed themselves into the Board of Commissioners[2].

In August 1876, William Hugh Dennett, honorary secretary to the Worthing branch R.N.L.I., was presented with a graceful tribute for his years of valuable service. He received a beautifully engraved and handsomely framed inscription of a minute passed at a special meeting of the national committee on 3 August, in which the the society acknowledged his long and valuable co-operation as the honorary secretary of the Worthing branch.

At this same time, Mr. Dennett also retired from his post as honorary secretary to Worthing's Infirmary and Dispensary after 40 years of devoted service.

The Bench dealt with many cases of drunkenness in 1876. Albert Grevett, a fish hawker, was fined 5s. with 9s. costs for being drunk in the highway. For his second conviction during this year, Albert Street received a heavier fine of 7s. 6d. with 9s. costs.

The sea went completely over the pier and flooded the Marine Parade. This lantern slide view, taken from the *Royal Sea House Hotel*, shows boats drawn up off the beach

The hardened carouser, George Davis[3], also described as a fish hawker, appeared for his fourth conviction this year and was penalised with a hefty 25s. fine and 9s. costs.

William (Bill) Freeman[4], described by the contemporary press as a violent and incorrigible drunkard, who had been convicted more than 30 times by 1871, was taken before Major Gaisford and Major Wisden on Monday 11 September 1876. He was charged not only with being drunk and riotous, but also with assaulting P.C. Stead.

It was revealed in court that on Saturday night 9 September, in consequence of his riotous behaviour, Freeman had been arrested and had become extremely violent whilst in police custody. After his conduct was described to the court as being like that of a madman, he was committed to prison for six weeks.

Worthing, which bore the brunt of many severe gales that attacked the south coast at this time, was fortunately more protected now due to the installation of more sea defences. But they still couldn't hold back the sea under the most violent of conditions.

On Monday morning 1 January 1877, waves being driven by a powerful gale were so high that they went right over the pier, tearing up wooden decking and causing considerable damage throughout the length of the structure. The sea rushed over the promenade and flooded Marine Parade, ran up Bath Place and half way up South Street, catching many shopkeepers unawares. Residents in Bath Place suffered badly as the water rose above their kitchen windows and streamed in through every crack and cranny in the lower part of their dwellings. Some half a dozen boats plied for hire and were kept busy for an hour or so in South Street and Marine Parade, carrying passengers to and from the Post Office and other places. As the knee-deep water subsided the proprietors cleaned up the mess and, within a few hours, were open for business again.

The sea flooded half way up South Street and boats were used to ferry customers to and from the shops

The beach was seriously damaged however, the worst of the erosion being to the east of the town, as usual. Higher tides were expected, and alarm spread through the town at the probable consequences should the wind increase again to the strength of the gale just experienced.

A few days later, Worthing weathered a heavy south westerly gale which caused only minor damage. But at 7.15 p.m., when the very rough sea had half ebbed, a Coastguard Officer spotted distress lights which he estimated to be three miles out to sea.

Conditions were absolutely dreadful and the lifeboat chairman and coxwain conferred with the coastguard to decide whether or not to risk the lives of the lifeboat crew. They decided to launch as the tide was on its way out, hoping that the breakers would gradually decrease in size, and fired the maroon to summon the crew.

While they were assembling and preparing for an arduous night, four horses arrived that had been sent for. In the event only two horses were required to pull the carriage as 25 men had volunteered to help position the craft for launching.

The volunteers waded into the sea up to their necks, experiencing considerable difficulty, in getting the *Jane* afloat, from the still-mountainous surf.

Eventually, at 8.30 p.m. the crew succeeded in putting off. They rowed and rowed in the direction of where the distress signals had been observed, but after searching for nearly two hours there was still no sign of a vessel so Coxwain Dean gave the order to return to shore.

The *Jane* landed at 11 p.m. opposite the lifeboat house, by which time the tide had completely receded, and the 25 helpers who had been waiting for almost three hours, soaked to their skin, waded in to the waves once more to pull the lifeboat 300 yards up the beach. The coxwain reported to the chairman, who was there waiting, that he thought the distressed vessel must have been carried further along the coast by strong currents instigated by the heavy gale.

The chairman immediately despatched telegram messengers to the next two lifeboat stations along the coast: Shoreham and Brighton, at a cost of 6s.6d., to warn them to be on the lookout for a distressed vessel.

A message received in reply, confirmed that the 578 ton barque *Ida* of Glasgow, owned by Denistown & Co., had been driven ashore at Brighton, cutting short its voyage. Captain Matthews had been taking the vessel, which was in ballast, from Le Havre to Pensacola.

In preparing his report on the service, Coxwain Dean recommended to the committee that the 25 patiently suffering assistants be paid 5s. each for their services. The new honorary secretary, Melvill Green, authorised it together with payment of 20s. to each of the following crewmen: Alfred Dean, coxwain; Charles Lee, 2nd coxwain; Reuben Ayling; George Goble; Luke Wells; W. Davis; Thomas Davis junior; W. Marshall; E. Bacon[5]; Mark Wingfield[6]; James Bashford[7]; and George Bashford[7] who was on his first lifeboat service.

The committee paid a total of £1 10s. for the hire of four horses: 10s. for each of the two required for launching; and 5s. each for the other pair.

The following morning at St. Georges Church, the Curate read a prayer for fine weather but, without apparently perceiving his mistake, he recited one for rain, to the concealed amusement of parishioners.

Five months later, Friday 1 June 1877 was a day long to be remembered by our fishing population. Many boats had brought fish to the town early that morning, and were anchored in the 'roads' off Worthing when a terribly strong south westerly gale sprang up.

Several broke their moorings and drifted towards the beach. Those vessels which were still manned, including Tom Blann's, hoisted sail to run for the safety of Shoreham Harbour, but some of the sails were torn to shreds as soon as they were raised.

Several unmanned luggers broke their moorings and were in danger of drifting in to the groynes and being seriously damaged. The R.N.L.I. branch chairman was aware of this and, in consultation with the chief boats officer of the Coastguard, ordered the lifeboat out to save what fishing boats she could. The lifeboat crew were already on hand and the *Jane* was launched at 12.30 p.m. in an extraordinarily heavy sea, which was four hours flood and running from the southwest.

It took them half an hour to reach a drifting and by now derelict lugger. She was the *Harkaway*, which belonged to William Benn. The master, Mark Benn, and his five crew had left the boat in ballast with the fishing nets and gear aboard, and gone ashore before the storm had materialised and the strength of the gale had broken her cables. Four of the 13 brave lifeboatmen managed to board the lugger, despite the perilous conditions, and successfully manoeuvred the valuable 15 ton lugger into Shoreham Harbour. In all probability she would have been wrecked but for the unselfish and courageous efforts of this lifeboat crew.

They also had orders to get alongside a half-decked boat and assist the five crew aboard. On reaching this vessel its occupants refused help in the swelling sea, but instead ran their craft ashore to save their lives, under the watchful eyes of the lifeboatmen as the *Jane* stood by. By the time this was accomplished the other boats had gone ashore. So the *Jane* dropped anchor off Lancing to ride out the ferocity of the storm.

There were no less than five luggers stranded within a mile of each other to the east of Worthing. Most of them had crashed into the groynes and stove in, severely endangering the lives of their crews.

One young man, sucked out to sea by the invisible powerful currents, was rescued by a well-known swimmer named Nichol. He had dashed into the breakers, risking his own life, and brought the lad ashore.

The violence of the breakers eased on the ebb tide, and at 4.40 p.m. the *Jane* ran safely ashore after breaking an oar. The crew sent a messenger to Worthing to inform the helpers waiting near the lifeboat station that they had beached at Lancing. Fourteen assistants clambered onto the boat carriage, pulled by two horses hired for £1, to Lancing.

Later that evening the *Jane* was returned to its house. Afterwards, the volunteers each received 3s.9d. for their valuable services, except two of them, Tom Belton and Stubbs, who were paid double. These two helpers were awarded 7s.6d. each, because they had bravely risked their lives in getting a rope clear of a post.

The twelve crew under Coxwain A. Dean were: 2nd Coxwain Charles Lee, J. Wells, L. Wells, W. Davis, G. Goble, S. Street, G. Bacon, F. Collier, H. Brown, F. Worley, S. Wingfield and G. Bashford. Some of our more experienced lifeboatmen had been out at sea and unavailable when the emergency happened. The last six afore-mentioned, drawn from the reserve crew, had not been off to a wreck in a lifeboat before. All 13 received 10s. each for their invaluable rescue work; and a record of the results was 'chalked-up' on the station's 'scoreboard'.

There had been great excitement in Worthing throughout the day, but at the end of it all, much sympathy was felt for our fishermen who had borne losses caused by the storm. It had been a hard winter for many of them, and this bad luck just at the beginning of the season hit them very hard indeed.

One Worthing fisherman, Newman, lost not only his boat but also his nets and all his gear, which would take years to save up enough money to replace them all. Another boat ran into her and she sank on her moorings. The Sally, a Brighton boat, was severely damaged and ran ashore near the Lancing tollgate.

To consider the best means of raising a fund to relieve the fishermen following the gale damage, a small group of gentlemen met at the Town Hall on Monday evening 4 June. Here it was revealed that one of the fishermen alone had sustained a staggering loss of £250. Without hesitation a committee was formed of W. Dawes, W. Harris and H. E. A. Dalbrack, with H. Hargood in the chair; and a subscription list was opened immediately with promises of nearly £40.

Three weeks later, when the fund stood at about £209 and claims totalling £250 had been received from agrieved fishermen, a further meeting of the committee was held at the Town Hall on Tuesday afternoon 26 June, to decide how the money should be distributed. As a result the committee voted £200 towards meeting the claims, and the balance to be paid to the Worthing Fishermen's Insurance Association.

To finalise their intentions, the committee met for the 3rd and last time, just one week later on Tuesday morning 3 July. Mr.Hargood submitted an audited statement of the accounts which showed that £194 2s.6d. had been subscribed; Mr. W. Paine had raised £17 4s.2d. from entertainment, and Mr. W. E. L. Trevor had collected £19 14s. in a similar manner.

After payment of expenses a grant of £160 was made to W. Newman, who asked for it to be deposited at the London & County Bank. Three other fishermen benefited from the fund: E. Edwards received £24 16s.; J. Searle, £8 and J. Dunford, £7 4s.

The balance of £16 14s.6d. was paid over to the Fishermen's Mutual Insurance Association, and the meeting concluded with a vote of thanks to the chairman for the exertionary way that he had fulfilled his duties.

Footnotes Ch. 7

[1] *Nelson Hotel* - The site on the east side of South Street is now occupied by Hammels.

[2] Board of Commissioners - A forerunner of Worthing Borough Council.

[3] George Davis - Previously a fisherman and lifeboatman, charged in 1871 with being drunk and disorderly.

[4] William Freeman - Previously a crewman on the Jane.

[5] E. Bacon - A relation of T. Bacon who crewed the lifeboat *Jane* during active service on 11 February 1866.

[6] Mark Wingfield - A relation of J. Wingfield who crewed the lifeboat *Jane* during active service on 24 March 1866.

[7] James Bashford and George Bashford - relations of H. Bashford who crewed the lifeboat *Jane* during a service on 11 February 1866.

Close Encounters 1878-86

It used to be said that immense catches of sprats betoken a hard winter. This old saying rang true in December 1878, after large quantities of these small fish were caught off Worthing. Sure enough, severe frosts followed, and heavy falls of snow enveloped the town. At Christmas, shops displayed their usual bright and bustling aspect, notwithstanding the apparent extremes of temperature and precipitation, which prevented many of the working classes from following their trades. Despite the lack of incomes in so many families, grocers and fruiterers all seemed to do excellent business, as well as butchers and wine merchants. While among the fancy traders, the turnover attributed to drapers was higher than at any previous Christmas.

During these Arctic conditions, it was accepted that the warmest place was in bed. For it must have been about this time that Alice Wingfield became pregnant by Harry Blann. Harry, my great grandfather, lived in a terraced house at 19 Clifton Road(demolished in 1960), and Alice lived with her parents at 18 Gloucester Place. After some stern advice from her father, Henry Wingfield, the two 20 year olds hurriedly married on 16 January. The ceremony at Broadwater Church was officially witnessed by Harry's sister Charlotte May Blann, two years his senior, with her fiance George Stephen Lingham, a 23 year old mariner of 2, London Street.

Nine months later, in September 1879, the baby who was to become my grandfather was born and christened Jesse Belville Blann. His middle name commemorated his great grandfather on his grand-mother's side, John Belville, who gave his life attempting to rescue those on the *Lalla Rookh* in 1850.

In 1881, Harry's younger brother Bill, aged 20, married Alice's younger sister, Elizabeth Wingfield, aged 21, also at Broadwater Church. The occasion was witnessed by Bill's younger sister Eva Eliza Blann and Charlie Wingfield. So now two Blann brothers had married two Wingfield sisters, all from Worthing fishing families.

In 1884, when my great great great grandfather Henry Blann was 79 years old, he was interviewed at his lodgings in Humphreys' Almshouse, by Edward Sayers a local historian - "When I was young I used to go, with old Tom Lindup the Ferryman, down to his boat at the water's edge, and several times on going down he would stop where there were some wooden stumps, about midway between the beach and low water mark, opposite Bedford Row, and putting his foot on one of the stumps would say 'This is where the old Sea House stood, I married my wife from there; she was servant there and came from Coombs," claimed Henry.[1]

When Henry became seriously ill in August 1886, he was taken from the almshouse to the home of his grandson James B. Steere, at 37 Gloucester Place, to spend his last days. He died there of chronic gastritis exhaustion on 1 September 1886, at the age of 81 years.

Infant mortality was still commonplace, and by 1886 Henry's grandson, Harry Blann, had lost two sons, and Harry's brother Bill, one.

Fishermen were poor and could not afford organised entertainment. To alleviate drudgery in the fishing community, several benefactors in the town took an interest in their welfare and paid for a special tea for them at Worthing's Christ Church on Thursday evening 13 January 1881. The large schoolroom was prettily decorated with flags, mottos and evergreens for the occasion. Messrs. Kettle & Son supplied an excellent repast, which was enjoyed by a large assembly of Worthing fishermen and their wives, totalling about 300 persons in all. After the Rev. F. Cross had addressed the gathering during the evening, he asked one of the benefactors, Mr. R. Loder M.P., to give a discourse. Both speeches were well-received, and the guests even burst forth with three cheers when their member of Parliament left. A ladies choir added to the entertainment and a thoroughly pleasant time was had by all.

Drink was the downfall of William (Bill) Freeman, an ex-lifeboatman and locally infamous character. Over the years he had been convicted of drunkeness on at least 40 occasions and was once again before the Bench on Wednesday 28 October. After pleading guilty to a charge of using obscene language, the chairman of the Bench, E. Henty, sentenced Freeman to 14 days hard labour.

At the same session, John Cooper, a sailor, was charged with being drunk and disorderly in the streets. In his absence he was fined 16s. with 11s. costs by the five-man Bench.

A prominent businessman and philanthropist in the town, Henry Harris, donated a large sum of money to the RNLI in 1880, and the local committee showed their appreciation by renaming the *Jane* the *Henry Harris.*

The lifeboat crew were drawn from experienced watermen on the front. The lives of these hard-working men were prone to occupational hazards, particularly during nasty weather.

But on Sunday 19 November 1882, which was a fine day, faulty equipment on the beach caused a nasty mishap. During the evening, Frank Burden and some other boatmen were hauling a small fishing boat up the beach in the usual way, by capstan. As they were rotating capstan using a long pole, the rope was unable to take the full strain of the boat and suddenly broke. The capstan swung violently round and the pole struck Frank's head, knocking him unconcious. He was immediately taken to the infirmary where he was examined by Mr. A. H. Collet. The doctor prescribed a short rest, after which he recovered and managed to resume his livelihood.

A view of the beach and the Parade from the pier, showing two capstans at the top of the beach

On Saturday 10 February 1883, a strong south westerly gale rendered a schooner uncontrollable off Worthing. The *Theresa* had left Guernsey two days earlier with a cargo of granite bound for London, and had not been long at sea when she encountered severe weather. Her main boom was carried away, and her mainsail rent almost asunder. During those two stormy days, the crew were unable to control the ship as the surging waves tossed it about like a cork at the mercy of the perilous gale.

At 5.30 p.m. when violent waves broke over the disabled vessel, its crew raised distress signals. An attempt to launch the schooner's boat failed. By now the crew were on the verge of panicking. But their skipper insisted that the frenzied sailors should await the arrival of help from the coast. Had the terrified crew left the ship they would surely have perished, for the small boat was quite unsuitable for this mountainous sea.

The coastguard acknowledged their signal by sending up rockets, while the lifeboat crew and horses were summoned. By 5.50 p.m. it became obvious that the unmanageable schooner was going to be driven right onto our coast by the powerful wind. Immediately Coxwain Charles Lee ordered the *Henry Harris* to be launched.

The sea was 3/4 of the way out on an ebb tide, and as the horses hadn't yet arrived, the crew and assistants ran the boat 400 yards over the sand to the water. In the rush one of the helpers, a gardener named Ayres, was knocked down and one of the wheels ran over his foot. Two of the others, fearing that he had sustained a serious injury, hurriedly carried him off to seek medical attention.

Meanwhile, these volunteers waded into the sea up to their waists, pulling the lifeboat and carriage with them. A large number of people, who had gathered to watch and experience the tense excitement, cheered the crew on their way as they rowed the *Henry Harris* through the breakers.

The lifeboat struggled through the heavy sea and reached the *Theresa*, which had since struck a sand bank, some 40 minutes later at 6.30 p.m.

The swell of the heaving sea was horrendous, and as soon as the *Henry Harris* was able to pull alongside the ailing *Theresa* and drop anchor, a terror-stricken sailor leapt from the deck into the lifeboat.

Just then a hawser parted and an anchor came loose, making it very difficult to keep the lifeboat alongside the Weymouth schooner.

But soon, Captain J. Hibley, who was part owner of the schooner, and his two other exhausted crew, one only a boy, were rescued by the lifeboatmen and taken, soaked right through, aboard the *Henry Harris*.

Nothing was saved except the crew's clothing which they threw into the lifeboat. Captain Hibley wasn't even able to reach his cabin where he had left £20 worth of gold locked up.

The *Henry Harris* returned and beached at Worthing at about 6.55 p.m. with the four shipwrecked mariners aboard. They were taken to Trafalgar House where they received every sympathy and warm hospitality from Mr. and Mrs. Strickland.

The lifeboat was now on the beach, waiting to be rehoused. But its carriage had been rendered useless following a mishap in the rush to launch the *Henry Harris*. Part of its ironwork had broken. It was now an exceptionally low spring tide and the lifeboatmen together with their helpers hauled the *Henry Harris* bodily over the vast expanse of sands and up the beach to the Parade. Coxwain Lee reported the damage to the chairman, Harry Hargood, who insisted that it be repaired at once, to be ready for any ensuing emergency.

It took the crew and helpers until 12.30 a.m. the following morning to repair the carriage, and return the boat on its conveyance to the boathouse. By this time they had all been on duty for a strenuous period of seven hours, and were quite relieved to return to their homes.

During the night, the *Theresa*, driven in on the tide, struck and damaged a groyne before stranding on the beach opposite St. Georges Church. Here it was exposed to the full fury of the lashing waves, and when the vessel was discovered at 12 noon, it had been reduced to a total wreck.

Lured by the sight of wreckage strewn along the beach, hundreds of sightseers went and gazed at the remains of the *Theresa*. They searched for valuables, the captain's gold in particular, but apparently nobody ever found it. The disappearing gold still remains a mystery today. Perhaps, if the tide covered it with sand, it could still be under the sea bed?

Later on that Sunday it was reported that Ayres' foot was not badly hurt, after his collision with the carriage, and was recovering well.

The committee considered that great credit was due to the Coxwain and his crew 'for promptitude and energy on this service':

Charles Lee-coxwain; Luke Wells - acting 2nd coxwain; James Wells; George Wells; George Goble; John Dunford; Fred Collier; Bill Marshall; Arthur Marshall; William Collier; George Riddles; George Parker Mugfield; Thomas Bridger junior. They each received the usual payment of 20s.

I consider that the crew performed exceptionally well on this occasion, especially as the last five crewmen on the above list had no experience as lifeboat crewmen on previous services.

This successful rescue of the *Theresa*'s crew was a most notable and exciting experience for the lifeboatmen and an entry of their proud deed can be found on the station's 'scoreboard'.

In the 1960's, part of the wrecked schooner was found to have been used in the construction of a shop's annexe at 20, Montague Street. It was Squire's menswear boutique, and beyond the main shop was an attached building used by staff. Its roof was supported by the 18 foot mast of the *Theresa*. Written on it were the words 'mast of the *Theresa*, schooner of Weymouth, wrecked off Worthing February 11 1883.' It measured more than one foot in diameter and along its length were thick iron rings to take rigging.

On Sunday 14 December 1884, the coastguard spotted a brigantine, about four miles to the west of the station, being blown towards the coastline at Goring by a strong south south westerly gale. At 9.45 a m the Chief Officer of the Coastguard, William L. Martin, notified the lifeboat coxwain, Charles Lee, who huriedly assembled his crew in the thick driving rain.

Two horses were fetched, which together with 29 men assistants, drew the *Henry Harris* on its carriage along the coast road, which was thick with heavy mud, to a spot about one mile west of the lifeboat station.

At about 10.15 a.m. when the tide was one hour's ebb, the carriage was backed down the beach to the water's edge and the volunteers helped launch the lifeboat. The crew sailed her out, tacking against the wind, for three or four miles, but, despite a lengthy search, they found no vessel. They eventually returned to shore, somewhat despondant, and beached at 12.30 p.m.

Apparently, it was afterwards ascertained that the brigantine had succeeded in reaching the shelter of Littlehampton Harbour.

The costs of this fruitless lifeboat service were: 5s. each for the hire of two horses in transporting the *Henry Harris* on its carriage to the launch site and back; 2s. each for the 29 volunteers; and 10s. for each of the 12 lifeboat crew. These payments were authorised by the local honorary secretary, Melvill Green, and the following lifeboatmen collected their remuneration:- Charles Lee (coxwain), M. Wingfield, St. Wingfield, T. Davis, G. W. P. Wingfield, George Riddles, E. Bacon, P. West, F. Collier, W. Wingfield, George Belton and Jo Street.

The crew were disappointed that their life-risking efforts were in vain; particularly for the last three men on this list, who had just experienced their first emergency lifeboat call-out.

To afford greater protection of the lifeboat house from high-spirited youths and the like, the local committee decided, in 1885, to install a pair of gates about 10 feet in front of the boathouse doors.

Worthing's third consecutive lifeboat house, on Marine Parade facing the sea. (The building survives today although it has been altered somewhat.)

On Monday 26 October 1885, there was an alarming rumour that three of our herring fishing boats had foundered off Shoreham when a gale had sprung up suddenly during the previous night; and that the crews were drowned. A telegram later that morning, however, explained that a Worthing boat belonging to Mr. Churcher had been driven ashore, but the crew had come to no harm. The other two boats, fortunately, had got safely into the harbour.

On Saturday 4 December 1886, two ships collided in the English Channel. The French barque *Edmund Gabriel*, a vessel of about 600 tons, struck the Guernsey brig *Never Despair*, about 15 miles off Cape Barfleur. The English crew of the brig, which was on an easterly course bound up the channel, had set every bit of canvas as the southerly wind was only moderate.

The drama began at about 3.30 a.m. when Captain Cooper on the deck of the *Never Despair* saw a green light on the starboard bow. About 10 minutes later the vessel got away on the port helm and showed a red light.

With the two vessels being so close, he knew as soon as he saw this port light that there would be a collision.

To ease the blow he starboarded his helm as the barque crashed into the brig abaft of the starboard fore rigging, with a force so great that the smaller vessel, the brig, was literally smashed in.

The master of the brig, realising at once the extent of the damage, called to his men to jump onto the barque whilst the two vessels were still jammed together. All but one, a young 22 year old man named Charles Winterflood from Guernsey, succeeded in boarding the French boat. Whether he was below at the time is not known, but he was heard shouting after the vessels parted; and within a short space of time the stoved-in brig went down.

The *Edmund Gabriel*, which was bound for Gaboon on the west coast of Africa with a general cargo of wines, spirits. silk, wood, coal bricks, salt and cement, also sustained considerable damage with her bow smashed in. As she started to take in water at a very rapid pace, the Master, Delaplanche, attempted to run her to the French shore. But when the wind shifted he found it an impossible task and changed course for England. The men of both crews were continually at work with the pumps, attempting to reduce the water level within the ship. But still the water in the hold rapidly increased.

At 12.15 p.m., the Coastguard spotted the barque, through a haze of thick rain, running ashore; and luckily, only a few minutes later, she ran aground about 1¼ miles east of Worthing pier, otherwise she would have sunk very soon, as the water had filled the hold to within three or four feet of the deck. Immediately, the coastguard telegraphed Shoreham for a tug, summoned the Worthing lifeboat crew by firing a mortar, and fetched four horses to draw the lifebat carriage.

Meanwhile, the two crews aboard the barque lowered its two boats, abandoned ship and rowed ashore.

The weather was rough with a fresh south south westerly gale blowing as the lifeboat was hurriedly trundled along the coast road on its carriage, forceably following the hoofsteps of four sturdy steeds.

When they arrived opposite the wreck, the *Henry Harris* was reversed down the beach and into the water. The carriage, not needed here anymore, was sent back to Worthing.

At 12.40 p.m., with the aid of 10 men, the lifeboat crew got afloat, and in 20 minutes, after a stiff row in the boisterous sea, reached the lee-side of the waterlogged wreck. Coxwain Lee ordered some of his crew to board her, fast filling with more water, and search the vessel. Having ascertained that she was abandoned, the lifeboatmen stood-by on the *Henry Harris* and waited for the tug to arrive from Shoreham. A considerable number of people gathered on the beach opposite the barque, expecting the vessel to break up, and spectators on the Worthing Parade evinced considerable interest.

The tug *Stella* arrived, and together with assistance from the Worthing lifeboat, tried all means to tow the barque off, but without success. The *Henry Harris* returned to Worthing, beaching at 6 p.m., having been on service for six hours. Twenty six assistants hauled the lifeboat up the beach and replaced her on the carriage, and returned both to the lifeboat house.

Worthing Branch committee paid out 1/6d. each to 16 of the men who helped with the *Henry Harris* on its return from the wreck; and 10 men, who asssisted with the launch as well as the return, each received 3s. The four horses were hired for 14s. each; while the lifeboat crew received the standard payment of 10s. per man. These payments, which totalled £12, were authorised by the honorary secretary George Piggott the next day. The 13 lifeboat crew were:- Charles Lee (coxwain), Stephen Wingfield, George Wingfield, Tom Wingfield, Fred Collier, William Collier, Frank Collier, William Groves, George Grevatt, George Irvine, Frank Burden, F. Bacon and F. Wakeford.

The coastguards made the necesary arrangements to accomodate the shipwrecked crews. The Chief Coastguard Officer himself entertained the two captains, while the sailors enjoyed comfortable quarters at the *Three Horse Shoes Inn*. Every possible assistance was rendered, not only by the Lancing Coastguard, but by residents who became aware of their plight. The Guernsey crew could not speak too highly of what was done for their comfort in such extreme circumstances, having lost everything when their vessel had sunk. Food and clothing were supplied, and some of them, wearing next to nothing, were kitted out completely.

The Frenchmen were later sent by the Swedish Consul, Mr. Brown, to the *East Street Arms* at Shoreham, to await instructions from the French Consul; while the seven surviving English crew were sent, at about 4 p.m., by the Coastguard to Southwick, where they were placed in the charge of the Shipwrecked

Mariners' Society, who provided them with lodgings at a private house in Adur Terrace.

On Monday afternoon, 6 December, the English sailors travelled by train to Southampton, where they caught the steam packet to Guernsey.

Although severely damaged the barque lay quite upright, firmly wedged on hard rock opposite the Lancing Coastguard Station. In addition to her bow being smashed in, it was feared that the bottom of her hull had also suffered a similar fate, as she had been running fast in the gale, and had struck land with great force.

Late on Saturday evening, the Superintendent of Customs at Shoreham sent two officers to take charge of the *Edmund Gabriel*. They boarded her and stayed during Sunday 5 December, whilst its cargo was transferred to two steam tugs, the *Stella* of Shoreham Harbour trustees and the *Mistletoe* which belonged to Captain Brazier. Gangs of men were engaged in taking off her cargo, a considerable proportion of which was spoiled. Hordes of people, from Worthing, Shoreham and the surrounding villages went to Lancing to look at the French vessel and watch the operations. Whilst at Kingston Wharf, crowds awaited the arrival of the cargo, which was landed quickly and taken away under the supervision of the Customs House officers.

Only one of the French crew of the *Edmund Gabriel* could speak English. He acted as interpreter for the others, when the Custom authorities, who took care of the crew's belongings, interviewed some of the ship's officers.

In the aftermath following the excitement of the shipwreck, the English sailors charged the French Captain with unmanly conduct, insisting that they could have saved their shipmate had not the French master denied them the use of his boat. Two of the French crew admitted that after the two ships had disentangled they could hear a man shouting from the brig, but said that in such boisterous conditions they could not have put down a boat, and furthermore it would not have been possible for anyone to survive in such a sea. They also insisted that it had been foggy at the time and that a S.E. wind had been blowing. They did agree with the Englishmen that the brig had remained afloat for about 20 minutes after the collision, but differed by insisting that nothing could possibly have been done to save the unfortunate man who, for some reason or other, had failed to scramble on board their vessel, as did his shipmates.

On the other hand, Captain Cooper denied that it had been foggy at the time of the collision, and stated that he had been able to see the barque for about a quarter of an hour before the crash. He further claimed that his own lights had been burning brightly, and that had the barque kept to her course no collision would have occurred. He also denied most emphatically that the wind had been very rough, or that the sea was heavy, saying that had the French Captain allowed a boat to be lowered, Winterflood might easily have been saved. When he had asked for a boat, he and his men were only too willing and anxious to man her, feeling confident that they could have saved their mate. But Captain Delaplanche had heeded not their entreaties, he had simply sailed away.

And so ended the desperate saga of a large French barque ramming a small brig, and the subsequent launch of the Worthing lifeboat which had answered the signal most promptly.

As by now a new up-to-date lifeboat had been ordered and was being built, this was the last time this particular lifeboat was launched on service. Under its first name the *Jane*, it had been launched for eight emergencies, rescueing six lives, between 1865 and 1880. After being re-named *Henry Harris* in 1880, three services saved four men.

Footnotes Ch. 8

[1] A reference to the original old *Sea House Inn*, a building where only the foundations remained, under the sea itself, which were visible betwen high and low water marks. Thomas Lindup married Mary Summer in 1777.
[2] There are still three very old capstans on Worthing beach today to the west of the Lido, and one near the *Half Brick Inn* to the east.

Ch. 9

Festive Times. 1887-8

The new lifeboat was completed by June 1887, and was ready for a ceremonious launching as part of the celebrations to commemorate the 50th anniversary of Queen Victoria's accession to the throne. Preparations and arrangements for the auspicious occasion had been taking place since Christmas, organised by a general committee of 52 local gentry including Mr. H. Hargood, chairman of the Worthing Branch R.N.L.I., who was in charge of the lifeboat and procession committee.

On Tuesday 21 June, in glorious weather, Worthing honoured this great event of the 19th century. This day was going to be a life-long remembrance for the citizens of Worthing. Early in the morning the church bells rang out a joyful peal, and most people were up early, busily engaged in completing the carnival decorations adorning their houses. The town had never before looked so cheerful, with all the public buildings and most of the private ones decorated with bunting, while strings of flags were suspended across the streets. A large number of tasteful and effective floral displays , which had taken a great deal of time and patience to arrange, were used. As well as the abundant use of bunting and flowers, many inhabitants expressed their loyalty by exhibiting appropriate devices and mottoes. All classes of people joined in to show their affection for their Sovereign.

The ornamental arch, erected at the pier entrance for the jubilee celebrations

The Jubilee Committee had decorated the entire length of the sea front with flags, creating a remarkably happy scene. An ornamental arch, erected at the pier entrance for the event, bore the words: 'Hail we thy jubilee', and 'Fifty years glorious reign'.

A full programme was planned for the day. At 8 a.m. the national anthem, sung by a choir of about 50 strong voices assembled on the top of the tower of Worthing's Christ Church, could be heard over most

67

of the town. Two hours later, short services of thanksgiving and prayer were held at all the churches and chapels in the town.

Liverpool Gardens where various public bodies gathered together for the parade

At 10.30 a.m. various public bodies assembled in Liverpool Gardens and adjacent roads to unite in procession. The procession, led by the band of the Royal Naval (Brighton) Volunteers and the Worthing Brass Band, started from Steyne Gardens at 11 o'clock. The principal thoroughfares were densely peopled, with many country visitors adding to the masses of excited local inhabitants, all crowding for a glimpse. Following the bands were the coastguards and H. Company of the 2nd Battalion Royal Sussex Regiment.

The new 34 feet long lifeboat, fully manned by a crew in cork lifejackets, was drawn on its carriage by eight horses along the very narrow Montague Street towards West Worthing. From some of the upper floors, instantaneous photographs were taken of the procession. Behind the new boat marched members of the Fishermen's Insurance Association, followed by the existing 32 feet long lifeboat which also had a full compliment of crew aboard, and was hauled by magnificent horses.

On reaching West Worthing the cavalcade, with members of the Jubilee Committee in Mr. Town's four-horse brake and the chairman and members of the Worthing Local Board in carriages, turned left, into what is now Heene Road, towards the Parade, returning by way of the seafront to the Steyne.

The procession, which included the Loyal Victoria Lodge of Oddfellows, the Ancient Order of Foresters, the Independent Order of Rechabites and the Worthing Medical Branch of Hearts of Oak Society, continued along Warwick Street. As they turned left into South Street, a drum and fife band followed close behind.

Also in the cortege were the two local volunteer fire brigades, from Worthing and West Worthing, with their engines.

After the two fire brigades came members of the two Worthing rowing clubs, the Amateur Boat Club and the Britannia Rowing Club, carrying their galleys. The procession was completed with the Ambulance Corps, Worthing Total Abstinence Union, St. George's Church of England, Temperance Society, and the Good Templars, while a brass band and the Cyclists' Club brought up the rear.

The carnival column, which had wound through the streets, halted near the pier and the new lifeboat was drawn onto the beach to the west of the pier.

The H. Company 2nd Volunteer Batallion Royal Sussex Regiment, under the command of Lieutenant

The Jubilee procession started from Steyne Gardens

W. S. Simpson, formed a line on the edge of the Parade opposite the Pier Bazaar. While a 1000 voice choir had assembled in an enclosure, specially erected for the occasion, on the beach to the west of the pier.

Mr. E. Henty J.P., chairman of the Jubilee Committee arrived with: Mr. & Mrs. Hargood; Rev. E. K. Elliott, Rector of the parish; Rev. S. L. Dixon, Vicar of St. George's; Mr. E. C. Patching, chairman of the Local Board, together with other members including the Clerk, Mr. W. Verrall. They seated themselves on a raised platform and the proceedings, arranged in connection with the launch of the lifeboat, commenced with the choir singing the National Anthem under the direction of Mr. W. H. Price, organist of the Chapel of Ease, and concluded with three hearty cheers from the massive ensemble of spectators.

Then the Coastguard fired a Royal Salute, and the Volunteers a feu de joie, followed by loud cheering as a mark of loyalty. Mr. F. Henty addressed the 10,000-strong assembly, congratulating them upon their presence to show their loyalty to their Queen, whose beneficent reign had extended over the long period of 50 years. After apologising for the absence of Mr. Graham, the District Inspector of the National Lifeboat Institution, who was to have officially presented the new boat to the town, and of Lady Fletcher, who had been expected to attend to christen the new lifeboat, Mr. Henty went on to mention that the first lifeboat stationed at Worthing was secured chiefly through the efforts of Admiral Hargood, father of the present chairman of the local Lifeboat Committee. He concluded by asking Mrs. Hargood to name the new lifeboat.

But before this was done, Mr. Hargood, on behalf of the National Lifeboat Institution, presented the new boat, built by Woolfe for £371, to the town. And, in the course of an excellent speech, spoke of the great services rendered by the fleet of lifeboats stationed around the coast of the United Kingdom and the Channel Islands. When he told the audience that, whereas in 1837 the number of boats connected with the institution was but 40, and the number of lives saved up to that time only 3,600, the Institution could now point to 291 boats and a grand total of 33,000 lives saved, it cheered rapturously.

The Rector of Broadwater read the following prayer, which had been used on the occasion of the first launch of a R.N.L.I. lifeboat. "O Thou great eternal Father, who inhabitest eternity, and hast promised to dwell with that man who is of a contrite spirit, we pray Thee to pour Thy blessing upon us and the work in which we are now engaged. Thou art of all power and might, Thou stretchest out the heavens like a curtain, Thou walkest upon the wings of the wind, Thou makest the clouds Thy chariot, Thou rulest the raging of the sea, and when the waves thereof arise Thou stillest them. In Thy hands are all the issues of life and death; but inasmuch as Thou art willing to act through human instruments, we beseech Thee to pour Thy blessing upon this lifeboat, which we now present unto Thee, and we beseech Thee that it may be serviceable in the preservation of the lives of our poor sailors, who, for the maintenance and support of their families, face the dangers of the ocean, and tempests of the stormiest sea. We know Thou willest not the death of one sinner, but rather that he should turn from his wickedness and live; we therefore pray Thee, Lord, to spare our sailors from a sudden death, for it is a fearful thing to enter Thy presence unprepared without a moment's warning. We need all the time that Thy mercy will grant unto us that we may prepare to meet our God, that we may repent us of our sins, and make up our accounts that we may render them to Thyself. We pray Thee for the crew. Grant that they may be Godfearing men, and not trust to the raging billows through the power of their own strength, or of their iron will, but that they may feel that it is not by might or by power, 'but by My Spirit saith the Lord', and that all their attempts are vain unless Thou givest the increase. Grant that they may be instruments in the hands of Thy Providence; and that many a wife may breathe the prayer 'God bless the lifeboat and their gallant crew', that many a Christian sailor may say from his heart 'For these and all ,Thy mercies O God, we thank Thee,' and that many a sinner, saved by this boat, may be brought to repentance. O Lord, we pray Thee to bless all those who have aided in this noble undertaking. Grant that they may have the reward of that promise 'Forasmuch as ye have done it unto one of the least of these My brethren, ye have done it unto Me. Spare their lives, bless them in their homes and in their families; and grant that when they are called from this world, they may enter into the joy of their Lord."

The new lifeboat, fully manned, was drawn on its carriage by eight horses

This was followed by a hymn for those at sea sung by the choir and the audience together:

Eternal Father, strong to save,
Whose arm hath bound the restless wave,
Who bid'st the mighty ocean deep
Its own appointed limits keep;
O hear us when we cry to Thee
For those in peril on the sea.

O Christ, whose voice the waters heard
And hushed their raging at Thy word,
Who walkedst on the foaming deep,
And calm amidst its rage did'st sleep;
O hear us when we cry to Thee
For those in peril on the sea.

Most Holy Spirit, Who didst brood
Upon the chaos dark and rude,
And bid its angry tumult cease,
And give, for wild confusion, peace;
O hear us when we cry to Thee
For those in peril on the sea.

O Trinity of love and power,
Our brethren shield in danger's hour;
From rock and tempest, fire and foe,
Protect them wheresoe'er they go;
Thus evermore shall rise to Thee
Glad hymns of praise from land and sea.

The cavalcade turned left into what is now Heene Road

The signal was then given and Mrs. Hargood christened the new lifeboat, "I name this boat the *Henry Harris*." Amid enthusiastic and animated applause from the tightly-packed crowds on the pier and the Parade the boat glided down the beach and into the sea, followed by a rapturous rendition of Rule Britannia.

Volunteer fire brigades in procession with their engines going past the *Steyne Hotel*. (The building survives today, but without the magnificent porchway

The new lifeboat had been paid for from a legacy bequeathed by the late Mr. Henry Harris of Streatham in London, who had started his business career from a shop in Warwick Street, Worthing. In 1845 he had become a partner in the firm of Maynard & Haines, Naval and military outfitters and general agents of the Port of London.

The new *Henry Harris*, official number ON 109, looked magnificent as she was put through her paces: the lifeboatmen capsized her and, being a self-righting craft, she immediately uprighted herself. Other tests followed, all of which were entirely satisfactory, for the benefit of the greatly interested spectators.

While the lifeboat trials were taking place, local rowing clubs competed against each other in five four-oared galleys, for a prize worth £5. The exciting race ended in victory for *The Minstrel*, crewed by E. Paine, H. Feest, J. Cove and A. Stubbs.

At 1.15 p. m., the aged poor and widows of Worthing and West Worthing were entertained at the new Assembly Rooms by the Dinner Committee under the presidency of Edwin Henty Esq. About 300 sat down to a substantial dinner of roast and boiled beef, mutton, ham and veal, with plum puddings and fruit pies for afters.

In the adjoining Drill Hall the Volunteers were regaled, at the invitation of the officers of the Company. While in the Minor Hall of the Assembly Rooms, Mr. Hargood provided a repast for his gallant lifeboatmen.

In the afternoon an immense concourse of people gathered in the People's Park (now called Home-field Park), where various sports were indulged in, competing for 1st, 2nd and 3rd monetary prizes. The first event at 2.30 p. m. was the 100 yards running race, followed by a sack race and a quarter mile race. A donkey race took place where no whips or spurs were allowed, and then a one mile tricycle race, a blindfolded wheelbarrow race, 100 yards bucket race, one mile bicycle race and a three-legged egg and spoon race. At the end of the lengthy programme a greasy pole competition took place, where contestants attempted to shin-up to the top of a slippery pole for legs of mutton.

While the races were proceeding, a concert was given in another part of the Park by a stirling choir composed of children from the various elementary schools. Assisted by their schoolmasters and mistresses and under the direction of Mr. H. Lea, several part songs, glees, anthems and choruses were efficiently rendered.

The dignitaries seated themselves on this raised platform erected on the beach to the west of the pier. Note the two recently-built pier entrance kiosks which replaced the single square-shaped one

At 5.30 p.m. about 2,100 children, all those attending the Day and Sunday Schools of Worthing and West Worthing, sat down to tea in the Park, and afterwards their teachers were similarly entertained. The children were very proud to receive a handsome Jubilee Medal each on such an exciting day.

Celebrations continued into the evening. From 7.30 p.m. the two military bands, that of the Royal Naval Artillery Volunteers and that of the H. Company 2nd Sussex R. V., played in the Park. At the same time the Rhine Band, which had accompanied the choir earlier in the day, performed on the Parade.

A grand display of fireworks by Messrs. Brock & Co. took place after sunset near the ornamental lake in the Park. The presentation began with a salute by aerial maroon at 9.30 p.m. followed by the ascent of two large baloons with magnesium lights and fireworks. At one time the grounds were illuminated by large Crystal Palace Lights, and by a great golden fountain flanked on either side by a revolving fountain of jewel jets. Rockets with multi-coloured stars went up, some discharging 'dragon flies'. Batteries of mines were exploded and shells 16 inches in diameter were discharged. A device called the Chromatrope Wheels, flanked on either side by two revolving suns, was particularly popular, which followed a curtain of fire, 30 feet long. An aerial wheatsheaf was produced by the simultaneous discharge of 80 large rockets, followed by a display of parachute and shooting star rockets. Some of the shells were 30 inches in circumference with C. T. Brock & Co.'s latest novelties. The finale included a portrait of Her Majesty the Queen in firework form and a special device whereby the words 'Worthing's Loyal Congratulations' were illuminated.

At 10 p.m. the town and the seafront were brilliantly lit up. . The Town Hall and other public buildings were ablaze with colours, as were Liverpool Gardens, the Convent, and numerous business premises and private houses. The seafront and the pier were illuminated from end to end by thousands of variegated lamps and Japanese lanterns; while on the sea a burning boat added to the effectiveness of the scene. The spectacle was a most imposing one and was viewed by many thousands of people.

The launching of the *Henry Harris* lifeboat at the naming ceremony

At 10.45 p.m. the exciting and exhilarating events of this special day were brought to a close when the bands united and played the National Anthem, after which the tumultuous crowds gave three deafening patriotic cheers for the Queen. Coincidentally, 21 June, being the longest day of the year, also heralded the longest procession that Worthing had ever seen. Even though this was even the largest programme of events ever staged in Worthing up until this time, the thousands of people who joined in the revelry were well-behaved: there was no disorder and no nasty incidents.

Later that year, the stalwart Worthing lifeboatmen were invited to the Lord Mayor's Show in London, where they crewed the new lifeboat for Huntstanton in Norfolk, the *Licensed Victualler*. Mounted on its carriage and manned by the Worthing crew arrayed in their oilies and cork jackets, it was a very interesting addition to the show, and evidently appealed to the sympathies of the crowd more strongly than some of the gaudier but less serviceable displays in the carnival.

The procession, on Wednesday 9 November, passed through Newgate Street, which was lined with eager sightseers. The Worthing lifeboat crew were received with great enthusiasm, which rose into a storm of cheers when they were handed a magnificent bouquet of Neapolitan violets. It bore the inscription 'To the brave Worthing lifeboatmen, as a mark of appreciation from their fellow townsman, T. H. Roberts of Sompting.'

Rain had fallen heavily during the previous night, and all through the morning persistent drizzle prevailed. It was seldom that such unfavourable weather was associated with the great City pageant, and was most prejudicial to the profuse decorations in the streets. Another effect of the miserable conditions was that many people, who would otherwise have gone to see the procession, stayed at home.

An important Metropolitan contemporary said that the men who looked really at home, and were quite in keeping with what might almost be termed a 'water procession', such as was once the civic custom, were undoubtedly the Worthing crew who, with their oilskins and sou'-esters, peaked their oars and stood beside the tiller, in the Hunstanton lifeboat. Their dress seemed so peculiarly appropiate to the dismal conditions of the day, that the crowd, amused and delighted, cheered the heroes of the sea. The men, who had been at their posts since 10 a.m., endured a great deal of discomfort during the six hour procession. But they were used to such conditions. Indeed, it was often far worse at sea.

In September 1887 a Worthing fishing boat was caught in a perilous position out at sea. The lugger *Heroine*, owned by Mr. W. Lucas of Richmond Road, had put off from Worthing on Thursday 1 September. But when she hadn't returned the following day as planned, her prolonged absence gave rise to grave fears by the relatives of the crew, as they had only taken three small loaves - enough provisions for one night.

The turmoil unfolded as the lugger had sailed eastwards, and the seven fishermen had cast the nets off Brighton on Thursday evening.

Spectators on the beach braving a shower of rain as they watch the lifeboat manouvres

Suddenly, a terrific gale blew up and drove the *Heroine* in towards Beachy Head. All the nets and ropes broke away and were lost; the bulwarks were washed in and the bowsprit broken; and the crew very nearly lost their lives.

After a hellish voyage, the exhausted and starving crew brought up the lugger at Dungeness for shelter, remaining there for the Saturday morning tide. Whereupon she proceeded to Ramsgate, where the master, S. Bacon[1], sent a telegram reassuring Mr. Lucas of the crew's safety. The damage to the boat and the loss of equipment represented a loss of £200. As Mr. Lucas was a member of the Worthing Fishermen's Mutual Insurance Association, he made a claim, but the amount he received was limited to only one third of the total damages.

One night during September an exceptionally high tide washed away three boats from Worthing beach and left their owners with serious losses. A public appeal was launched to purchase three replacement craft, but it only realised a fraction of the sum required.

Exceptionally severe gales at the end of September blew out the dials on the Town Hall clock and smashed some of the large windows at the *Royal Hotel*. Boatmen drew their craft up from the beach and out of harm's way before the sea washed over the Parade.

Throughout Great Britain generally, splendid service had been rendered in the saving of life during 1887 by gallant coxwains and crews of R.N.L.I. lifeboats. But for the timely aid given, resulting in the rescue of 368 persons, many would have drowned. In addition, no fewer than 10 vessels had been saved, by the lifeboats, from total destruction or had been helped by them into a safe haven. Besides launches resulting in the saving of life, the lifeboats had put out to sea 89 times in reply to signals of distress, only to find that their aid had not been required, or that the signals had been made in error.

In the year, the Society had also given rewards for the saving of 204 lives by means of shore boats, fishing boats and other means; resulting in the Institution having been instrumental in rescuing a total of 572 lives in 1887. This brought the total number of lives saved since the founding of the Institution to 33,243.

At this time the main committee of the R.N.L.I. made an urgent and special appeal to the British public for funds to enable them to replace a considerable number of their 291 lifeboats stationed around the coastline by new improved boats. They had already been compelled, in furtherance of this project, to draw on the Institution's capital to the extent of nearly £18,000.

Five four-oared galleys from Worthing clubs preparing for the start of a race.

Worthing had been fortunate in having its 21 year old lifeboat replaced, by a new model of the latest type, in the middle of the year, and would soon be launched on its first active service.

It happened during the fourth week of January 1888. At about 3.30 a.m. on Wednesday 25th, the brig *Albert H. Locke*, carrying coals from Shields to Littlehampton, had lost its way and ran aground during thick foggy conditions when visibility was extremely poor. The crew, of the ship stranded on the sands about ½ mile opposite the *West Worthing Hotel*, sent up a rocket, which was perceived and promptly answered by the Coastguard. Lifeboat officials were informed, but their help was not required as the sea was quite calm, so the lifeboat crew were not summoned. But the Coastguards did go off to the brig's assistance in their own galley.

Later in the morning two steam tugs arrived from Shoreham, but their aid was not soon enough to be of any help, because the tide had fallen considerably. It was decided to lighten the 206 ton brig of Sunderland in the hope of getting her off, should the weather keep fine.

But during the night, the drama became more intense when a strong westerly gale lashed the stranded vessel and she drifted eastward.

In answer to a distress signal from her crew at 6.30 the following morning, the honorary secretary, George Piggott, ordered the lifeboat to be launched, and the gun was immediately fired to summon 12 crewmen. The tide was almost in full flood, and within 15 minutes, the *Henry Harris* was afloat in the heavily running sea.

At 7 a.m. under a cloudy sky the lifeboat reached the vessel and her master, William Booth, five crew and four others were taken on board from the brig, fearing that it would break up.

The *Henry Harris* returned to shore, performing very well, and safely landed the 10 survivors at 8.15 a.m., transferring them to the charge of Mr. J. Burt, the honorary secretary of the Shipwrecked Mariners' Aid Society, who made arrangements for their accommodation at the *King's Arms Inn*, to recuperate before being sent home by train the following day.

The lifeboat, however, was slightly damaged. Part of the steering mechanism had broken and the gunwhale was chipped, necessitating immediate repairs.

Remuneration for those who took part in the service was paid accordingly. The honorary secretary authorised payments of 10/- for each of the crew, 3/- for each man who assisted in launching and hauling up the lifeboat, and 5/- each for the hire of four horses in transporting the lifeboat to the site of the rescue.

Meanwhile, fear began to spread among the large number of sightseers who had accumulated on the beach, that the combination of strong wind and high tide would drive the stranded brig still further east, and could endanger the pier. The service of the tug *Mistletoe* of Shoreham was again called upon and she attempted to tow the vessel off, but again found it impossible to move her.

The ornamental lake in the People's Park (now called Homefield Park)

During this high tide the *Albert H. Locke* was knocked by the swell some 500 yards in a north easterly direction. Seeing the danger threatening the pier, Mr. H. Hargood drew the attention of the pier directors to the situation. At a hurriedly arranged meeting of the directors, the brig's captain agreed to instruct the lifeboat crew to lay out one of the bow anchors to try and hold her in position, and the Pier Company would settle the cost thus incurred.

Yet Thursday night's tide carried the brig 400 yards still further eastward, bringing her close to the beach opposite Augusta Place. The tug again tried her best, but the ship was labouring very heavily and straining with every movement of the sea, and the tug's efforts were to no avail.

Here the brig stayed. An examination showed that she was completely waterlogged and unseaworthy in every respect. After being condemned, she was officially taken charge of by the Coastguard as a wreck.

Carts were employed removing coal from the stranded brig, which belonged to George Judson, about 30 tons being landed and deposited on the Parade at West Worthing. And men busily engaged themselves in dismantling the craft, watched by large crowds of onlookers with avid interest.

This first service launch of this new *Henry Harris*, turned out to be its first successful rescue. The lifeboat crew very proudly chalked-up '1888 Jan 26th, Brig. *Albert H. Locke* of Sunderland, 10 lives saved', on the station scoreboard.

Footnotes Ch. 9

[1] S. Bacon - a relation of E. Bacon, the lifeboatman.

The Town Hall where the clock was damaged by very high winds

Ch. 10

Leisure, Litigation And Lives Lost. 1888-90

A three-masted brig, the *Arabian*, on a voyage from Shields to Plymouth with a cargo of coal, ran aground off Worthing on Monday 16 April 1888. Early in the morning she was spotted opposite West Buildings, and, fortunately, she was soon towed off without sustaining any damage. Her master, a Mr. Patten, was only too pleased that she didn't suffer the same fate as the brig *Albert H. Locke*, which was wrecked after running ashore in the same area the previous year.

Another type of event that had happened here before occured again on Saturday 14 July, the capture of a large shark by Worthing fishermen. The 600 lb fish was caught 11 miles off Worthing, hauled on board the *Lizzie* fishing lugger by a pulley and affixed to the mainmast. The boat, under the command of its master, Mr. Benn, returned to Worthing with its haul of dogfish and one shark, whereupon the 8 feet long creature was exhibited on the beach opposite Bath Place. Many people who subsequently went to see the huge shark were amazed by its huge bulk, three feet across the fins.

The beach opposite Bath Place with the pier in the background

From heavy fish to heavy fishing boats. As luggers weighed several tons or more, care was necessary when manoeuvring them on the beach. On Tuesday 31 July, when several fishermen were lifting the lugger *Reform*, in the course of routine maintenance, one of them was seriously injured in an accident. They had lifted it in order to place a barrel under its side, but when the barrel took the full weight of the lugger it burst, and the boat fell on Mr. W. Miles. The fisherman was taken to his home in Marine Place and a doctor was called. He soon arrived and diagnosed severe internal injuries as well as several broken ribs.

Those fishermen, who increased the danger in their lifestyle by doubling as lifeboat crew, launched the lifeboat on quarterly practises to keep themselves ready for emergencies. The full compliment of crew drilled regularly, four times a year, regardless of the weather or the state of the sea.

The lifeboat itself was the subject of yearly inspections by the district inspector of the R.N.L.I., Mr. C. E. F. Cunningham. Arrangements for each visit were made some time in advance, and every time the *Henry Harris* was launched for testing, come hail or shine.

The Worthing lifeboat was not called out to a vessel, wrecked some distance westward along the Channel, but the prevailing wind subsequently washed some of its flotsam ashore on Worthing beach. This was the result of a collision off Bognor at 1 a.m. on Thursday 7 March 1889 involving the 1,420 ton barque *Vandalia*. It collided with a craft, whose identity was at first unknown, but which went down with all hands.

The *Vandalia* of St. Johns, New Brunswick, had been bound for London with a cargo of petroleum from New York, when the encounter took place. At the moment of impact one of the watch, stationed as lookout on the bows, was killed by a falling anchor. This barque was badly damaged, and, as a precautionary measure, its crew took to their boats, but remained by the vessel. At about 4 a.m., when The Vandalia appeared to be sinking rapidly, the shipwrecked crew in their two tiny craft rowed away from the mother ship. They experienced some rough times in their ordeal, endeavouring to reach land. Finally, one boat went ashore at Aldwick and the other at Middleton.

The 1,420 ton barque *Vandalia*

Meanwhile the barque did not sink but drifted eastward and eventually grounded off Brighton. Almost immediately its decks began to break up, and the cargo of hundreds of petroleum casks was soon floating in the water. Locals waded into the sea up to their armpits to retrieve some of these floating barrels.

One man, Richard Cook, for many years in the employ of Captain Fred Collins, suddenly dropped dead in the water. It was widely believed that the combined effects of cold and excitement had been too much of a shock.

Another man was remanded for stealing a cask of petroleum from Brighton beach.

When the hold of the *Vandalia* was searched on Thursday night only two or three hundred casks remained out of a total of 9,916. Many of them had been driven along in the heavy sea by the strong wind, which had veered round to S.S.E., as far as Worthing and Goring.

Great excitement abounded here on the Friday as a large number of barrels and miscellaneous wreckage floated about in front of the town. Pieces of piano and a quantity of wreckage bearing the name *Duke of Buccleuch* were washed up in the vicinity of Worthing.

This steamship, which had been on an outward bound trip with an assorted cargo from Antwerp, and was known to have passed Dover between 4 and 5 p.m. on Wednesday, was considered certain to be the vessel with which the *Vandalia* collided and went down with all 47 hands still on board.

Fishermen and others were busily engaged in bringing the escaped cargo, which included a great amount of paraffin barrels, ashore. By Monday, the total number of barrels secured on the beach opposite the Coastguard Station was 700, extending from West Street to Queen's Road. At 9 a.m. on 11 March a cover from a seaman's box, marked *SS Duke of Buccleuch* and with the commercial code of signals on it, was picked up on Worthing beach.

A representative of the Eastern Steamship Company, owners of the doomed steamer, travelled to Worthing to identify some of the miscellaneous wreckage, including: a case containing 20 packages of cloth, a case of glass globes, a lug sail, three ship's ladders, two large gratings, a few books and a looking-glass. A door bearing the name *Duke of Buccleuch* and a mallet with the recent inscription *Vandalia* on its side needed no identification. All of this wreckage was taken charge of by the Chief Officer of the Coastguard, Mr Billett, pending its transfer to the Receiver of Wrecks. It was not yet known at this stage what amount of salvage money would be distributed among those who had assisted in securing the wreckage, as it depended on certain contingent expenses. The loss was immense, for the value of the steamship which was roughly estimated at £10,000 and the value of the cargo at £8,000 were only partly covered by insurance.

The badly damaged *Vandalia* stranded off Brighton

On Friday 15 March the wreck of the *Vandalia* was sold by auction for £640, and its new owner carried out essential repairs to enable it to be floated off. At midday on Tuesday 30 April it was towed past Worthing, on its way to Southampton, to complete her repairs. After refitting her, the new owner resold it for £6,000, which produced a handsome profit of about £4,000 after expenses. Not a bad investment!

On Monday 8 April, Messrs. Robert Lyon & Co., under an order of the High Court of Justice, Queen's Bench Division, auctioned 8,000 barrels of petroleum, part of the cargo of the wrecked *Vandalia*, at the Old Ship Hotel in Brighton. The room was crowded and competition was rather keen for the lots, which included a quantity of empty barrels and miscellaneous items. The barrels themselves were sold in lots of 20 and 40, and the successful bidders, of which a Mr. Wiber of Chapel Road, Worthing was one, paid an average price of 13s. per barrel.

The lots being auctioned were those secured by the following Coastguard Stations: Kingston, 73 barrels; Goring, 601; Worthing, 924; Lancing, 1,959; Fishersgate, 204; Brighton & Hove, 2,634; Blackrock, 402; Portobello & Rottingdean, 718; and Newhaven, 344.

An enquiry was held into the collision between this three-masted sailing vessel and the larger 3,010 ton gross screw steamer *Duke of Buccleuch* of Barrow. Mr. Justice Butt was of the opinion that no blame was to be attached to the master of the *Vandalia* for abandoning his ship, that he had properly navigated her, and that his certificate should not be dealt with. And the Court also exonerated the late Captain Langlois of the *Duke of Buccleuch*.

The owners of the *Vandalia*, however, were insistent that the skipper of the steamer had been negligent. Represented by Mr. Cohen Q.C., Mr. Mayburgh Q.C. and Dr. Raikes, the barque's owners went to the Court of Appeal, and on Saturday 7 December the Master of the Rolls and Lords Justices Lindley and Lopes reversed the earlier decision of the Court of Enquiry, deciding that the 380 foot *Duke of Buccleuch* was alone to blame for the collision. Sir W. Phillimore Q.C., Mr. Barnes Q.C. and Mr. Laing for the respondents were naturally disappointed by the decision.

The *Duke of Buccleuch* which went down with all 47 hands after a collision with the *Vandalia*

In 1988 a small group of local divers found the wreck of the *Duke of Buccleuch*, 18 miles off Littlehampton. Examination of the hull revealed that there was a break amidships, where she must have been struck by the bow of the *Vandalia*. It would now appear in the light of this latest evidence that the barque was to blame for the collision.

Among the general cargo on the ship, these divers found a large quantity of porcelain plates and drinking glasses. Also recovered have been a number of portholes, some with brass deadlights on them. An unusual characteristic is that they have the ship's name embossed on the inside face of the deadlight.

The summer of 1889 brought mixed favours: from a heavy thunderstorm to good catches of fish, and even steamboat trips.

A heavy thunderstorm, which lasted nearly an hour, and the violence of which had probably not been paralleled in local experience, broke over the town between 4 p.m. and 5 p.m. on Thursday 6 June. Considerable alarm was caused by the fierceness of the storm when at its height, 'The Bays' in Lyndhurst Road, a detached villa occupied by Mr. J. V. Shaw, was struck by lightening, one of the chimney pots was completely shattered, and part of the cement work below carried away. The house of Mr. H. Best in Newland Road was also struck, slates torn off the roof and a stove in the laundry below displaced. At Messrs. Barnwell and Magness's nursery in Crescent Road, a chimney on the stokehouse was struck, causing considerable damage to the building and apparatus for heating the greenhouses.

While a couple of week's later, large quantities of fresh herrings found their way into mackeral nets. The fish, of excellent flavour, realised good prices.

Two special steamboat trips were announced for the *Queen of the Bay* from Worthing Pier to Eastbourne and back, on Tuesday 6 August and Thursday 8 August, departing at 9.15 a.m. and returning at 7 p.m. The return fare was 5s., and passengers were also conveyed to Brighton.

At the beginning of July, local rowing clubs engaged in a series of races to the delight of thousands of spectators on the beach and lining the pier. The four main events included a race for four-oared galleys and one for novices.

The Worthing Amateur Boat Club and the Britannia Rowing Club from Worthing were represented in two of the events at Newhaven Regatta on Monday 5 August.

A steamboat arriving at Worthing Pier from Eastbourne. Note the newly erected pavilion at the southern end of the pier. This view was reproduced from a rather crinkly photograph

The Amateur Club crew, E. Paine, F. Dean[1], G. Paskins, A. F. Corney(stroke) and Corney(cox) started in the contest in their new *Clasper*, but unfortunately collided with the Eastbourne boat, inflicting serious damage on their handsome cedarwood galley and getting a good ducking themselves. The crew and their boat were picked up by a steamer.

The Brittania captain was wise in not using their new galley. His crew, H. Feest, J. Newman[2], E. Long, W. Pacey,(stroke), and Belton[3](cox), secured second prize in the race for junior amateur fours, being beaten by a Newhaven crew who had by far the best berth. They won four inkstands with a total value of £3; and the win counted as one point for the South Coast Challenge Cup.

This was the only prize brought home to Worthing, although they were represented in the junior amateur pairs as follows: J. Newman[2] and E. Long, Britannia; H. Feest and W. Pacey, Britannia; and A. F. Corney and G. Paskins, Amateur.

The prize of £20 for professional four-oared galleys was won by Southsea, Portsmouth coming second; and in the international four-oared galley race, a Brighton Excelsior crew was first, and St. Leonards second.

Postponed from 14 August on account of the unfavourable weather then prevailing, the Worthing Annual Regatta was held on Monday 2 September, under somewhat more favourable conditions of wind and tide. The air was close in the early morning, but as the day advanced the heat was agreeably tempered by a breeze that momentarily acquired force, and made its influence felt over the surface of the sea as the tide gradually came in. Sunshine was of comparitively brief duration, and its total disappearance was succeeded by a condition of gloom that presaged a coming storm. When the programme was partly through rain did actually fall, albeit in exceedingly minute proportions and then stopped. There was a lowering of the temperature, but this was more an advantage than otherwise to the spectators.

The freshening breeze was of the greatest possible assistance to the sailing boats as they sped over the triangular course. But those who took part in the rowing heats would have wished for a little less swell, the lumpiness of the water increased the effort of the oarsmen, and almost submerged some of the frailer craft.

Never before in the long history of this annual meeting had so many sightseers been brought together:

special trains had been laid on to enable people from Town to visit. A steamer arrived from Ventnor, and two from Brighton, with crowds of spectators. A boat from Bournemouth was expected but did not arrive, due to the rough weather on that part of the coast.

Annual Regatta with packed crowds upon the pier and on the beach

In accordance with a well-recognised custom, the leading business establishments in the town closed for the afternoon, thus enabling their employees to join in the fun and excitement of the occasion.

When the proceedings were at their height, the scene was most animated: the largest collection of spectators on the pier, on the beach and in boats on the sea, that had ever yet witnessed the Regatta. Four thousand people trod the pier deck that day.

On the Parade were vendors, and street entertainers who performed tricks. People were entertained by music in three places: the Rhine Band in the centre of the pier; Mr. T. Binstead's brass band to the west; and Mr. G. F. Wright's brass band to the east of the structure.

There were 13 events and nearly £90 was bestowed in prizes: the professional watermen, most of whom were lifeboatmen, received their prizes in cash, whilst the amateurs received theirs in kind, from various tradesmen.

At 2 p.m. proceedings commenced with a race for Worthing watermen in lug sail boats not exceeding 17 feet in length: J. Hutchinson won the first prize of £3 in the 16 foot *Seagull*; A. Beck[4] took away the 2nd prize of £1 10s. in the 13 foot *Mystery*; the *Ebenezer* came 3rd winning 15s. for F. Burden; the 4th prize of 10s. was won by a Mr. Hutchinson in the 16 foot *Here We Are*; while G. Belton in the 15 foot *Ada* and T. Clark[5] in the *Lord Beaconsfield* were unplaced.

In the second event, for licensed quarter boats belonging to Worthing watermen (fishermen and boatmen), the *Myrtle* came home first with a long lead for S. Wingfield who collected £2 prize money. But there was a very close gap between the 2nd and third boats, the *Arthur John* piloted by F. Burden having less than a length in its favour over Bill Marshall's *Lily*. Bill's brother Harry won the 4th prize of 10s. in the *Lily of the Valley*, and J. Churcher's *Cock Robin* was unplaced.

In the second heat of the junior amateur pairs, E. Easton and R. Blann (a distant relation of mine), representing Newhaven Rowing Club, came a poor third, being beaten to second place by H. Feest and W. Pacey for the Worthing Britannia Rowing Club (B.R.C.). The latter went on to win the third prize in the final of goods to the value of 15s. E. D. Paine and F. Dean for the Worthing Amateur Boat Club (A.B.C.) came fourth, while Southsea took first prize and Littlehampton came 2nd.

After Worthing teams finished unplaced in the sailing boats race and the one for senior amateur sculls, the crowds of spectators were delighted when Worthing B.R.C. crews, in boats not exceeding 30 feet, came first and third in the junior amateur fours. The winning team, H. Feest, J. Newman, E. Long, W.

Pacey(stroke), Belton(cox), romped over the finishing line even before the 2nd boat had reached the eastern buoys, to qualify for the 1st prize worth £6.

During the course of the afternoon, there was a youths swimming race, other aquatic sports, and greasy pole walking.

In the event for Worthing sailing boats not exceeding 15 feet, the 1st prize of £2 10s. went to R. Clarke[5] in his 12 foot *Kittie*; 2nd was W. Sayers in the 12 foot *Iolanthe*, winning £1 10s.; J. Belton[3] achieved 3rd place in the 11 foot 6 inch *Star*; and C. H. Aldridge was fourth in his 12 foot *Gazelle*.

Then followed an event for second-class three-oared boats belonging to Worthing watermen. The four boats that entered all kept well together throughout, and the difference that distinguished them at the finish was comparitively slight, the second and third boats being especially near to one another when the gun was fired.

All four winners were lifeboatmen. Charles Lee , in the *Rapid*, was awarded the first prize of £2; G. Belton in *Alcey* came 2nd, winning £1 10s., third was Bill Marshall in *Pansy*, taking away £1 in cash; and F. Burden was last in *Florence*.

Then followed the senior amateur pairs and the Challenge Cup Race, where the winning positions were filled by teams from other towns.

Worthing A.B.C. came 2nd and 4th in the junior amateur sculls, C. R. Ramsay and J. Cove respectively.

Worthing, Eastbourne, St. Leonards, and Hastings had entered for the novices' race, but all failed to appear at the starting point apart from the Worthing team. Accordingly another Worthing crew was hastily assembled to make a race. A close contest developed between the two Britannia boats, the winners having but a very slight advantage at the finish. The runners-up were Feest, Poland, Knight, Botting(stroke), and Belton(cox) who had fouled the buoy-line, which deprived them of a decided advantage which up to that time they were enjoying. The winners, Biggs, Slaughter, Muller, Butcher(stroke) and Feest(cox), took away the first prize valued at £4.

Seven lifeboatmen entered the final race of the day, for pair-oared boats belonging to Worthing watermen. It was won by Fred Collier in *Mabel* and he collected £1 10s. prize money; Harry Marshall in *Thistle* came second, winning £1; Frank Collier in *Grace Darling* was next, to receive 10s; Steve Wingfield was placed fourth in *Daisy* winning 5s.; George Belton in *Ethol*, fifth; Bill Marshall(Harry's father) in *Rosie*, sixth; and Charles Lee in *Fred*, came last.

The prizes were distributed without any ceremony whatsoever, the winners were quite simply required to present themselves at Sumner House, the secretary's residence, to receive their awards.

At 7.30 p.m. the gates of Beach House Park were opened to admit the many hundreds of people who flocked to witness the customary display of fireworks, and for whose entertainment selections were played alternately by the Rhine Band, Mr. T. Binstead's band, and Mr. G. F. Wright's band before the show of pyrotechnics commenced. The best items were a figure of a fiery man who performed somersaults to the great amusement of the spectators, and a really capital set piece 'Britannia rules the waves'. At about 9.15 the last one was discharged and the Regatta was over for another year.

A few weeks later Worthing watermen enjoyed a successful rural excursion in one of Mr. Town's four-horse brakes. The outing, arranged by Mr. W. J. Butcher, started at an early hour leaving Worthing on the London road. They enjoyed the drive through Ashington and Adversane to Wisborough Green, where dinner was provided for them; and with local preparations in progress for the annual fair at the latter village they appreciated the happy atmosphere. They then returned to Adversane for the rest of the day where some dancing took place, before returning to Worthing at 8 p.m.

From happy sunny summer days I will now move forward to the winter when a succession of high tides culminated in an overflowing of the sea, on Thursday 23 January 1890, when Worthing shared in the havoc caused by a terrific gale that swept the south coast.

For some time before high water, sightseers gathered in considerable numbers on the seafront, and when the probability of an overflow became imminent, townspeople went down to witness the unusual sight. They were certainly rewarded for taking the trouble, in the grandeur of the spectacle before them, which had had no parallel since New Year's Day 1877, when a similar visitation had occassioned serious damage.

The sight of the waves rising high was incredibly outstanding and by 12 noon, assisted by a fierce westerly wind, the sea began to come over the Parade, casting shingle and seaweed in every direction. The pier stood the test exceedingly well, protected to a certain extent by the substantial landing stage.

For some time the roadway between the *Royal Hotel* and the *Marine Hotel* was impassable, and South Street shopkeepers made hasty preparations to protect their premises. But although the water went just beyond the junction of South Street and Montague Street, it did not remain in the road long because several of the Local Board employees were engaged in keeping the surface drains clear.

Rough Sea at Splash Point, Worthing.

Townsfolk experiencing the excitement of watching the violently powerful sea

It was estimated that the total amount of damage to the Worthing sea defences was not less than £400 and the repairs were scheduled over a lengthy period. In consequence of damage to the beach, the issue of permits for the removal of material from the foreshore was temporarily suspended.

Six weeks after the storm, the District Inspector of the R.N.L.I. visited the Worthing Lifeboat Station for his annual inspection of the lifeboat. It was launched at 3.15 p.m. on Friday 14 March in a calm sea and was put through various evolutions under the instructions of the inspector, Mr. Cunningham Graham. Hundreds of spectators had gathered on the pier and along the beach to watch the coxwain, Charles Lee, and his 12 crew in their familiar red caps and cork lifejackets putting the *Henry Harris* through its paces for 45 minutes.

The next day the inspector, together with the Worthing lifeboat chairman, Mr. H. Hargood, went on to Shoreham to assist in the ceremonial launching of a new lifeboat, the *William Restell.*

On the following Wednesday a Worthing lugger, owned by Alfred Beck[4], was wrecked off the French coast. The *Secret* had left Shoreham Harbour at about 11 a.m. in moderate weather, making for the French coast to dredge for scallops, with a crew of six. Four Worthing fishermen: John Tester[8] (master), George Belton and Jo Street(both lifeboatmen) and Seth Street; and two Shoreham seamen.

The saga began about 12 hours into the voyage, when the skipper was about to take his turn on deck. The two Shoreham crew, who were both acquainted with navigating the coast, told him that they could not discern some lights.

Something was wrong!

John Tester ordered his crew to lay-to, but one of them declared he could hear the sea breaking on the shore. He was sent forward to investigate and, although visibility was poor, returned with the message that he could see land.

At that moment the smack struck a tremendous rock. More sail was hoisted in an attempt to keep away from the land. But to no avail, as the tremendous force of the sea drove the craft ashore.

The mainsail was lowered to steady the vessel, because of the fear of somebody being knocked over-board.

The *Royal Hotel* and the *Marine Hotel* (just out of view on the right)

The *Henry Harris* being launched in a calm sea from the beach on the east side of the pier during an annual inspection by the District Inspector

The sea poured in on them and they were compelled to abandon ship, alighting on a shingle beach.

After a time they returned with a lantern, and with the approach of dawn they endeavoured to save the dredges, warp, and sails, as well as some of their clothing which they had put in a cavern beneath the cliff.

At daybreak they attempted to find their way beyond the cliffs, or double-cliff as the skipper expressed it, that towered above them. The huge rocks rose to a height of four or five hundred feet, and in the absence of a footpath the ascent was most perilous. John Tester feared that it would be an impossible task, but at length he succeeded, but only by robust determination and being utterly exhausted when he reached the summit.

The first human being seen by the shipwrecked crew was a shepherd tending his flock, but they found it difficult to communicate with him because their fishermen's French was not that good.

However, they eventually reached the town of St. Jouin, and by the direction of the local 'maire' they were accommodated at the Hotel de Normandie, where the hospitality they received was second to none.

In the afternoon (Thursday), they were driven 15 miles in horse-drawn conveyances to the British Consul at Havre, who had been notified of the shipwreck. By his instructions they were taken to the Sailors' Home, a useful institution presided over by the benevolent Lady Beeching, sister of Lord Radstock; and during their brief stay there they visited Jo Street's relation, Mr. E. Street.

By appointment they went to see the Consul again on Friday, and he told them to be prepared to leave for Southampton that night. But beforehand, the two Shoreham men obtained berths, one on a Shoreham boat and the other on a Worthing vessel, leaving just the four Worthing crew to return as directed.

They left Havre that night by the South-Western steamer *Wolfe* and after a good breakfast during the voyage, were landed at Southampton on Saturday, being taken by the Inspector of Steamboats to the Board of Trade at that port, as the Consul had ommitted to issue them with passes. The fishermen were then sent home to Worthing by rail, courtesy of the Shipwrecked Fishermen and Mariners' Royal Benevolent Society, who paid all their expenses.

A considerable loss had been sustained by the skipper and his crew, who had heavily provisioned the boat at their own expense, and in addition to the loss of their supplies they all sacrificed some of their personal belongings. The *Secret* itself, which was owned by Mr. Beck, was insured in the local Fishermen's Insurance Society for the sum of £30, but this was only about one third of its value, the maximum portion allowed under the rules.

The day after the shipwrecked fishermen returned home the notorious Belton family had a fracas within their own ranks. Harriet Belton went to 'the Cupboard' (the *Victoria* beerhouse) at 2 p.m. on Sunday to fetch her husband when her brother-in-law, Alfred Belton, made a remark about his brother, her husband Charlie, allowing her to come for him. She replied to him, Alfred struck her in the eye and she returned the blow. Alfred was then held by the landlord, Mr. Cutler, whilst a witness fetched the police.

At about 10.30 that night, Alfred, who had been creating a disturbance in King's Row, went up to his brother's front door, swore and declared that he was ready for the — — pair of them. When Harriet opened the door he knocked her down and, while a man by the name of Steve Ede was picking her up, Alfred struck her again.

On Wednesday 26 March in the Petty Sessions before five gentlemen including Mr. H. Hargood at Worthing Police Court, Alfred was charged with being drunk and disorderly in King's Row. He pleaded guilty and was further charged with assaulting his sister-in-law, Harriet Belton. Steve Ede, who was called as a witness for the complainant, supported the defendant's case in its entirety, stating that when Mrs. Belton went into the beerhouse she used fearful language and struck at the defendant, who simply acted in self defence.

The complainant, who herself had been requested by the defendant on more than one occasion to speak the truth, told the Worthing Police Court: "He's taken a very false oath," at which there was laughter.

Charlie Belton, the complainant's husband, said his wife came to the beerhouse saying "It's dinner-time mate," and the defendant, his brother, then remarked, "I'd like a — — woman to come for me."

The complainant had said she did not come for him, whereupon he struck her in the eye, and she scratched his face in self defence.

Frank Ballard was called as a witness by the complainant, but he refused to testify against Alfred, saying that he knew nothing whatever of the case. This witness, who had changed his tune at the last moment, was not sworn in, but instead was dismissed.

When the defendant complained, "They're swearing black's white and red's yaller," the court burst into laughter. He alleged that his sister-in-law 'bully-ragged' him when she came into the beer-shop.

Alfred's father, John Belton, who was called as a witness on his behalf, denied that any blows were struck when the disturbance occurred in the evening.

At the close of the case, which had caused considerable amusement, the Bench fined the defendant 5s. with 9s. costs for the first offence, but dismissed the charge of assault, and called upon Mrs. Belton to pay 10s. costs.

At a Licensing Meeting on 12 September 1888, boatman Steve Wingfield, a lifeboatman, was fined £2 plus costs for taking to sea more passengers than his boats *Florence* and *Minnie* were licensed for.

During the evening of Sunday 3 July 1890, a sad boating fatality ocurred off Goring, within sight of the shore. A visitor to the village, the possessor of a small sailing boat, had gone to Littlehampton in the morning, having engaged a local man, Chris Newman, to navigate the craft. Mr. Benjamin Dorrington, a merchant living at 11 Gunterstone Road, South Kensington, had been staying at Goring for the past three weeks, and was the owner of the lug-sail boat measuring 13 feet by 4½ feet, which Newman informed him was registered to carry seven persons.

At 7 a.m. Newman started to sail the boat containing Mr. Dorrington to Littlehampton and Arundel, accompanied by John Bennett, a seaman living at Ferring, and Arthur Hutchings, a wheelright, living at 1, Malthouse Cottages, Goring. The wind was against them and they tacked seven times, arriving at Littlehampton at 4 p.m., when they abandoned their intention of going on to Arundel.

When they started the journey back to Goring at 4.55 p.m., Newman described the wind, which was then in their favour, as puffy.

Although they had been out for seven hours, only a little beer and spirits had been consumed during the whole time, and Newman was perfectly sober.

The drama unfolded on the return journey. When they were only about ¾ mile from the shore at Goring an accident happened, while only the lug sail was being used. In the space of ten minutes the south westerly wind freshened and Newman told Bennett to 'stand by', informing the other two that he was about to 'shift' and lower the sail.

When Newman got up to take up the rope attached to the sheet there was a sudden gust of wind, the sail went towards the mast, the rudder in his other hand shifted violently and the boat instantly capsized, shooting it's four occupants into the sea.

They all rose to the surface together and scrambled onto the upturned hull, where two of them remained for scarcely two seconds. Newman looked round and then started swimming for the beach with Hutchings, while the other two remained with the boat.

Within 10 minutes Hutchings, a strong young fellow, reached the sand, but Newman who had been about 15 yards behind, had disappeared some 25 yards from the vessel.

The watchman at the Goring Coastguard Station had been watching the boat through his glass and when the craft had capsized he informed the chief boatman, Patrick Creemin who, with another coastguard, put off in their boat to the rescue.

It took them about 25 minutes to reach the distressed craft, during which time they saw nothing of Newman, but succeeded in saving the two occupants clinging to the boat.

Three hours later, at about 8.45 p.m., Newman's body was discovered by James Pollard Wilkins, a commissioned boatman stationed at Goring, in the sea about 150 yards east of Goring Lane. He recovered the corpse and reported the discovery to the local policeman, P. C. Frank Wilton, stationed at Goring, and with assistance they conveyed the body to Newman's house. A search of his pockets revealed his watch, which had stopped at 6.15 p.m. , 11 pence in money, a pipe and tobacco box. The only noticeable sign of injury was a slight scratch on the face.

An inquest was held at the *Bull Inn*, Goring, on Tuesday afternoon 5 July, by Mr. A. W. Rawlinson, Coroner for West Sussex. Mr. R. T. Hyde was chosen foreman of the jury, and they were absent for about 15 minutes while the body was viewed at the residence of the deceased. After returning to the inn and hearing evidence from the survivors a verdict of Accidental Death was returned. The jury and witnesses put in claims for their expenses totalling 18s.

The late Newman, who was the son of one of the 11 Worthing fishermen drowned in the *Lalla Rookh* disaster, had been a steady and industrious man, but his sudden departure had left his poor family to fend for themselves. The charitable jury and witnesses at the inquest very kindly instructed that their 18s. fees be handed to the widow for the support of her four children.

To raise more money for them a 30 minute open-air show by the Musical Bohemians was held on Saturday evening 26 July on the Parade. During this, their eighth annual visit to Worthing, the sum of 13s.8d. was collected for the cause.

Footnotes Ch. 10

[1] F. Dean - A relation of A. Dean who had been coxwain of the lifeboat *Jane*.
[2] J. Newman - One of the Newman family who lost four of their family in the *Lalla Rookh* disaster.
[3] Belton/ J. Belton - A relation of George Belton the lifeboatman.
[4] A. Beck - A relation of Bill Beck the lifeboatman.
[5] T. Clark/R. Clark - A relation of J. Clark the lifeboatman.

A Cautionary Story Of Diminished Vigilance. 1890

On Sunday 27 July 1890, when a young man, John Newman[1], was strolling along the beach a gin bottle on the stones opposite the west end of Heene Terrace caught his attention. On closer examination he discovered that it contained half a sheet of notepaper. Written in pencil on the back was:'C. C. Hide. Ship went down March 30th, S.S.O. Name, *Hecla*, from Liverpool. Please write to my friends, 8 Grenville Road, Kilbern, London.'

Newman reported the discovery to Mr. Billett, the officer in charge of the Worthing Coastguard Station, who dispatched the note to the Receiver of Wrecks, as was the normal course of action.

Meanwhile, Newman's employer, Mr. A. Crouch, wrote on the Monday to the address given in the message, and investigations during the course of the following month revealed that the supposed writer of the missive, a Mr. C. C. Hide, was safe in New York. The 'farewell note' was shown to be the work of some unknown humourist.

On Friday, 25 July, John Newman was in a race between Worthing Britannia Rowing Club(B.R.C.) crews, to test the merits of the professional crew that had been chosen by the B.R.C. captain, William Paine. The professional team was comprised of fisherman Bacon and three boatmen - the Marshall brothers - Harry, Bill and Mark, in the *Minstrel*. Newman's team, H. Feest, E. Long, and W. Pacey were the previous year's successful juniors, and ranked this year as senior oarsmen, in preparation for the coming regatta.

A Regatta day view showing a marquee erected for the occassion on the beach to the east of the pier

The Worthing Regatta was scheduled for Thursday 21 August, and conditions early in the morning were fairly indicative of a tolerably fine day with one or two slight showers. Some glimpses of sunshine were experienced and, but for the prevalence of a strong westerly wind, the outlook during the morning was not altogether unpromising. But towards noon things looked somewhat ominous, the wind force increased, making the sea choppy.

Despite the fact that for two years in succession the weather had been unkind on Regatta day, a huge number of people converged on the town. Captain Lee brought a number of passengers from Brighton in the *May* and, an excursion train from London brought a considerable complement of passengers who added to the crowds that had gathered on the pier and along the beach. Throughout the day in excess of 3,300 promenaders paid for admission to the pier. A display of flags on the pier conveyed the knowledge that the occasion was one of some importance, but the display of bunting ashore was a meagre one, scarcely calculated to profoundly impress the visiting population.

Some changes were made this year: the colours of the competing crews were of a more distinctive character; and in place of a committee boat moored off the pier, the judges and other officials were accommodated in a specially constructed stand of lofty elevation at the foot of the beach, just to the east of the pier.

Mr. A. H. Collet, Committee Chairman, acted as starter as he had done for many years; the judges were Mr. C. C. Cook (rowing) and Mr. J. S. Smith (sailing); the secretarial duties were carried out by Mr. W. Paine; and the remainder of the committee who assisted with the arrangements were Messrs. W. J. Harris, W. S. Simpson, E. T. Cooksey, A. Crouch, E. Tucker, C. Fibbens, A. Hewer, and E. D. Paine.

Owing to the fact that it was an early tide, 2.34 p.m. , it was necessary to commence operations at noon, a couple of hours earlier than arranged. The weather then was bright, but not as favourable as was really desired, but nevertheless the starter was ready and in position. The first batch of boats, however, were not at the post and 50 minutes passed before it was decided to proceed with the 2nd event on the programme, for Worthing watermen.

The Licensed Quarter Boats belonging to fishermen and boatmen raced once round the course, only four of the five boats entered reaching the finishing post. First past the post was Arthur Marshall in *Lily* who won £2; 2nd was Steve Wingfield, a lifeboatman, in *Myrtle*, awarded £1 10s.; and Frank Burden, another lifeboatman, came in 3rd in *Arthur John* to collect £1.

The Lug Sail Boats event, for craft not exceeding 17 feet, for Worthing watermen, was over two laps. A. Beck[2], in his 13 feet *Mystery* took first prize of £3; and Hutchinson was runner up in the 16 feet *Seagull*, winning £1 10s.

A sailing boat braving the choppy sea off the pierhead

The Junior Amateur Pairs in rowing craft not exceeding 18 feet went only once round the course, and although two heats were originally arranged, the competitors were all dispatched together as there were only five of them. The winning crew from Littlehampton came home with a long lead to collect £3 10s., the other boats being greatly distressed by the roughness of the sea. E. D. Paine and F. Dean[3], for Worthing, made a bold bid for 2nd place but were unfortunately wrecked at the eastern marker buoys and had to be rescued, making way for a Newhaven pair who came second to win £2. A. Hewer and Feest, for B.R.C., came 3rd, saving Worthing from humiliation and qualifying for a prize worth £1.

Sailing Boats not exceeding 22 feet were to race twice round the course for three prizes worth £10 10s. in all but, as E. P. Ashmore's *Pollywog* and Messrs. Crapps and Voysey's *Favourite* were the only craft to appear, the race was cancelled and the boats immediately returned to Shoreham.

Unfavourable conditions added to the difficulties experienced, in particular by the rowing boats. This became increasingly apparent and ultimately the committee found it necessary to hold a hurried consultation as to the advisability of postponing the meeting, but did eventually decide to carry on with the programme.

The afternoon's events continued with the Junior Amateur Fours in boats not exceeding 30 feet racing two laps for prizes totalling £14. This event was to some extent disappointing, inasmuch as only four of the eight boats entered actually put to sea, and one of these, the Newhaven craft, quickly filled with water and was taken ashore, her crew being rescued by some watermen. The *Charman Dean* also had a mishap just before the start when one of her crew broke an oar. Three teams, Worthing Britannia, Worthing Amateurs and Eastbourne, eventually started the race, but by the time half of the course was completed both of the Worthing boats had shipped considerable quantities of water and at length went ashore.

After discharging their cargo of water, however, the Britannia crew again embarked to continue the race, the Eastbourne men having meanwhile, to the great astonishment of the spectators, awaited their reappearance. What sporting gentlemen!

The two rival boats then commenced the remainder of the course, but the Britannia crew once again went ashore off the western buoys, and Eastbourne obligingly made a further protracted halt.

When a further start was effected Eastbourne displayed no anxiety to win the race, but crawled home second, the Britannia crew being declared the winners.

The Amateurs put off again with a view to securing the 3rd prize of £2, but in rounding the western buoys their frail craft was swamped and they were taken ashore in a boat.

Another delay now occurred, while the committee deliberated at a hastily convened meeting. At length it was announced that it had been decided to postpone the remaining events until Saturday afternoon. This was the only prudent course of action to take, for the occupants of so many of the slightly-constructed boats had come to grief that the risk to life and limb had become very serious. The frequent immersion of the oarsmen appeared to be regarded by many of the spectators as a peculiarly amusing feature of the afternoon's diversion; but the element of danger was so great that the more thoughtful section of the crowd was deeply concerned for the safety of the men. In consequence of the peculiar nature of the last event they further decided that a fresh series of prizes should be offered for another race for Junior Fours at the adjourned meeting.

By this time, in an animated scene, a crowd numbering some thousands had gathered on the pier and along the beach. The announcement of the postponement, as may be supposed, created much disap-pointment, but the spectators did not readily disperse. Attention was simply transferred to the auxiliary attractions: the Rhine Band, Mr. T. Binstead's brass band, Mr. G. F. Wright's brass band, and itinerant troupes of minstrels. Stalls lined the beach to the west of the pier and there was a walk-the-greasy-pole contest.

Pickpockets were said to be present in considerable force, one lady being relieved of some £6. These depredations occurred despite the vigilance displayed by the augmented police force commanded by Superintendant Long.

Although the racing had been abandoned for the day, it was decided to hold the promenade concert and fireworks display as planned in Steyne Gardens. Some thousands of spectators assembled both within and without during the evening to watch the display of fireworks which included Messrs. Brocks new whistling rockets to the amusement of the crowd.

When Saturday arrived a further postponement of the remaining events in the regatta was found to be necessary. The morning opened very boisterously with rain descending and a fierce south westerly wind blowing. Under these circumstances a meeting of the committee was held at an early hour, and as there did not then appear to be the remotest prospect of holding the regatta that day, it was decided after consultation to postpone the fixture indefinitely.

The annual Hove Regatta, entered by some Worthing oarsmen, had been fixed for Friday 22 August, but was consequently postponed to the following Monday because of rough weather. Conditions looked promising in the morning and a start was made at 2 p.m. on a tolerably rough sea, but after three events it was impossible to continue. The only races decided were one for sailing luggers, the Junior Amateur Pairs Open where the Littlehampton crew beat the Brighton Excelsior by a length, and a race for Coastguard Service Boats in which the Brighton crew took the first prize and Hove the second.

In the Junior Amateur Pairs Open the Worthing Britannia crew, A. Hever and W. Feest, won the 3rd prize of £1, while the Worthing Amateurs, E. D. Paine and F. Dean, took in so much water they were unable to complete the race. This race, for which each of the five teams had paid an entrance fee of 2s.6d. , was rowed under the greatest difficulty. The Newhaven boat was also swamped and did not finish the course.

Both of our local rowing clubs were represented at Hastings annual regatta on Wednesday 20 August, and the honour of the town did not suffer in their hands. In the race for Junior Pair-Oared Skiffs the representatives of the Amateur Boat Club, F. Dean and E. D .Paine, obtained the 3rd prize valued at 10s.

In the Senior Four-Oared Race, the winner of which scores one point for the South Coast Challenge Cup, the Brittánia crew came 2nd to St. Leonard's to collect a prize valued at £4. The crew were H. Feest, J. Newman, E. Long, W. Pacey(stroke) and Belton[4](cox).

Nine boats started in the Amateur Junior Fours, the Brittania Club winning 1st prize worth £6. The winning crew consisted of A. Hewer, E. Knight, Hayward, W. Feest(stroke), and Belton(cox); the Dover team was 2nd; Eastbourne 3rd. Other competing crews in this race were Hastings, Brighton, Folkestone, Newhaven, St. Leonards, and the Worthing Amateur Boat Club represented by J. N. Lawten, E. Hanmore, E. D. Paine, F. Dean(stroke) and Hubbard(cox).

Worthing oarsmen performed in the Portsmouth and Southsea Regatta which took place in magnificent weather off Southsea beach on Thursday 11 September, witnessed by thousands of spectators. In the Amateur Junior Pairs open race the Worthing B.R.C. came 3rd represented by A. Hewer and W. Feest. These two crew, together with E. Knight, A. Howard and Belton(cox), took 2nd prize in the Amateur Junior Fours for W.B.R.C.

Steyne Gardens where the promenade concert and fireworks display were held

On Monday 10th November a young lad, William Riddles who had celebrated his fourteenth birthday less than three weeks earlier on 22 October, drowned in a fishing accident at East Worthing. He could not swim and had not been out fishing regularly, although he had been 'off' perhaps five or six times.

The boy had wanted to go out fishing on Sunday night with his uncle, Alfred 'Fatty' Belton, who did anything for a living and was now a coal porter. But as the weather had looked a little forbidding he had been told to go home with the promise that if Monday was a fine day he would take him out to sea.

Monday, as it happened, was a beautiful and still day with no 'air of wind'. At 2.15 p.m. Fatty from 7, Field Row went off in a 16 ft. 6 in. fishing boat belonging to his cousin Jack Belton, together with William and an ex-mariner and former licensed boatman named George Joseph Inkpen, now a painter and plumber living at 4, Sussex Road. They rowed about 2½ miles out and, when they had finished shooting their nets, they were off the *Half Brick Inn.*

After making a fire and having tea they hauled in the nets at 8 p.m. to examine their catch, but as they had only caught a few fish they returned the nets to the water to increase the numbers.

After sunset the wind gradually increased until, at 8.30 p.m., they were struck by a squall. It passed off and nothing further happened until about 10.15 p.m. when another squall suddenly came up. Inkpen suggested that they should get to work bringing in the nets with the increased catch. Inkpen rolled William up in a coat, which completely covered him, to keep him warm, and put him aft. They put everything in order, Fatty went to the net room and Inkpen went forward and grabbed hold of the swing-rope, which attaches the nets to the boat.

Inkpen shouted, "Look out! here comes a nasty sea." The wave struck the boat, the strain breaking the swing-rope, and before they could manouvre the craft's bow round to the wind another wave struck them and the boat capsized.

All three of them were thrown into the water. It was high tide, they were about 3/4 of the pier's length(50yds) from the beach and somehow, scarcely conscious, Fatty who could not swim managed to struggle ashore. Inkpen swam to safety but found no trace of William who could not swim either. Inkpen and Fatty had been in the habit of going off together, and had been afloat in rough weather before without incident.

When his father, William Riddles,(although he did 'any mortal thing' he was, at that time, a hire carter) returned home from work on Monday night, he was surprised to hear that the lad was not in bed. Directly his wife told him that the boy had gone off fishing he said, "It blows three parts of a gale, and if he is on the sea you will never see the boy again."

A startling allegation of gross neglect came from Richard Knott, Chief Officer of the Lancing Coastguard, who, having saved his life on two previous occasions, considered Inkpen to be too venturesome. The Chief Officer had been called by one of his men at 9.30 that night, because he thought the boat was in danger. Although it was not a very clear night he was still able to see the boat which was about ³/₄ mile offshore. It appeared to him to be anchored, waiting until the tide slackened, even though there was a gale of wind blowing from the S.S.E. with a heavy sea breaking on the beach.

The craft appeared to Chief Officer Knott to be in very great danger but he did not give the order to launch the coastguard galley to go to their assistance because he felt that the conditions were unsafe.

He said that looking through his glass he saw two men in the boat who were behaving quite leisurely, sitting by the fire, as though there was nothing the matter, instead of making preparations to get out of danger.

About 10 p.m., when it was high tide, the boat drifted rapidly to the west according to Knott, who followed it up, sending Robert Bowden, one of his coastguards for the life-lines and a civilian for the rest of the crew. The force of the gale, with the ebb tide, carried the boat bodily across the groynes, with the nets still attached, but the men still made no effort to save their lives.

The nets fouled the groynes, bringing the boat to a standstill, which the Chief Officer considered was very fortunate for them. The net-line was carried away while their nets were caught on the groyne, causing the vessel to beat in between two groynes. And the two men stood in the boat, still making no effort to get out the oars. For an hour this had been going on, till the boat capsized.

When the boat got between the two groynes the men went forward, leaving the poor little boy in the stern-sheets to the mercy of the waves.

In about two minutes after the rope was broken the boat capsized. Richard Bolt, a Lancing labourer, rushed into the water to assist the two men, and the boy's body was found in the wash about 20 minutes later, and brought ashore by Bowden and a civilian. They took him up on the beach and tried for an hour to revive him using the Dr. Sylvester's method of artificial respiration. But when they found no sign of life the body was taken to the *Half Brick Inn.*

An enquiry into his death was held by the Coroner for West Sussex, Mr. A. W. Rawlinson, at the *Anchor Inn,* High Street (now the Jack Horner) on Thursday afternoon 13 November. After searching investigations and a lengthy summing-up, the jury returned a verdict of Accidental Death and unanimously agreed that a severe censure should be passed upon the two men in charge of the boat.

The Coroner told them both, Inkpen especially, that they were guilty of great carelessness and recklessness in not returning to shore when signs of bad weather set in, even though other boats did. The jury took a very merciful view of the case; had they taken another view which the evidence might have supported, both Inkpen and Belton could have found themselves committed on a manslaughter charge.

At the close of the enquiry the jurors donated their fees to William Riddles senior.

A public appeal for subscriptions in aid of the bereaved parents received a satisfactory response. Mr. G. H. Hunt of the *Royal George Hotel* in Market Street (since demolished to make way for the Guildbourne Shopping Centre) who undertook to raise the money, collected £4 3s.5d.; and after Mr. Hubert E. Snewin had audited the accounts, a seperate donation of 5s. was received from a Mr. W. Walter, making a total of £4 8s.5d. contributed. The expenses incurred in the interment of the deceased were met from the fund, and the balance of £1 8s. 6d. was given to Mrs. Riddles.

Footnotes Ch. 11

[1] John Newman - one of the Newman family which suffered badly in the *Lalla Rookh* tragedy.
[2] A. Beck - A relation of Bill Beck, the lifeboatmen.
[3] F. Dean - A relation of A. Dean, coxwain of the lifeboat *Jane*.
[4] Belton - A relation of J. Belton, the lifeboatman.

Twice In A Day. 1891

There were so many non-swimmers among Worthing's population of 16,606 that a preliminary meeting was held at the Young Men's Christian Association in Warwick Street on Monday evening 16 February 1891, to consider the desirability of forming a swimming club for the town. A Mr. C. B. Cook explained the objective to some 30 intending members who attended.

A formal resolution was passed approving the formation of a club, and, after considerable discussion in which, among other matters, the desirability of purchasing a dressing tent and a diving board was considered, a provisional committee of eight, Messrs. Gibbs, Ash, Courtney, Botting, Mitchell, Cowley, Johnson, and Gazelle, was appointed to prepare a scheme for the successful working of the club.

New members were initiated at a general meeting on Monday evening 13 April at their headquarters, the same room at 41 Warwick Street, increasing the club's strength to 51. Mr. E. W. Morecraft presided over the meeting where Mr. Sartain was unanimously chosen as club captain. At the meeting concessions were arranged for members: Mr. W. J. Butcher, a bathing machine proprietor, offered special terms; and $1/2$ price admission was arranged to the West Worthing baths (in Heene Road, now the site of a petrol station and an insurance company office block).

1752 Worthing The Baths and Tennis Ground

Half-price admission was arranged to the West Worthing Baths

The very first annual ball of the Amateur Boat Club was held at the Assembly Rooms on Wednesday evening 7 January 1891. Only seven club members turned up but, as the committee had worked energetically and managed to secure a tolerable amount of outside support, the total strength of the company was about 60. A concession, largely appreciated by those responsible for the arrangements, was that the committee of the County Ball, held in the same building the preceding evening, had kindly allowed the elaborate decorations used on that occasion to remain.

The hall was under the patronage of many dignitaries, including Sir Henry Fletcher M.P., Mr. G. Wedd J.P. (President of the club) and Mr. H Hargood J.P.(lifeboat chairman). Dancing to the Rhine Band commenced soon after 9 p.m. and continued with much spirit until about 4.30 the following morning. A good time was had by all, especially since they had an extended drinking licence.

The ABC committee purchased a new boat from Messrs. Pickett & Son of Southampton at the beginning of May for £12 10s. The boat was clinch built of cedar, with sliding seats and swivel rowlocks, originally for the Bros. Rolls of Bournemouth, but the boatbuilder had been unable to meet their deadline leaving him with the craft to dispose of.

At the Newhaven Regatta on Monday 3 August Worthing Britannia Rowing Club representatives secured two prizes: one in the Junior Fours and the other in the Junior Pairs. In the first event E. Isted, E. S. Pearse, E. Feest, and Steve Wingfield(stroke), a lifeboatman, all won a tankard worth £1 10s. each. The other Worthing winners were E. Feest and Steve Wingfield who were awarded jam pots, together worth £2.

The Shoreham Regatta was held on Tuesday 11 September and, although the weather could have been described as fine, a fresh breeze which blew off the sea could have materially affected the competitors if it had taken place in the open sea instead of in the western arm of the harbour.

Several successes were scored by Worthing representatives: H. Feest and W. Feest for Britannia came third in the Amateur Senior Pairs for skiffs not exceeding 18 feet, winning 10s.; E. D. Paine was third in the Amateur Junior Sculls in the same size craft which rowed to Kingston and back; in the Amateur Junior Four-Oared Galley event for vessels not exceeding 30 feet, Worthing A.B.C. took the second prize valued at £2, represented by E. D. Paine, F. C. Cook, H. J. Carpenter, F. Dean and A. Belton (cox); following them was E. Isted, E. S. Pearse, E. Feest, Steve Wingfield, and E. Burgess (cox) for B.R.C. who took the third prize valued at £1; B.R.C. was 2nd in the Challenge Cup for Amateur Senior Fours in galleys not exceeding 30 feet producing a prize worth £3 which was shared among J. Newman, W. Feest, E. Long, E. Paine, and E. Burgess (cox); and the last prize to be won by a Worthing team was that of 2nd place in the Amateur Junior Pairs when H. J. Carpenter and F. C. Cook for the A.B.C. shared a prize valued at £1.

Worthing's annual aquatic festival, the Regatta, took place on Wednesday 12 August. One o'clock was the hour chosen for the opening event, and as that time arrived the wind freshened as the tide rose. Over £100 in all was being offered in the shape of prizes, and in the 15 events of which the afternoon's sport consisted exactly 100 entries had been received. This year the course was altered slightly: the western buoys were brought nearer to the pier, while those to the east were anchored opposite the A.B.C. building, so that the two sets of buoys were almost equidistant from the pier.

The results of the Lug Sail Boat event for Worthing watermen, all of whom had 16 ft. craft, were as follows:

Sea Gull,	J. Hutchinson	1st	£3
Mystery,	A. Beck	2nd	£1 10s.
Dolly,	T. Wingfield	3rd	15s.
Lancashire Lass,	G. Wingfield, a lifeboatman.	4th	10s

The five other entries were: *Dawn of Day,* Bill Marshal; *Here We Are,* J. Hutchinson; *Nelly,* G. Wingfield *Never Can Tell,* Harry Blann (my great grandfather); and *Rambler,* J. Gentle.

There were four entries from Worthing watermen for the Licensed Quarter Boats Race but as they came to the post some dispute arose in regard to the *Albatross,* and they all returned to the shore without ever starting the race, Bill Marshall's *Lily,* his brother Harry's *Lily of the Valley,* Steve Wingfield's(a lifeboatman) *Myrtle* and J. Hutchinson's *Albatross.*

A team from Worthing Amateurs won the Junior Amateur Pairs event for boats not exceeding 18 ft., while Worthing Britannia came third. In the Junior Amateur Fours Worthing took away the 2nd prize valued at £4.

Worthing watermen raced in another event, this time it was for Second Class Three-Oared Boats, with the following results:

Pansy,	Bill Marshall	1st	£2 10s.
True Blue,	Steve Wingfield	2nd	£1 10s.
Yum Yum,	J.Davis	3rd	£1

Elsie, G. Belton (a lifeboatman); *Mabel,* Fred Collier (a lifeboatman); and *Rapid,* S. Lea, were unplaced.

Worthing watermen's sailing race

The Challenge Cup Race

The Challenge Cup Race, for senior amateur fours in boats less than 30 feet long, was considered the most important event of the day: one point being scored by the winner for the South Coast Challenge Cup in addition to a first prize worth £10. On the return from the western buoy Hastings held the lead; the Britannia and Bournemouth crews, neck a neck, were well up. The other boats posed no threat as they were far behind. Bournemouth on turning increased its lead, while Hastings in its turn drew away from the Britannia boys, and Eastbourne gave up. Before they reached the pier again Hastings had secured the lead, Worthing retaining its place, though in a somewhat less favourable position compared with the second boat. Dover came last, and after the final turn there was, curiously enough, yet another reversal of first and second positions. Bournemouth once again secured the lead, and after a capital race home, won by barely two lengths. Worthing was a bad third, but this was due to some extent to a mishap on the part of the cox, E. Burgess, at the eastern buoys. Otherwise the Britannia men went well.

Probably for the first time in the history of the Regatta, there was a little ceremony to present the prizes; his Worship the Mayor distributed the awards in the Pier Pavilion immediately after the close of the races.

During the evening, in accordance with the custom that had prevailed for many years, the Regatta proceedings concluded with a promenade concert and a grand display of fireworks in Steyne Gardens. It had been intended to hold this spectacle in the grounds of Warwick House on this occassion but they were not available.

The first of a succession of smoking concerts was given on Thursday evening 3 December by the Amateur Boat Club, in an attempt to foster the social side of the organisation. In the event this gathering in the Steyne Assembly Room was a success, bringing the members together in the dull and dreary season in which aquatics found no place in the recognised round of sports and pastimes.

Some new light-signalling apparatus, called the comet signal, was delivered to Worthing Lifeboat Station in January. Our local lifeboatmen experimented with this new invention on Thursday evening 29 January. During that day Captain Cunningham Graham, the Eastern Divisional Inspector of the R.N.L.I., made his annual inspection of the *Henry Harris* and the boathouse. The boat was launched for exercise with Capt. Graham and Mr. H. Hargood, the chairman, forming part of the crew.

The 505 German iron barque, *Capella* of Hamburg

Raising money for the R.N.L.I., which has always existed on voluntary contributions alone, was a never ending task. Cash was given in various ways: for example £8 0s.3d. was raised at a concert given in the Pier Pavilion on 1 September. And on a national basis, Lifeboat Saturdays started during this year as a means of collecting contributions from members of the public, to help support the large number of lifeboat stations around the coast of the British Isles, which by now had grown to 300.

The Worthing lifeboat was called out on 11 November in a raging south south westerly gale. The powerful wind tore off slates, chimney pots crashed to the ground and yet another face of the Town Hall clock was smashed - this time it was the western face. The storm had started in the small hours of the morning and during the early part of the day included torrential rain. The full force of the wind was felt on the seafront with many people being blown down.

At 9.30 a.m. the lifeboat coxwain, Charles Lee, saw two vessels being blown dangerously close to the shore, and knowing that their grounding was unavoidable, he fired the lifeboat gun to summon his crew. The first victim of this unusually ferocious Channel gale was the 505 ton German iron barque, *Capella* of Hamburg which, after being battered for two days, struck the beach opposite Heene Terrace, just as the maroon went off on the Parade opposite the lifeboat house.

Fourteen fishermen and watermen, including my great grandfather Harry Blann and his brother Bill, helped the lifeboat crew to get the boat out of the house and launch a rescue. There were lives at stake and although it was never expected that the *Henry Harris* would get away in the violent water, it was only by the plucky efforts of the gallant coxwain and crew that it took only 16 minutes to get her off.

Coxwain Lee decided that the crew of the other vessel, the *Kong Karl*, were in greater immediate danger than the crew of the iron-built *Capella* because the wooden schooner could be dashed to pieces. So instead of going to West Worthing the lifeboat went eastward to assist the schooner which was in difficulties, leaving the barque to her fate for a time as they could not attend both ships simultaneously. It was just after high tide and the gale was whipping the sea into such a frenzy that the *Henry Harris* was swamped at least six times, filling with water, on its way to rescue the 230 ton, three masted schooner off Lancing.

Meanwhile, at West Worthing, heavy seas were breaking over the *Capella*, which was flying a distress signal. As the barque's 12 crew might all be drowned, Harry Blann and his mates decided to launch the ferry boat to rescue them. A ferry boat had been used in an attempt to rescue the crew of the barque, *Lalla Rookh*, some 41 years earlier with disastrous results and the thought of his drowned grandfather, John Belville, Harry pushed to the back of his mind. It was highly dangerous trying to get a plain open boat off in crashing breakers, but they had little choice.

Many townsfolk helped to drag the ferry boat along to West Worthing and the plucky band of 14 fishermen and boatmen managed to get away in the violent sea.

They rowed with all their strength towards the *Capella*, but were tossed about and cast ashore like a cork. They launched her three times in all, and tried their hardest to get the crew off the barque, but without success. Each and every man gave of his best until they were completely exhausted and thus forced to abandon further attempts.

The *Henry Harris* reached the Norwegian schooner, *Kong Karl* of Christiana, at 11 a.m. and stood by until she foundered; then lifeboatman Harry Marshall, Worthing lifeboat's first official bowman, threw grapnells with lines attached, from the lifeboat to the schooner. The ropes were used to haul the lifeboat alongside the schooner and temporarily secure her in this position while the schooner's seven crew jumped from the vessel into the lifeboat as the two boats reciprocated with the force of the swollen waves. As the last man clambered aboard, the lines were immediately disconnected, allowing the *Henry Harris* to return ashore with her human cargo.

The lifeboatmen safely landed the rescued crew ashore at Lancing at 11.45 a.m. watched by a large crowd of excited spectators who gave three hearty cheers of welcome to the ship-wrecked foreigners and for the courageous Worthing lifeboat crew who had stood by to succour them. They were received at the Lancing Coastguard Station and were subsequently sent on to Mr. Brown, the Swedish-Norwegian Consul at Shoreham Harbour.

The drama had begun two weeks earlier. Manned by Captain Jornson, a mate, four men and a boy, the *Kong Karl* had left Liverpool on 28 October with a cargo of coke bound for Christiana. She had lost her way in the Atlantic due to the severity of the weather, and had been proceeding up the channel when the gale arose. After what Captain Jornson later described as the roughest night that he had ever passed at sea, an unsuccessful attempt had been made to clear Beachy Head. On putting about, the craft had lost her foretop-gallantmast, and then all efforts to control her had been wasted. She had subsequently drifted around until she had been spotted by the coastguard about ½ mile west of Lancing, and eventually crashed into the beach between Lancing Tollbar (near the present-day Brooklands Boating Lake) and Lancing Coastguard Station. The next day she was found to have been driven further up the beach and the elements began battering her into a thousand pieces of matchwood.

Lancing Coastguard Station. (The site is now occupied by a block of flats, Seaview Court)

Having just brought the shipwrecked Norwegians ashore, the lifeboat crew had no time for a break. Knowing that the *Capella* was ashore at West Worthing Coxwain Lee ordered Bowman Marshall, assisted by the volunteers to connect the chain and winch the lifeboat back onto the carriage as quickly as possible and proceed to Worthing.

The wind had increased to hurricane force by now and the courageous assistants managed to launch the *Henry Harris* once more at 1 p.m. and the brave lifeboatmen reached the stranded vessel at about 2 p.m. Five of the shipwrecked mariners had already landed in their own jolly boat, and, in the excitement, many people had rushed into the water to help drag the boat through the surf; but Captain Martens and his six remaining crew had to be rescued by the *Henry Harris*.

The saga had developed after the barque had left Marseilles for Tyne in ballast and had come ashore at Worthing after being blown off course. This was the only time that two ships of this calibre had been stranded at Worthing on the same day.

After the last of the crew of the German vessel had been rescued, she began to drift eastwards: the heavy iron-hulled craft creating a potential danger to the Pier. Consequently the Pier directors were called together for a conference with Mr. Hargood, the Lifeboat Committee Chairman, and burly, bearded Coxwain Lee; with the result that the latter received instructions to board the boat and put out her anchors. This was done at low tide, and early next morning two tugs arrived from Shoreham, and in the gaze of a large crowd, pulled the *Capella* off the sand and out to sea just before 8 a.m. They had intended to tow the barque to Shoreham, but when they encountered some difficulty in entering the harbour, they towed her to Newhaven.

The 13 brave lifeboat crew who effected this double rescue with great stamina were remunerated with 10s. for each of the two services, totalling £1 each man. They were:-

Charles Lee (cox)	Jack Elliot	William Collier
Fred Marshall	Fred Wakeford	Tom Wingfield
George Wingfield	Peter West	Luke Wells[1]
George Belton	Frank Burden	Steve Wingfield
Harry Marshall(bowman)		

A signalman was paid 5s. for each of the two services making 10s. in all.

After foundering off West Worthing the *Capella* drifted eastwards, narrowly missing the pier.
The *Capella* bore a resemblence to this vessel which was photographed opposite the *Steyne Hotel*.

The 30 assistants who helped to launch and haul up the *Henry Harris* in connection with the *Kong Karl* rescue were paid 3s. each; while it took 50 helpers to assist with the lifeboat for the *Capella* rescue because the *Henry Harris* had to be hauled in from the low water mark.

On both services six horses were hired to pull the lifeboat and carriage to the launching positions at a cost of 6s.6d. per horse for each service, even though the distance travelled for the *Kong Karl* was twice as far as that for the *Capella*.

Those who were best qualified to judge described the services of Coxwain Lee and his crew as most courageous and meritorious, and their self-sacrificing efforts received the grateful acknowledgement of his Worship the Mayor, Alderman Patching, on behalf of the townspeople. In recognition of their gallant services Charles Lee and his crew were generously entertained at the Minor Hall on Monday evening 16 November by the Mayor himself.

They were joined by Piermaster Belton and his deputy, Mr. Blunden, and at the request of the Mayor, the company was presided over by Councillor Butcher, the contractor who supplied horses for the lifeboat, and was also signalman.

An excellent and substantial dinner was served by Mr. George Field of Montague Street. After the meal, clay pipes and a liberal allowance of tobacco were distributed to the men. Among those who sang during the evening was Mr. Hargood, and a recitation from the Coxwain was efficiently rendered.

A noticeable absence from the occassion was the crew of local watermen who had manned the ferry boat in an unsuccessful attempt to rescue the crew of the *Capella*. They had not been invited.

However, there was much praise attributed to them throughout the town and many people were keen to give them a donation by way of encouragement; especially as with the weather being so bad, these fishermen had been unable to go to sea or earn any money at all for their wives and children, and the coming weekend looked like being another poor one.

So Harry Blann and his fellow fishermen consulted one of the most influential gentlemen in the town who wrote the following for them: 'The attempts made by 14 Worthing watermen and fishermen during the height of the gale on Wednesday morning last, to rescue the crew of the stranded barque off West Worthing seem to call for some slight acknowledgement, and subscriptions are therefore respectfully invited to form a fund for the purpose of giving each of the men a small gratuity for their praiseworthy and plucky endeavours to render assistance. Worthing, November 12th 1891.'

The subscription list was headed by his Worship the Mayor, followed by Mr. John Roberts, Councillor Sams, Mr. Digby, Mrs.Gresson, and many other ladies and gentlemen who were fully conversant with the facts, with the result that the 14 fishermen each received 9s.3d. Harry, Bill and their brave colleagues were very satisfied and thankful to their kind friends who had subscribed.

The 14 Worthing fishermen and watermen were:

Harry Blann	Charles Lambeth
Bill Blann	William Poland
John Riddles	Charlie Stubbs
Jo Street	Frank Collier[2]
Mark Marshall	James Medhurst
Arthur Marshall	Tom Giles
James Tester	Richard Cusden

On 9 December a photographer, Mr. E. Pattinson Pett, presented each member of the lifeboat crew with a mounted copy of a group photograph he had taken a week or two earlier.. This photograph was reproduced in the illustrated weekly, The Gentlewoman, accompanied by the following verses:

The photographer presented each member of the lifeboat crew with a mounted copy of this photograph.
Standing: Peter West, Fred Wakeford, Tom Wingfield, Fred Marshall, George Belton. Sitting: George Wingfield, 2nd Coxwain William Collier, Coxswain Charles Lee, Harry Marshall, Jack Elliot. On floor: Steve Wingfield, Luke Wells, and Frank Burden.
William Collier, the assistant coxwain, can be seen here delirious and supported by colleagues. Two different folklores survive to explain this: one maintains that Collier was struck by an oar; the other that he was suffering from severe physical and mental exhaustion after the extremely hazardous rescue.

A GALLANT LIFEBOAT CREW

Oh! men of Worthing town,
That in the salt sea sail,
Where the breeze from Findon down
Swells on to meet the gale.

Oh! men of Worthing town,
That fear no sea-born wind,
You smile at Neptune's frown,
And count the storm too kind.

Oh! men of Worthing town,
To you the well-won palm;
Long may ye sail and fear no gale,
To end your days in calm.

While all this was going on, a local photographer, Mr. E. B. Blaker of the Borough Studio in Ann Street, took some views of the wrecked *Kong Karl*, and sold them from the studio in postcard form priced 6d. each.

The committee of the R.N.L.I., at a meeting in London on Thursday 10 December, decided to present the silver medal of the Institution, accompanied by a copy of the vote inscribed on vellum and framed, to Charles Lee, the gallant coxwain of the Worthing lifeboat, for his courage in rescueing the two crews during the recent gale.

The lifeboat crew chalked-up another two rescues on their station's 'scoreboard' showing 14 lives saved in one day. It was a truly remarkable feat: not only did they crew the lifeboat on two seperate launches to two seperate ships; but also went out a third time, to anchor the iron-built *Capella* which was threatening the pier structure. I firmly believe that the stamina and courage displayed by these Worthing watermen in the face of this gale, a gale so strong that none of them had experienced one stronger in their lifetime, were much greater than is the expected norm today.

These qualities were captured in this poem written by Davidson:

THE WRECK OF THE *KONG KARL*

I was sitting in my vicar's room,
When I heard the Coastguards' dreadful boom,
It was the summons to obey,
And there and then the lifeboat men
Dashed in the leaping, foaming bay.

What a dreadful day it was that day;
The town was filled with a wild dismay-
A wreck! a wreck! oh can it be?
And with the throng I ran along
Down to the heaving, boiling sea.

The sky was dark with an awful frown,
And the blinding wind and rain came down,
Mountainous waves came rolling in;
With mighty roar they lashed the shore,
And then died with a fearful din.

Many a brown waving hand was seen
To cheer the hearts of the brave thirteen,
Many a cheering word is thrown,
As on they go, breasting the foe,
To save men's lives and risk their own.

Just like a chip the lifeboat is toss'd,
Now on a wave and now as if lost,
The very billows fail to check;
Still on they ride o'er raging tide,

On, on to the wreck! to the wreck!

Fiercer and fiercer the tempest grew
Over the heads of the noble crew,
The very heavens seem to rend,
And with a shock, as on a rock,
The Worthing lifeboat stood on end.

The cry goes up, She's lost to sight!
And then a murmur, All is not right!
Good Lord protect the lifeboat crew!
We see the wreck, all hands on deck,
Waiting, praying for the rescue.

She's there! She's there! and their eyes they strain,
And they shout Thank God, she rides again!
Down on the wreck she's heading fast,
O'er hissing wave still mounts the brave,
Three cheers, she's gained the wreck at last!

The crew is safe in the Worthing boat,
And the wreck is left to sink or float;
Back, back they come with full bent oar,
And now a cry reaches the sky-
The shipwrecked crew are safe on shore!

A momento, in the form of a figurehead taken from the wreck of the *Kong Karl*, can be seen in Worthing Museum; together with Coxwain Lee's silver medal.

During 1891 the services of the R.N.L.I. had been constantly requisitioned: the total number of service launches nationally was 334, resulting in 551 lives being saved. The lifeboat crews were also instrumental in saving a great deal of valuable property, including 24 vessels from partial or total destruction.

In addition to these launches, the lifeboats were out 188 times in response to either signals of distress, or what were presumed to be such, but their services were not ultimately required on those occasions.

During the year, the institution also gave rewards for the saving of 168 lives by means of fishing boats, shore-boats, or by other means, so that altogether in 1891 it granted rewards for the saving of 719 lives.

In all, a grand total of 36,162 lives saved could be wholly or partially credited to the institution since its establishment in 1824.

Footnotes Ch. 12

[1] Luke Wells – his grandaughter, Miss M. Monery, lives in Worthing.
[2] Frank Collier – a lifeboatman on the service to the *Edmund Gabriel* in 1886.

Ch. 13

Competition and A Nostalgic Dinner. 1892 - 3

On the first Sunday in February 1892, just after 8 p.m., a distress flare was spotted coming from a vessel close in-shore. About two minutes later another flare was seen coming from the craft, and again a couple of minutes later the procedure was repeated.

The lifeboat crew were summoned and the horses ordered to be in readiness. It was misty and the weather was rough with a fresh westerly breeze making the sea very choppy, too much so for ordinary boats.

Just when the lifeboat was to be pulled out of its house, the distressed vessel went about and disappeared. The lifeboat crew, who by this time had assembled, were kept on watch in case the craft reappeared needing assistance. An hour passed without sight of the vessel and without any further incident, and so the crew were dismissed. They were: Charles Lee (cox), Harry Marshall (2nd cox), F. Marshall, Harry and Bill Blann, Frank Collier, Fred Collier, George Wingfield, Steve Wingfield, P. West, S. Bacon[1], and Luke Wells. Mr. W. J. Butcher would have acted as signalman.

Harry Marshall signed on as 2nd coxwain replacing William Collier, who stood down to be a basic crewman as he had been unnerved by the dangers faced while fulfilling his responsible position as 2nd cox. during the *Kong Karl/Capella* double rescue three months earlier.

During the rest of 1892 the *Henry Harris* was launched quarterly on its usual regular practices to keep the crew up to scratch. These ever-popular events were always watched by a considerable crowd of spectators who enjoyed the thrill and excitement of the blue and white boat being rushed into the water and the subsequent manouevres on the sea.

It was during one of these exercises, on Wednesday afternoon 16 March, that one of the reserve crew collapsed and died.

The death of 47 year old George Riddles was reported to the coroner, Mr. A. W. Rawlinson, who directed that a post-mortem examination should be carried out by Dr. Van Buren. This took place on the following Friday, and as the results revealed that death was caused by heart disease, an inquest was not deemed necessary.

The funeral for Riddles, who was married but had no children, on Monday afternoon 21 March, was witnessed by a large number of people. His final farewell was in true patriotic style befitting a lifeboat man. The coffin, draped with the Union Jack, on which wreaths and crosses had been placed, was borne from Montague Cottage in Portland Road to the cemetery in South Farm Road by the deceased's lifeboat comrades, attired in blue jerseys and red woollen caps, in relays of four. The lifeboat men were:-

Charles Lee (cox), who was in charge.	Harry Blann
Harry Marshall	Bill Blann
F. Marshall	T. Wingfield
W. Collier	G. Wingfield
Frank Collier	Steve Wingfield
Fred Collier	T. Bridger
S. Bacon	F. Wakeford

Relatives and friends followed in mourning coaches. On reaching the cemetery, the service was conducted by the Rev. C. E. Haynes, Curate of Broadwater.

As a result of Riddles death during a R.N.L.I. training excercise, the R.N.L.I. Committee of Management decided to donate to Mrs. Riddles the magnificent sum of £30, which in those days was a large sum of money.

About 10 days after the widow's bereavement, the following paragraph appeared in a publication entitled 'Truth':

'A correspondent sends me an account of a melancholy occurrence at the practice of the Worthing lifeboat a few days ago, when one of the crew was taken ill and died of heart disease shortly after landing. It is suggested to me that, as such an occurrence when the boat was out on business, instead of for practise, might have had very serious consequences, steps ought to be taken to ascertain that every

107

member of a lifeboat crew is equal to the strain involved in the service. This is all very well, but - apart from the unexpected ways in which the hearts of even the strongest men break down - it is not easy to obtain the fittest men under the present system. For the same reason that you must not look a gift horse in the mouth, you can hardly put a volunteer lifeboatman through a medical examination. If we are to have our lifeboats manned on the same principle as our Army and Navy - and even there the personnel are not by all accounts exactly perfect - we must assimilate the conditions of the service to those in the Army and Navy, and begin by paying for the men we want.'

Another member of the Worthing lifeboat crew died suddenly on Good Friday morning at home, 17 Surrey Street. His wife had gone downstairs to brew some tea for him, as he had difficulty in breathing; and on her return to the bedroom she found that he was dead.

The circumstances were reported to the Coroner by his officer, Mr. Lindfield, and instructions were given that a post-mortem examination should take place. This was performed by Dr. Coxwell at the Mortuary on Monday 18 April, and the cause of death was found to be syndcope. This result was given to the Coroner, who deemed it unnecessary to hold an inquest. The deceased, who was 53 years of age, was a fisherman by occupation, supplementing his income by occasional employment as a chimney sweep.

After the tragic deaths of two Worthing lifeboatmen, the fishing community was enlightened with the birth of a son to one of the lifeboat crew. Bill Blann was blessed with a son, who was christened with the same name, William (Bill). A recruit-to-be in the lifecycle of lifeboatmen.

To help pay for the lifeboat service, occasional concerts were given locally in aid of the R.N.L.I. One such nautical concert took place on Wednesday 31 August with one performance in the afternoon and another in the evening.

St. Botolph's Church offertory was devoted to the R.N.L.I.

The programme included the Pier Orchestra, conducted by Mr. G. W. Collins, the popular Alzando Glee Singers, and Miss Jennie Franklin with her original comedy sketches.

Although unfavourable weather reduced the number of patrons attending the two performances, the £5 profit for the Institution, realised from the admission prices of 2s.6d., 1s., and 6d., was handed to Mr. Piggott, the honorary secretary of the Worthing Branch.

Local churches also gave money to the charity: the offertories at St. George's and St. Botolph's, on 11 September, were devoted to the R.N.L.I.

Some relatives of Worthing fishermen were elected to the committee of the Britannia Rowing Club during its annual meeting at the *Spaniard Hotel*(which was demolished to make way for Boots department store in Portland Road) on Thursday evening 7 April. The new committee was comprised of Messrs. A. Crouch, J. H. L. Hine, W. H. Sawle, G. Pacey sen., J. Hutchinson, E. Long, J. Newman, E. Hearsey, W. Pacey, J. E. Knight, F. Butcher, E. Isted, and Burtenshaw.

At the meeting a favourable report was presented: a long list of rowing successes was submitted; and the previous year's deficit was shown to have been considerably reduced. New members were accepted by the club: Messrs. J. Steere, G. Poland, J. Head and F. Blann (a distant relative of mine).

At the conclusion of business, a vote of thanks was accorded to the President, Mr. Wedd, for his kindness in coming down to the meeting and encouraging a band of working men in their rowing exercises. The President spoke of the pleasure it gave him to attend the meeting, to show them in person that his sympathies, and those of other gentlemen, were with the working men quite as much as with one another. They worked quite as hard in different ways, and felt they had their interest at heart as much as their own. No one class of the community could prosper without the other; they were bound up together. If they wanted to build up the edifice of society in the most solid way, they could only do so by the unity of the classes. He hoped as education advanced it would be felt more and more that they could not carry out any selfish plan to the disadvantage of other classes without receiving injury themselves.

A few representatives of the Britannia Rowing Club attended a special meeting called by Mr. W. J. Butcher and Mr. J. G. Davis in an endeavour to arrange a local regatta for the watermen and oarsmen of Worthing only. The gathering at the Spaniard Hotel on Saturday evening, 7 May, attracted some members from both rowing clubs and men connected with pleasure boats, comprising a total of about 20.

Mr Davis was anxious that it be understood that this local regatta would not be at all antagonistic to the existing annual regatta, but would simply be for the encouragement of local oarsmen and watermen.

He explained that other south coast towns had additional local regattas - why not Worthing?.

Those at the meeting agreed to hold a local regatta and over the course of the coming weeks the necessary arrangements were organised.

Worthing's first Local Regatta took place on Monday 15 August during seemingly favourable weather. There were nine principal events, six of which were for rowing boats, with a prize list representing a total value of £75.

The sun was shining brightly, but at 2 p.m., when the programme was due to start, a fierce westerly wind blew up and greatly disturbed the calmness of the water.

It was 3/4 of an hour later before it was deemed expedient to make a start and appease the waiting spectators. The customary enormous regatta crowd were on the beach and esplanade, and over 3,600 people paid for admission to the pier during the day. Excursion trains, specially laid on by the railway company, brought some 400 people from London itself and a further 200 were collected along the line to Worthing.

For the entertainment of spectators the Ceylon Band from Tunbridge Wells was engaged, giving performances alternately on the Pier and then on the Parade, creating a distinctly favourable atmosphere.

Traditionally, some of the events were specifically for Worthing watermen. Most of these fishermen and boatmen were connected with the lifeboat in some way. Those who were not in the first or reserve crew would volunteer to help launch the lifeboat.

The results of the these watermen's races are listed at the back of this book.

In a somewhat calmer sea, but with a rapidly diminishing attendance both on the pier and the beach, all seven in the quarter boats race started well, but the number was soon reduced; the *Cosby* suffered a broken oar and had to drop out almost immediately after the start. The *Lily* had a long lead when the pier was passed on the eastern journey, and after the western buoys had been passed the race resolved itself into a virtual procession, with the *Lily* maintaining its advantage to the finish.

Walking the Greasy Pole Contest was won by Jo Street who was awarded a leg of mutton and 10s.; W. Grant was second winning 10s.; and T. Wingfield won the third prize of 5s.

The presentation of prizes took place at 8.30 p.m. on the lawn fronting the Royal Hotel (now the site of the Arcade). Rows of lanterns that had been hung in the grounds lit beautifully, but a device that had been created on the front of the balcony using bucket lamps would not work properly. The letters V R were shaped but the contents obstinately refused to ignite, and this small item in the scheme of illuminations had to be abandoned as impractical.

A powerful ray of light was cast upon the crowd below by a lime-light operator who was positioned in one of the upper windows of Mr. Haywood's offices, which adjoined the hotel; the mellow light occasionally gave way to pretty and effective tints.

The Ceylon Band played a selection of music and gave occasional vocal performances as a variation of the programme, on the lawn where regatta officials and fund-subscribers had assembled. And although the attraction was not that great, several thousand people had gathered in the roadway outside and on the esplanade to witness the prizegiving.

The next Worthing maritime festival, the very first annual Swimming Club Gala, was held on Monday afternoon 29 August off the Pier head. The Mayor and other local dignitaries attended the occasion, and altogether more than 1300 people were admitted to the pier.

For the convenience of competitors, a tent was erected on the east side of the landing stage, and 10 events took place in a somewhat turbulent sea, including:

88 yards handicap for boys under 14
440 yards handicap open
300 yards handicap for Worthing Swimming Club members only
120 yards ditto
150 yards consolation scratch

Two other attractions were: a duck hunt in which six entrants competed to secure a duck; and the well-known Greasy Pole Contest, won by Jo Street again, who won a similar competition two weeks earlier, and who was awarded a leg of mutton. H. Proctor came second winning some ham, while other entrants were T. W. Lucas, T. Wingfield, W. Grant, Nicholl jun., and A. Street.

The town's Annual Regatta was due to be held on the following day, Tuesday 30 August; but during the morning a powerful south westerly wind arose, creating a succession of white-crested rolling waves that threatened to destroy any small craft that left the safety of the beach. Consequently the big occasion was postponed for a fortnight until 13 September.

On this dull September morning a strong wind again threatened to cause the fixture to be postponed, but in the afternoon the sun shone brightly. The sea was quite rough, and although only one crew were willing to venture out in the Junior Fours, and the local Four-Oared Galley Race was postponed to a future date, the Regatta was held that afternoon.

As was usual on Regatta day there was a large number of spectators on the Pier and upon the Parade, where Mr. Wright's popular Brass Band performed selections during the afternoon, the Rhine Band being similarly engaged on the Pier.

In the Lugsail Boats Event, for Worthing watermen in Worthing boats not exceeding 17 feet, the *Seagull* took a long lead soon after the start and won easily with the following results:

J. Hutchinson	*Seagull*	1st prize	£3
George Wingfield	*Lancashire Lass*	2nd	£1 10s.
F. Wakeford	*Petrel*	3rd	15s.
T. Wingfield	*Dolly*	4th	10s.
Bill H. Blann	*Never Can Tell*		
A. Marshall	*Dawn of Day*		
E. Bacon[1]	*Ellen & Margaret*		
W. J. Hutchinson	*Here We Are*		
A. Beck	*Mystery*		

Chief Coastguard Officer Billet was the official starter of the races including the rowing contests, which were particularly troubled by the rough sea with many boats being either swamped or sinking.

There was a large number of spectators on the pier and upon the Parade

Worthing watermen had another race all to themselves, the First-Class Pair-Oared Boats Event. The first and second boats were dead level when they passed the Pier, but Wingfield managed to pull away, winning by four lengths. Three lengths separated second and third; but poor Harry Marshall's boat was a long way behind. The results were as follows:

C. Wingfield	*Daisy*	1st prize	£2
A. Marshall	*Oruba*	2nd	£1 10s.
Fred Collier	*Mabel*	3rd	£1
G. Belton	*Lady Anne*	4th	10s.
F. Collier	*Grace Darling*		
Harry Marshall	*Thistle*		

By the time the last race started, owing to long delays between the races, the tide had receded some distance from the beach and the start was made from almost the end of the pier. In this final event, which was for coastguard galleys, the Worthing and Lancing crews kept almost level for most of the course, but just before the finish the Lancing men put on a last desperate spurt, drew away and won by four lengths. The results were:

Lancing	Mr. Knott, Chief Officer	1st prize £4
Worthing	Mr. Billett, Chief Officer	2nd £2
Goring	Mr. Petty, Chief Boatman	3rd £1

Prompted by his connection with the Magisterial Bench, ex-Mayor Alderman Cortis entertained the local police together with the local lifeboat crews and lifeboat committee on Thursday evening 23 March. A total company of nearly 60 persons was invited to dinner at the *Spaniard Hotel*.

The commencement of a race

Members of the police force were attired in the familiar blue, but the appearance of the sons of the sea in their cork jackets and scarlet caps imparted a touch of colour previously lacking.

Coxwain Charles Lee was proudly wearing his medal awarded to him by the R.N.L.I. Mr. H. Hargood J.P. , chairman of the lifeboat committee arrived late because he had had to preside at a lecture in connection with the Mission to Deep Sea Fishermen.

After toasts to the Royal Family and the Armed Reserve Forces, a toast to 'The lifeboat crews and executive' was next submitted by Alderman Piper, who remarked that there was something very grand and very noble about a lifeboat and its crew; but when they came to deal with the Worthing lifeboat crew there was something very chilling about it, because some of them knew how the first lifeboat at Worthing came to be established. Forty years earlier the boatmen of that time had put off in an ordinary beach boat to the rescue of the barque *Lalla Rookh*, but they had not returned in the same manner as they had gone out, shoulder to shoulder, in the full vigour of their manhood. Instead they had come home one at a time simply to find their last resting place in God's Acre at Broadwater, where there is a monument recording the heroism and bravery of that gallant band.

They had that night gathered before them the descendants of those men - worthy sons of worthy sires - they had in the lifeboat crew men who in the past had shown that in the hour of danger they were ready to risk their lives to save those of their fellow men; and what they had done in the past they would do in the future.

Alderman Piper continued, "We have been told by pessimists – by men whose livers were out of order, for they were synonymous terms – that England has seen its best days. We have been told that the power and influence of this dear old land had passed its meridian; that it's star was on the wane, and that before long it would set, and this old land of ours be only remembered in history as ancient Carthage, Rome or Greece; that we should be simply looked upon as having a grand history, but no future, and scarcely any present. It was false; it was a slander; let them not believe it. So long as we had this sea-girt island of ours."

His speech was interrupted by a shout, "What about the Channel Tunnel!"

"We would never have the Channel Tunnel," replied Alderman Piper to the approval from the audience. He hoped our statesmen would be wise enough to see, and, if they were not, he hoped the people would be wise enough to make them see, that we did not want any Channel Tunnel.

Other guests found this all very amusing - a Channel Tunnel? - surely it was only fairy tale stuff.

The Alderman concluded, "We want this island of ours to remain a sea-girt isle, and so long as it can produce such men as those to whom I have alluded, and so long as we are true to ourselves, we can depend upon it that there is no fear that this land of ours would ever take any position but that which it now occupies among the nations of the world."

His speech met with the approval of the gathering and was rapturously applauded.

The toast was replied to by Mr. G. Piggott, Honorary Secretary of the Worthing Lifeboat Committee, who said he had been with the lifeboat crew under all circumstances – at practise sessions, on services, during festive occasions, and at sorrowful times – and had always found them ready and willing, and thoroughly well-behaved. A better body of men he was quite certain could not be found. He could not speak too highly of Coxwain Lee; they had only to look at the medal on his chest, which had been given to him for the number of lives he had been instrumental in saving, to be assured of his fitness for the post he held in the lifeboat. He did not believe there was a better coxwain to be found around our shores; they might have found one as good, but they would not have found one better.

Mr. Piggott praised the Executive, saying they were a body of gentlemen who worked together most harmoniously, and always did their best for the Institution.

Coxwain Lee replied saying that when the boat was needed the crew were never found wanting.

In proposing The Royal National Lifeboat Institution the Mayor mentioned that there were 304 stations around our coast similar to the one in this town, dedicated to the one objective of saving life at sea. Last year (1892) the Society's boats saved 836 lives, besides assisting to rescue 33 vessels from destruction; and in addition, 220 lives were saved by shore boats and other means, making a grand total of 1,066 lives saved during the year.

At this point loud cheers went up from the guests.

They now had men as brave as those who went out to help the *Lalla Rookh*, and it was due to the Institution that it was possible to do this work with the minimum potential risk that human ingenuity and skill could devise.

Mr. H. Hargood, who had been connected with the Institution for more than 30 years, replied to the toast, mentioning in the course of his speech that since 1884 the boats of the Institution had been instrumental in saving no fewer than 6,672 lives.

This statement was greeted with loud hand-clapping.

Year by year the expenses increased, for there was never any invention brought out that might add to the safety of the boats, and by that means protect the lives of the noble men who manned them, that the Institution was not ready to provide. In the previous year (1892) the income derived from subscriptions and donations, and interest on invested funds, was deficient in meeting the expenditure by £20,880; and he therefore thought the Committee were justly entitled to issue an appeal throughout the length and breadth of the land, asking for clergy and ministers to establish a Lifeboat Sunday, thus giving everybody an opportunity of contributing to support the Society's noble work.

Further applause errupted from the guests before Captain Holmes R. N., one of the R.N.L.I. inspectors, said a few words, disclosing that more than 37,000 lives had been saved by the boats around the coast since the Institution was established.

Mr. Melvill Green proposed 'The Chairman,' to which toast a most enthusiastic reception was given by the company present.

The chairman, who was the Mayor, explained that in giving an invitation to dinner, it was usual to ask some congenial friends to meet one's guest, and he thought he could not do better than ask the lifeboat men to be present.

All of the songs and recitations, to relieve the speeches during the evening had a distinctly military or nautical flavour. Coxwain Lee sang 'The Queen and the Navy forever'; and Mr. T. Wingfield, facetiously referred to as 'Jumbo', probably attracted most attention, with an occasional vocal flourish of Pom-tiddly-om, being introduced with great brevity and received with loud laughter.

When the clock chimed eleven, a hearty round of cheers was voiced by those present for their genial host, Alderman Cortis, and the singing of the National Anthem brought a pleasant gathering to a close.

In furtherance of the national appeal for R.N.L.I. funds hitherto mentioned, the following letter appeared in the 19 July issue of the Worthing Gazette.

'A Lifeboat Saturday at Manchester resulted in the collection of £5,000, and one at Leeds in the handing over of £2,000 to the Institution. The service is still however in dire need of funds, having this year a deficiency of many thousands of pounds. If the noble example above-mentioned is followed by other centres of population they will simply be upholding a voluntary service that we cannot possibly do without. There is not the slightest doubt of the endeavour proving a success; the harvest is there, and it only wants reaping.

One has but to stand on this dangerous coast, watching the alabaster thunderclouds gather with the oncoming of the storm as one listens to the distant peals of thunder and watches the flashes of lightning dart before one's eyes penetrating the heavens, and to see the storm increase in its fury and the tempestuous sea dash with terrific force against the surrounding reef. Presently the masts of a merchantman in distress are visible, from which rockets are being fired, and she is seen hoisting signals of distress; fast is she being driven to her ruin on our rugged and dangerous coast. No life is apparent, save what is lashed to the rigging, for the deck has long been cleared, and night is fast approaching. From the shore comes the familiar cry of Man the lifeboat! The small but well found schooner, under close-reefed topsails, is, before the eyes of anxious lookers, being fast hurried to its doom in this tumultuous and seething sea, the turbling and troubled waters and boiling and foaming spray almost reaching the top-gallant mast. What anxious moments! The lifeboatmen kiss their wives, their sweethearts, and their daughters, and bid them Goodbye.

Is it a forlorn hope? When all seems gloom and despair the familiar blue-and-white boat of mercy leaps out of the darkness into the midst of the foaming surf. The huge roaring waves, breaking with terrific force with a noise as of the most appalling thunder, seem to defy the efforts of the brave lifeboatmen. On she goes on her errand of mercy, the fury of the tempest beating upon her bow, the blinding flashes of lightning permeating the brave little craft. The roaring sea, rising mountains high, dashes with thundering roar upon the surrounding reef, the huge waves at times seeming to almost engulf the boat. Even the brave hearts of those who form the gallant crew cannot now fail to be impressed by the mighty power and majesty of the forces of nature. Amidst all this the wreck is cleared of every living soul, and the brave and fearless hearts return from their perilous adventure and errand of mercy with the rescued (some indeed breath their last before the shore is reached), amidst a thousand cries of "Well done, ye noble warriors of a briny deep!"

Can Englishmen see these lion-hearts, who court what seems to be certain death at every storm, in dire distress? No! One has but to read some of the touching and ineffaceable incidents of the imperishable annals of the nation's heroism to have his heart stirred. Cannot Sussex do something in aid of the funds of one of the prides and glories of this the first maritime nation in the world? With what force the following words bring unto our minds deeds of days gone by:

> O pilot! 'tis a fearful night,
> There's danger on the deep.
> But,when the stormy winds do blow,
> Ye gentlemen of England,
> That live at home at ease,
> Ah! little do you think upon
> The dangers of the seas.

Surely Englishmen are still proud, and not wanting in appreciation, of the heroic services and noble work of the Royal National Lifeboat Institution! What can Sussex do for it?'

Footnotes Ch. 13

[1]Bacon - A member of the Bacon family that suffered a tragic loss in the *Lalla Rookh* disaster.

Ch. 14

Praise From An Earnest Visitor 1893-4

Here in Worthing we had a thriving fishing industry that was more productive than Southwick and Shoreham put together. According to a government return issued in April 1893, the value of fish landed at Worthing during the previous year was £2,536, compared to a combined total of £1,601 for Shoreham and Southwick.

The fish market on the beach to the east of the pier during a quiet day

A well-known fish salesman, Tom Burtenshaw, died at the beginning of April, at the age of 82, which was considered at that time to be quite an advanced age. He was buried on Thursday 6 April at the Broadwater and Worthing cemetery in South Farm Road, where his coffin was carried to the grave by four of his friends: Charles Lee, coxwain of the lifeboat, Steve Wingfield, Harry Blann and Bill Blann, in the presence of several other people from the fishing community.

The unusually hot days of spring 1893 were followed by a drought which baked and split the ground.

During the second week of May a dreadful fever struck Worthing, now inhabited by 17,000 people. Sixty were diagnosed as suffering from typhoid. The following week a further 42 were affected.

While this was happening, my great grandfather, Harry Blann, was on a fishing expedition somewhere towards the eastern end of the English Channel.

During his absence the fever visited the Blann family and killed one of his children.

As fishermen were gone for weeks at a time capturing their perishable stock, my great grandmother, Alice, sent an urgent message to Harry, informing him of the tragic visitation.

On receipt of the melancholy news the fishermen abandoned operations, hauled in their nets and sailed for home.

But on his return he learnt that, since the tragic news had been despatched, another of his youngsters had died from the fever.

Thirty people in the town died of typhoid by 9 June, out of 284 reported cases of contracting the disease.

Folk were now boiling water and milk as a precaution, and only one or two new cases were reported the following week.

'The epidemic may be considered at an end.'

This statement, which had been signed by the Mayor, the Town Clerk, the Medical Officer and the Chairman of the Sanitory Committee, was announced on 16 June.

Townsfolk stopped boiling their water; and during the first three weeks of July the disease infected 548 residents.

The railway company even took the unprecedented step of stopping all excursion trains to the town from 23 July. Rich people moved up country to avoid contamination; leaving their villas empty and shuttered, and their normally well-kept gardens to fall into a state of neglect.

They tried to sell their expensive homes, but found that the bottom had fallen out of the market.

Forty businessmen made a 'killing' by purchasing properties at drastically-slashed prices and reselling them after the fever scare was over at a greatly increased mark-up, or so it was thought.

Water was brought in from the neighbouring West Worthing Water Works and Shoreham Water Works in 100 gallon tanks when 1,000 typhoid cases had been reported and 100 persons had died. Those who were still healthy collected their water supplies in jugs and buckets which they filled from these large tanks perched on carts in the streets.

Drinking water was brought in from the neighbouring West Worthing Water Works and Shoreham Water Works in 100 gallons tanks

It was not until after the origin of the epidemic was officially realised as being the impure water supply 'fed by a watercourse travelling under fields hitherto used by the municipal authorities as a sewage farm,' that leaflets were distributed warning people to still boil all drinking water, and reminding them that the water in the tanks was not intended for use by horses and cattle.

Fever troubles affected annual festivities in the town. The Local Regatta Committee mooted the idea of including a lifeboat competition in this year's events and set about raising the £30 - £40 required to stage the race. But due to the disruption caused by the epidemic a -total of only £11 was subscribed by supporters and the Local Regatta had to be abandoned for this year. After meeting their liabilities of £9, the committee devoted the balance of £2 to the benefit of Worthing watermen.

In the depressed state of affairs caused by the typhoid outbreak a diminished interest in the Annual Regatta was inevitable, the competition being open to entrants from south coast towns.

It was many years since so small an attendance of spectators was seen at this very popular occasion. Very few visitors came in from neighbouring towns to witness the sport provided, and the beach was practically deserted. Only 1,073 people paid to go on the pier, 2,645 fewer than the previous year when 3,718 passed the turnstiles.

The attendance at the Annual Regatta was very poor this year

In one respect, that Thursday 17 August was particularly favoured, the weather was magnificent, in marked contrast to previous years, and the sun did literally shine upon those stalwart supporters who did turn up.

The crews from Worthing rowing clubs were unplaced in every race, a sombre reflection of the mood of the town.

In the Lug Sail Boats Race for Worthing boats not exceeding 17 feet, no centre boards or false keels allowed, watermen's craft were placed as follows:

Marquis of Salisbury	A. Beck	1st
Lancashire Lass	G. Wingfield	2nd
Dolly	T. Wingfield	3rd
Dawn of Day	Bill Marshall	4th

But as there had been no wind to fill the sails all the competitors had cheated by paddling vigorously, and some of their friends had even rowed out from the beach to assist them. The race would have to be re-run.

The committee decided to sail the race on the following afternoon when fortunately there was a good breeze to help the craft. All went well until the *Marquis of Salisbury* turned too sharply round the eastward spot buoy, keeled over and sank in 15 feet of water. The three crew, Frank Burden (a lifeboatman), W. Wells and H. Brown, received a good ducking, but were picked up by the *Curlew* and another boat in the race. The results of this re-run were: *Dawn of Day*, 1st; *Lancashire Lass*, 2nd; *Petrel*, 3rd; the Blann brothers' *Never Can Tell*, 4th; *Dolly*, 5th.

Two lifeboatmen received prizes in the traditional Walking the Greasy Pole competition. Jo Street came first again, as in recent years. He was awarded 10s. The 2nd prize of a leg of mutton went to J. Davis.

Immediately after the close of the Regatta the prizes were distributed without formality in the committee room at the *Marine Hotel*. As it was feared that the sound of explosives might distress some of the many invalids in the town suffering from typhoid, the customary display of fireworks by Messrs. Brock & Co. was dispensed with for this year.

The number of new cases of typhoid eased off during September. The worst of the epidemic, which had claimed 168 lives, was over, but residents remained cautious and uneasy.

People's wariness persisted the following year. On Thursday 31 May 1894, when the lifeboat underwent its periodical inspection by an inspector of the R.N.L.I., the familiar large crowd was not there to watch.

The *Henry Harris* was drawn from its headquarters in Marine Parade by a team of six horses supplied by the signalman, Councillor W. J. Butcher, and the launch was effected in such an admirable manner that the Inspector was afterwards led to remark that in only one other of the 150 stations he visited had he found the horses take the water in thoroughly good style, that other station being Mablethorpe on the Lincolnshire coast.

Under Coxwain Lee the crew rowed the lifeboat out past the pier head, where they hoisted the sail and began to put the boat through its paces.

On completion of the exercises, everything was found to be in order by the Inspector, who declared that the station was among the best on the coast. He also acknowledged the interest displayed by the local committee in the welfare of the Institution.

Another excitingly unusual craft was launched on 18 June 1894: a new yacht built by John Belton at his yard in Library Place. The vessel named *White Wings* was constructed for Mr. G. F. Smith of West Worthing, who was a member of the Mosquito Yacht Club. Mr. Smith designed a new dropkeel for the racing yacht, which superseded the *Isobel*, with which its owner won 11 out of 14 first prizes.

Beltons Yard also built the *Jolly Sailor* which was used for taking out rich holidaymakers on pleasure trips by its owner, boatman Harry Marshall[1]. His brothers used the *Ariadne* for the same purpose and herring catching as well. Built by Beltons, it was named after the Greek town of Ariadne, which was one of the many places around the world that Harry Marshall had seen, having been a deep sea sailor since the age of 14.

Also built by Beltons were four unusually large luggers which were kept by their owners shored up on the beach opposite Western Place.

Watermen's Regatta spectators on the beach, where a marquee was erected opposite the *Pier Hotel*

The local fishing and boating community, the majority of whom were associated with the lifeboat service, held their Watermen's Regatta on Thursday 9 August. Gathered on the beach and on the Pier were a considerable number of spectators. In addition to season ticket holders on the pier, 2,410 paid for admission during the day.

In bright, clear conditions a powerful westerly wind assisted the sailing boats in speeding over the course, but the oarsmen found their task a very laborious one. Owing to the difficulties encountered, the slowness of proceedings taxed the patience of the onlookers. The first race commenced just before 3 p.m. and the last race was not completed until past 6 p.m., by which time only a comparatively small number of spectators remained.

During the afternoon Mr. G. F. Wright's Band played its customary melodies on the east side of the pavilion at the Pier head.

The meeting, under the auspices of the Regatta Committee, had been organised by a sub-committee which included three boatmen: Charles Lee, A Beck, and Harry Marshall. C. R. Ramsay, Wm. Paine, E. F. Collet, Captain Fraser and W. Paine completed the panel.

William Paine, Captain of the Britannia Club, acted as starter for the races, the results of which are listed at the end of this book.

A rescue race was staged on this occasion. Five boats were beached opposite the Country Club in readiness for an 'accident' which had been arranged. A 'lady' in a boat near the Pier was thrown overboard, and when the mishap was observed from the shore, the five boats put off, the rescue being successfully effected by the *Oruba*.

Greasy Pole:

Jo Street	1st prize	10s.
J. Groves	2nd	5s.

In the evening the prizes were presented in the Pier Pavilion (at the southern end of the Pier) by the Mayoress Mrs. Piper who was accompanied by the Mayor.

The contest did not pass without disagreement. Mr. T. Clark objected to the *Southern Cross* receiving second prize in the Sailing Race, on the grounds that she fouled the south spot boat, and another protest was lodged in respect of the Pair-Oared Race. Both of these matters were reserved for consideration by the Committee.

A vote of thanks to the Mayoress for kindly presenting the prizes was proposed by Alderman Cortis and carried by acclamation.

Acknowledging the compliment on behalf of his wife, the Mayor said he could assure the company that it was with very great pleasure that the Mayoress went there to distribute the prizes. When he looked round and saw such a large number of visitors present, and when he saw, as he did that afternoon, so numerous an assemblage along the front and on the Pier, he felt that he ought to tell them that evening how warmly they welcomed the visitors to Worthing at the present time.

The crowd applauded and he continued, saying that he could not help feeling either that they had been influenced this year by knowing that the town wanted them, knowing the terrible disaster of last year, they felt that the town was ripe to receive them. He assured them that the townspeople generally appreciated their coming amongst them so soon after the event of last year; and he hoped they and their little ones would go back better than they had come, thoroughly recovered in health, so that they would be able to tell their friends that Worthing was not only one of the prettiest towns along the coast but also one of the healthiest.

After a further round of applause the Mayor proposed a vote of thanks to the officials of the Watermen's Regatta and the proceedings came to a close.

Watermen in a wider sense of the word were the topic of the day at St. Botolph's Church on Sunday 19 August 1894. At each service on that day the vicar spoke about the lives of sailors in his sermon; after which a collection was made for the 'Missions to Seamen' by uniformed Worthing Coastguardsmen together with their newly appointed Chief Officer, Henry Lang, who had taken over the post from Chief Officer Billett on his retirement four months earlier.

Following the after effects of the typhoid epidemic Worthing held a maritime event which was unprecedented on the south coast. A Lifeboat Day was held on Wednesday 22 August 1894, with the dual purposes of adding another attraction to the Worthing season and creating a wider interest in this little watering place on the South Coast. But the primary purpose of the demonstration was to stimulate greater interest in the work of the R.N.L.I. and collect funds on its behalf. England was the maritime supremo of the world, and her very existence depended on this supremacy. The Institution had been instrumental in saving 38,000 lives but their expenditure at this time had surpassed their income by more than £26,000 , leaving them in urgent need of money.

Mr. Hargood was the main organiser, assisted by the Mayor, Alderman Robert Piper, who was chairman of the General Lifeboat Day Committee. Brilliant weather favoured the occasion which was patronised by some very distinguished guests: the Marquis of Abergavenny K.G. , Lord Lieutenant of Sussex; the High Sheriff of Sussex, Mr. C. J. Fletcher; His Grace the Duke of Norfolk, E.M., K.G. ; His Grace the Duke of Richmond and Gordon K.G. ; the Right Hon. Lord H. Thyne; Sir Henry Fletcher, Bart, M.P.; Admiral of the Fleet Sir G. Phipps Hornby G.C.B.; Mr Gerald Loder M.P.; and Mr. Bruce Wentworth M.P.

As a prelude to a busy afternoon, the Mayor entertained a numerous company to luncheon at the *Royal Hotel*, to the strains of the Rhine Band which played on the lawn.

Shops closed for the afternoon. Lines of flags hung across the streets while lavish decorations adorned the principle thoroughfares. The Parade and the Pier were decorated with bunting whilst, at the bottom of South Street, a triumphal arch formed of firemen's ladders and appliances was a conspicuous feature.

An imposing cortege, scheduled to move off at two o'clock, had been forming in what was the new part of Shelley Road. The order of procession was as follows:

H.M. Coastguard, Worthing.
1st Sussex Artillery Volunteers, No. 8 (Shoreham) Company preceded by their band.
H. (Worthing) Company 2nd Volunteer Batallion Royal Sussex Regiment under the command of
    Major A. Henty preceded by their band.
Fire Brigades commanded by Captain Crouch of Worthing.
L. B. & S. C. R. (London Brighton & South Coast Railways) Brigade with steam engine.
Littlehampton Volunteer Fire Brigade with a manual.
Worthing Borough Fire Brigade: No. 1 manual fire engine.
                                     No. 2 manual fire engine
                                     No. 3 manual fire engine
                                     No. 1 hose reel
                                     No. 2 hose reel
Broadwater Volunteer Brigade with hose reel, Chief Officer R. R. W. Hyde in charge.
Band of the Brighton Volunteer Fire Brigade.
Band of *H.M.S. St. Vincent.*
The Brighton Lifeboat of the R.N.L.I.; Coxwain Maynard.
The Shoreham Lifeboat of the R.N.L.I.; Coxwain J. Humpries.
The Littlehampton Lifeboat of the R.N.L.I.; Coxwain Pelham.
The Worthing Lifeboat of the R.N.L.I.; Coxwain Charles Lee.

The most interesting feature of the procession was the lifeboats, fully manned, and each drawn by six horses. The fire engines were also well horsed, and the entire procession was one not to be readily forgotten, with 85 collectors plying for funds along the route. The cavalcade proceeded westward along the entire length of Shelley Road to Heene Road, returning by way of Marine Parade to the Steyne, along Warwick Street and finally down South Street towards the Pier.

When the procession arrived in South Street, the soldiers and sailors marched into an enclosure reserved for the lifeboats, followed by the firemen who had dismounted from their engines.

For the first time, races for lifeboats had been arranged. The four lifeboats were drawn on to the beach to the east of the Pier, and shortly after 3 p.m. the massed bands played the National Anthem; the signal to launch was given, and the lifeboats glided simultaneously into the sea to the loud cheers of the spectators and the sound of Rule Britannia played by the bands.

At this time the Parade between Bath Place and Bedford Row was jam-packed with people, as was the landward half of the Pier.

The placid sea was dotted with small sailing and rowing craft, one of which was occupied by Mr. Oscar Wilde, who was visiting Worthing at the time. The summer toillettes of the ladies afloat and ashore gave an additional note of charm and colour.

The four red, white and blue lifeboats formed a very pretty sight with their blue and white oars, as their crews in their cork jackets and vivid scarlet caps made their way seawards.

The four lifeboats being drawn in procession past the *Marine* and the *Pier Hotels*

A beautiful scene was apparent, looking inland from the Pavilion, which was near the Pier head: dense crowds lined the shore, rising up to the handsome houses and gardens of the Parade, with the distant sweep of the South Downs forming a charming background.

As the day advanced the beauty of both sea and shore were enhanced by a lovely, distant, but particularly clear view of Brighton and the cliffs beyond, as far as Beachy Head, which under the rays of the setting sun, stretched out along the horizon in a long low line of white, accented at intervals by gleaming spots of silvery light.

The Pier was now crowded from end to end. There was to be two races: one rowing and the other sailing. The starter in both cases was Mr. H. Hargood J.P. and Mr. T.U. Thynne R.N. , Judge. The course for each race was from the Pier to buoys off West Buildings, returning off the head of the Pier, round buoys off York Terrace and back to the Pier.

Positions had been previously drawn in public at the luncheon by Lord Henry Thynne and the Mayor: Brighton had been alotted the number one position at the shore end; Shoreham, number two; Littlehampton, number three; and Worthing, number four, sea berth.

The rowing contest, which took place first, and Worthing's win by a good two lengths, were received with tumultuous cheers by the spectators. Shoreham came second, about a length ahead of the Littlehampton lifeboat, and Brighton was a very bad fourth.

The fine, still weather was unkind to the sailing race, and in the absence of the necessary breeze oars had to be resorted to over part of the course. Worthing had an easy win over Shoreham, followed by the Littlehampton boat while the Brighton crew were last back to the Pier.

When the exciting events on the seafront had been brought to a close, a new source of diversion was created in South Street, where a large body of local and visiting firemen, under the chief command of Captain A. Crouch, enacted a most interesting series of drills. The brigades had constructed in honour of the occasion, a triumphal arch, formed of two fire escapes with ladders laid across, from which buckets, flags and hoses were suspended. Here the Old Bank formed a useful base for operations, the exercises consisting mainly of using the domestic fire escape, carrying down the escape, life-line drill and using the jumping sheet.

The lifeboats preparing to launch from the beach to the east of the pier

Then when the wet drill started the crowd got really excited, and the spectacle of a woman and child within range of a tremendous shower from a hose reel being soaked, afforded great delight to the assembled onlookers. These wet drills from the hydrants effectively doused the dust of South Street and had the effect of scattering the crowd.

Policeing arrangements for the day were the responsibility of Superintendent Long, who directed an additional force of about 20 constables, drafted from other divisions in West Sussex.

During the afternoon the band from *H.M.S. Vincent* played on the Pier head; and the band of the H. Company of Volunteers, on the Parade opposite the *Steyne Hotel*. The band of the Brighton Volunteer Fire Brigade played on the lawn of the *Royal Hotel* and, during the fire brigade drills, opposite the Town Hall.

At tea-time a nautical concert took place in the Pier Pavilion near the Pier head. Those who contributed to the programme included the Pier Band, Miss Edith Chaplin, Mr. Armstrong, and 30 boys from the Richmond Road School dressed as young sailors, under the direction of the headmaster, Mr. A. W. Woolgar. In their smart naval attire they attracted much attention in the streets on their way to the pier.

Prizes totalling more than £15 were presented after the concert by the Mayoress: ranging from £3 18s. for first place in the lifeboat rowing race, to £1 6s. for fourth (last) position in the lifeboat sailing event.

As a fitting conclusion for an eventful day, a grand illumination of the Pier, by Brock & Co. of the Crystal Palace, took place in the evening, when the town and Pier looked even more charming, where the long line of shore lights was met at right angles by rows of coloured lamps which ran out seaward.

The *Henry Harris* being launched to the strains of the National Anthem played by the bands

A total of £60 was raised for the R.N.L.I. on the first Worthing Lifeboat Day and forwarded by the Branch Committee to the headquarters in London.

Another new attraction for visitors to Worthing was the hastily arranged Water Carnival which took place on Thursday evening 13 September 1894. The entire length of the pier was brilliantly illuminated for the occasion with Japanese lanterns and bucket lamps, and over the gateway at the Pier entrance was a device in coloured lights which read 'Go it, Worthing!' Among those who helped with the lights were Messrs. H. E. Snewin, F. G. Blaker, G. Ewen Smith, A. Newington, W. H. Elsworth, E. G. Pope, R. Floate, W. C. Amore and Ward.

As well as the Pier being lit, establishments on the seafront, including the Royal Hotel, the Pier Hotel and Stanhoe Hall, were effectively illuminated.

The chief feature of the evening's entertainment was a procession of 20 illuminated boats, some owned by Worthing boatmen, competing for prizes offered by the committee. The entries were:

Caprice	Mr. C. R. Ramsay
Surprise	Mr. Kellett
Coast Guard Galley	Mr. Lang
The Balli	Mr. Charles
The Dawn of Day	Mr. Marshall
The Seagull	Captain A. Fraser
Ina	Mr. Andrews
Monica	Messrs. J. Haywood and Const
Dolly	Mr. G. Ralli
Tunach	Mr. Lawton
Hilda	Mr. Aldridge

Young William	Mr. Brandon
Pride of Worthing	Mr. Johnston
The Don	Dr. Le Riche
Helen & Margaret	Messrs. Attree and Rouse
Britannia	Mr. William Paine
Edith	Mr. C. Vores
The Primrose	Mr. De Mierre
Lily of the Valley	Miss Dunn

A lifeboat race starting from the pier. The lifeboat with a flag in the bow and nearest the camera is the *Henry Harris;* and shoreward are the Littlehampton and Shoreham lifeboats, with the Brighton lifeboat nearest the beach

The promoters were favoured with a beautiful night, and the pretty spectacle was witnessed by some thousands of people on the Parade and on the beach; while on the Pier, where the ordinary tolls were suspended for the evening and a charge of 6d. made for admission, 1,330 people congregated.

The competing boats assembled opposite Warwick Buildings, the start was signalled by a rocket fired from the Pier head, and the pretty boats proceeded westwards in a line, headed by Mr. Wright's band, mounted on a steam launch.

Some novel designs were displayed in the illumination of the boats: coloured fire was produced and fireworks discharged along the course; while Mr. Ralli's boat contained one of the latest pieces of equipment, a powerful electric searchlight, which was flashed across the water and was panned along the beach.

The pier pavilion at the southern end of the pier

The fire brigades' triumphal arch in South Street

Voting cards, which had been issued for spectators to mark the three best boats, were collected by the committee who counted them and announced the following results:

Mr. C. R. Ramsay   1st
Mr. G. A. Ralli   2nd
Mr. Marshall   3rd

In the Pavilion the Pier Band played a selection of music; and Mr. H. Binstead's Band was stationed about halfway down the Pier.

At the close of the spectacle a concert was given in the Pier Pavilion, and the prizes were distributed by Mr. Oscar Wilde, who was still here on his visit.

He congratulated Worthing on the extremely beautiful scene of that evening. Worthing, he said, had arranged other extremely pretty shows, such as the exceptionally delightful Lifeboat Demonstration.

He could not help feeling the change that had taken place this year in the town, and expressing the great pleasure it gave visitors to return. He considered that such a charming town would become one of the first watering places on the south coast. Mr. Wilde amused his audience by saying that the area had beautiful surroundings and lovely long walks, which he recommended to other people, but did not take himself.

His humour came through again in a reference to Worthing's now excellent water supply, saying that he was told that total abstainers who visited the town were so struck with the purity and excellence of its water that they wished everybody would drink nothing else.

Above all things, he was delighted to observe in Worthing, something very apt at the time, the ability to offer pleasure. To his mind few things were so important as a capacity for being amused, feeling pleasure, and conveying it to others.

Once more he made them laugh by saying that he held that whenever a person was happy he was good, although, perhaps, when he was good he was not always happy.

He told the listeners that there was no excuse for anyone not being happy in such surroundings; and although this was his first visit it would certainly not be his last. His speech was applauded after having been so well received.

Captain Fraser proposed a vote of thanks to Mr. Wilde for his kindness in presenting the prizes, and the entertainment following the Water Carnival drew to a close.

Footnotes Ch. 14

[1] Harry Marshall - Bowman on the *Henry Harris*.

Ch. 15

Action and Inaction 1894 - 5

The sinking of a Worthing lugger at Ramsgate on Tuesday 23 October 1894 caused great excitement and concern. The craft, the *Elizabeth & Mary* belonging to Mr. E. Edwards[1], had just returned from a mackerel voyage with her first good haul of the season. She was heavily laden with 20,000 fish, which had an estimated value of between £50 and £60.

The drama unfolded as people on shore noticed that she was labouring heavily before a strong south east wind. There was a nasty sea running when a giant wave broke over the small vessel.

She staggered under the tremendous force of the impact, and then struck on a shoal to the east of the pier, sinking almost immediately in full sight of a large, concerned crowd which had gathered on the beach.

A strong wind carried the crew's urgent cries to the onlookers, and people at once ran down to the pier, where they witnessed a gallant deed by a man named Little.

This man, who appeared to be near the scene of the accident, got in a boat and rowed vigorously to the spot where the disaster occurred. His plucky effort was rewarded with success, as he managed to rescue all six fishermen from the ill-fated lugger.

The greatest enthusiasm was shown when the half-drowned fellows had been brought safely to land. Little's bravery, shown in rescueing these Worthingites, was recognised by a testimonial.

The Worthing lifeboat *Henry Harris* being launched for its traditional practice

The Worthing Lifeboat *Henry Harris* was launched for its customary practise and inspection on Saturday afternoon 10 November 1894, the horses taking the sea in fine style. After the customary excercise, the crew, under veteran coxwain Lee, pulled ashore at Lancing, where the boat was landed and brought home on its carriage. Captain Holmes R.N., the Institution's Inspector, expressed his complete satisfaction with the result of the afternoon's work.

Four days later, on Wednesday 14 November, when Worthing was experiencing its worst storm for three years, the lifeboat crew were on the beach within a few hundred yards of the boathouse, keeping a good look out, in murky conditions and with visibility limited to 300 yards, for any vessel in distress. The lifeboat horses were harnessed and kept all day in readiness in Walter Butcher's stables at Western Place, only 150 yards from the boathouse.

The gale whipped up the waves at high water, just before noon, to such an extent that parts of the Esplanade were swamped. It was a grand sight witnessed from the seafront, and some of the more highly spirited onlookers went on to the end of the Pier to experience an even better view of the magnificent waves. One of those at the Pier head, Mr. F.W. Patching, was blown down by the sheer force of the wind and sustained a somewhat severe cut over one eye.

At 3.30 p.m., the lifeboatmen and Coastguard received their first news of a distressed vessel, a ship's lifeboat, which had already been driven ashore opposite Lancing pay-gate on the Worthing/Lancing boundary. Within 15 minutes Chief Officer Lang of the Worthing Coastguard turned out all hands and took extra precautions.

Enquiries revealed that the little craft had been sighted about midday by people watching the storm from the Pier and Parade. Many people followed it as it drifted eastward. One of them, a fisherman named Charles Stubbs, who lived in Ann Street, was in no doubt that there was a man aboard her. When the vessel was off the Lancing border, about 300 yards out to sea, it capsized and not long afterwards the boat was washed ashore, keel uppermost, with the name *Zadne* painted on it.

Stubbs, who later registered as a salvor, was helped in securing the heavy whaler-built lifeboat by other men including Norman, Riddles, Tupper, Head and Bull. While being landed in the turbulent foaming surf she struck a groye which stove a small hole in the port bow.

There were six rowlocks in the black-painted boat when she was recovered, but only one pair of oars, one of which was broken. A rudder and a boathook were washed in at the same time. The 21 feet long boat contained a cask of water lashed amidships: a survival requirement rigidly enforced at that time when ships left harbour. She was handed over to Chief Officer McGregor of the Lancing Coastguard, as Deputy Receiver of Wrecks.

Meanwhile wreckage was coming ashore all afternoon – doors, panels, hatches, drawers from chests, and other moveable items which had obviously come from a very large vessel.

Although a large number of people, about 150, had seen the ailing lifeboat, not one of them had deemed it necessary to report their sighting to official quarters.

The arrival of the deserted craft could only be interpreted as a very sad message indicating the fate of the steamer's crew. Even more conclusive evidence of a disaster was forthcoming later, when, during Wednesday night and the following morning, eight bodies were washed ashore, together with some wreckage.

All but one of the bodies were found separately on the beach in the vicinity of the *Half Brick Inn* at East Worthing, at various times during Thursday morning by John Barns, Frederick Parsons, John Watts, Henry Scrace and John Head, who reported their findings to the police and assisted in their removal to the mortuary. The other was found by Edward Small, a bricklayer living at Ham Arch, at 6.30 that same morning at the top of the beach. The body had been washed up and left by the receding tide about 300 yards west of Lancing Tollgate. This discovery Small reported to the Lancing Coastguard.

The bodies were covered in seaweed and their clothes filled with sand. The sheer force of the sea had ripped the clothing, on several of the bodies, into shreds, leaving cut and horribly disfigured limbs exposed. The bodies were strangely clad: one was wearing boots but no trousers. In fact they were all wearing boots, two of them high sea boots and the others, Bluchers (low boots favoured by Field Marshall Blucher, a Prussian). Two of the men brought in were found to have their coats half off; and one of them, apparently a stoker, wore only his underclothes, having possibly left his engines without stopping for his clothes.

Seven of the bloody corpses, of sailors between the ages of 20 and 60, were laid in the Worthing Public Mortuary, in the yard of the old Waterworks. The eighth, having washed ashore on Lancing beach, was kept in the neighbouring parish. In some cases their features were so battered and bruised as to make identification extremely difficult.

Investigations took place which revealed that the *Zadne,* a steamship of 700 ton gross belonging to the Europa Shipping Company, had left the harbour at Briton Ferry, South Wales at 4 p.m. on Saturday 10 November with a full cargo of coal destined for London. She had been due to reach that port today, Thursday, and had last been heard of sheltering under Lundy Island from the bad weather on Sunday.

She had carried 14 hands, the Master, two mates, four seamen, three firemen, a donkeyman, two engineers and a steward, mostly married men from North Shields.

The Coroner came to the *Anchor Inn*, High Street at 1 p.m. on Friday 16 November to open an inquest on the seven men lying in the mortuary. Members of the jury were sworn in and Councillor W.J. Butcher was appointed foreman. During the proceedings the Coroner's Officer, Alderman F.C. Linfield, remarked that the question had been raised as to whether or not the Worthing lifeboat ought to have gone out. The Coroner said this was among the points that he had not yet been touched upon and postponed the inquest until 3 p.m. Thursday next at the Town Hall.

Immediately after the preliminary Worthing inquiry the Coroner drove to Lancing in his horse-drawn vehicle, and opened an inquest on the eighth victim at the *Three Horseshoes Inn*. During this latter inquest accusations were made against the Worthing lifeboat crew and the coastguards.

Elements of the local seafaring community, who were present, were outraged at these allegations.

The Coroner insisted that the maritime rescue services were not on trial at this inquiry and that it would be emminently unfair anyway as there was no evidence for or against. The inquest returned a general verdict on the body, 'found drowned'.

Public concern increased as professional evidence given at the inquest had suggested that, as the bodies were all washed ashore on a comparitively narrow section of beach between the *Half Brick Inn* and the Lancing boundary, the *Zadne* must have gone down within a mile of the coast.

Gossip around Worthing implied that the lifeboatmen and coastguards had been cowardly in not launching a rescue. But their families joined with those of the fishing and boating fraternity, back to back, united in their counterclaim that their men were not faint-hearted.

On the Monday a large portion of the main-deck water ways of a vessel was brought in by the tide, some 40 feet long and roughly $3\frac{1}{2}$ inches thick. Earlier that morning, between six and seven o'clock, four more sandy bodies were found by John Head, labourer Charles Belton of 4 Cranworth Road, and gardener George Hutchings from Warwick Road, on the beach between St. George's Church and the *Half Brick Inn*. Various items of clothing were also discovered. The police were informed and the gruesome, shockingly disfigured bodies were taken to the mortuary.

The Coroner was informed and an inquest was held at 3 p.m. that same day at the *Anchor Inn* with the same jury and foreman as previously. Various testimonies were heard and then the inquest was adjourned until Thursday 22 November to coincide with the adjournment of the other, preliminary Worthing inquest.

View from Railway Bridge, towards Broadwater and the Downs.

1288. 12.

A view looking north from Broadwater Bridge, over which the funeral procession travelled

A mass funeral of 11 of the victims took place at Broadwater on Tuesday 20 November. The other sailor's body was taken by relatives to be buried in his home town in South Wales. Eleven coffins were placed on the two lifeboat carriages and each was drawn by three horses in a cortege led by the local Salvation Army Band. Worthing and Shoreham Lifeboat crews and fishermen walked on either side of the two carriages. After the relatives and mourners came the Coastguards, paying their last respects as the procession left the Mortuary in High Street and wound its way over Broadwater Bridge past crowds of sympathising onlookers.

At the church the lifeboatmen bore the coffins, of their fellow seamen, each draped with a Union Jack, through the west door and placed them in a line which extended from the door almost to the tower.

Leaving by the north door of the church, the cortege proceeded to what was known as the New Cemetery in South Farm Road, where an enormous gathering of people had collected to witness the burial. Never before had so many people attended a funeral; it was estimated that almost 5,000 had turned out. Separate graves had been dug, almost in the centre of the burial ground, for each black coffin. When the coffins were about to be lowered, a pretty cross, made from dried seaweed, was laid above one of the sailors who had not been identified.

Members of the Worthing Lifeboat crew who acted as bearers included: Coxwain Charles Lee, 2nd cox Harry Marshall, bowman Steve Wingfield, Thomas Wingfield, George Wingfield, Tom Wingfield, Bill Blann, Harry Blann, Mark Marshall, Tom Bridger, William Collier, Fred Collier, Frank Collier, S. Bashford, G. Bashford, Stephen Bacon, William Cousins, Frank Burden, George Belton and Peter West.

The Worthing Lifeboatmen placed a handsome tribute on the coffin of Captain Farrell, the master of the *Zadne,* with the inscription 'With deepest sympathy from the Worthing Lifeboat Crew'.

Relatives and friends of the deceased sailors were very touched by the immense sympathy shown by everybody, regardless of class, who gave generously to collections for the dependants.

Controversial rumours were still circulating in the town as to the reasons why the *Henry Harris* did not put to sea to rescue the shipwrecked sailors from the *Zadne.* The local seagoing community were deeply grieved at some of the suggestions being expounded. Lifeboatmen and coastguardsmen alike closed ranks.

32 WORTHING. — The Town Hall. — LL.

The Town Hall where the enquiry was hold

In an attempt to stop the rumours circulating, Mr. H. Hargood J.P., chairman of the Worthing Branch R.N.L.I., issued a statement declaring that no news of a wreck had been received before the *Zadne* lifeboat had been drive ashore; and called for a public inquiry into the catastrophe.

This inquiry was held at the Town Hall on Wednesday afternoon, 21 November, exactly one week after the tragedy and only the day after the mass funeral. Mr. Cunningham Graham, Deputy Inspector of the R.N.L.I., attended the inquiry, the purpose of which was to determine whether there had been any failure of duty on the part of the Worthing Lifeboat crew to render assistance to the shipwrecked sailors from the *Zadne.*

Lifeboatmen and coastguards, eager to support their colleagues, crowded into the Town Hall.

Coxwain Charles Lee, who had been connected with the Worthing lifeboat for 20 years, told the inquiry that he had been watching out on the beach for the whole of that fated stormy morning, for any sign of a distressed vessel. The lifeboat crew, in fact two crews if necessary, were ready at a moment's notice, if there had been any sign or had they received any message of a craft in difficulty.

A Mr. Edward Tucker of Chesswood Road, called as a witness, said that he first saw the drifting ship's lifeboat when it was off the Navarino, and it was some time before anyone thought there was possibly a man standing in it: a lady on the Pier thought she saw a man, but others around her put it down to her imagination.

A Mr. Gerald Rouse gave evidence that a man named Alfred Swain said he thought there was a boat off the College. In the poor visibility it was almost impossible, even through binoculars, to see the boat, which was about 200 yards from land. But as they thought they might have seen somebody in the craft he sent Swain to inform the lifeboatmen and coastguard.

Alfred Swain told the inquiry that he misunderstood Rouse and thought he had to report to the fishermen, Stubbs and Riddles.

Charles Stubbs told the sitting that he took no steps to report the matter to the lifeboat crew.

Mr. G. Piggott, Worthing Branch Secretary of the R.N.L.I., stated that he had remained at home all the morning in order that, if any messages or telegrams had come, no time would have been lost. He had not heard of the loss of the boat until the afternoon, when he told Harry Marshall, 2nd coxwain of the *Henry Harris,* that the lights at the boathouse had better be lit and an all-night watch kept.

Alfred Downer, who had been on the beach when the boat came ashore, had first seen it off the *Half Brick* about 400 yards out with a man it, he thought; and believed that Swain had raised the alarm.

The inquiry's chairman, Mr. H. Hargood J.P., who was also Worthing Branch Chairman of the R.N.L.I., said that the lifeboat committee took every precaution they could to make the Worthing lifeboat efficient, and that the lifeboatmen themselves were always ready, day or night, to do their duty. After this statement loud applause, particularly from those who engaged in maritime pursuits for a means of support, filled the Town Hall. The inquiry then recessed for 30 minutes for the inspector to prepare his report.

When the sitting resumed, and before Mr. Graham read the document, he made it clear that it was not the duty of lifeboatmen to watch the coast. That was the coastguard's responsibility and the lifeboatmen's duty started when they had received a call.

The inspector then read his report, which was a most complete exoneration of the lifeboat crew, and which greatly excited and pleased the crowded public gallery, resulting in rapturous acolade.

The Town Hall was used the next day, Thursday 22 November, for the adjourned inquest on the 11 bodies washed ashore within the borough boundary. Although the preliminary investigation had been held at the *Anchor Inn,* a larger venue was necessary to accommodate the considerable number of people who displayed a great interest in the proceedings.

Councillor W.J. Butcher was again foreman of the jury and Alderman Melvill Green was there in the interest of the R.N.L.I. Among others in the hall were: Mr. H. Hargood J.P., Chairman of the Worthing Branch R.N.L.I.; Mr. G. Piggott, Honorary Secretary of the local branch; Supt. J. Long; Mr. A.R. Dawson, Receiver of Wrecks, Shoreham; Chief Officer Lang of the Worthing Coastguard; Chief Officer McGregor of the Lancing Coastguard; E. Snewin and Coxwain Lee of the Worthing lifeboat.

One of those giving evidence was Mr. Alfred Swain who had been on the Parade on the 14th. He revealed to the jury that two children had drawn his attention to a boat, some 300 – 400 yards off St. George's Church with what appeared to be a man standing up in it, although some thought it was a small mizzen mast. Swain explained how he had run in the direction of the Pier, facing wind and rain, jumping railings and a wall, to the end of the Parade (Splash Point), where he had stopped, exhausted. There he had told Stubbs, Riddles, Lawman and a group of boys of the impending emergency, that there was a man in a boat requiring assistance.

Swain insisted to the jury that he had thought news would get to the lifeboatmen when he saw the boys running in both directions along the seafront. But Stubbs had had another priority on his mind: he wanted to claim salvage on the boat and had given instructions to the others to report nothing until they had recovered the craft.

2001 Worthing   Rough Sea

Swain had run, facing wind and rain, jumping railings and a wall, to the end of the Parade

Henry Scrace, a brickmaker, said he had been with Swain at the time that they had seen the vessel with it's standing occupant. Scrace had followed the boat eastward while Swain had gone to inform the lifeboatmen. The boat had remained afloat until it reached a point, above low water mark, about a mile east of the Pier, where it capsized, throwing its occupier into the murky sea. Scrace told the jury that he had seen this distinctly and had seen the man gain the boat and cling to the life line, only to be washed off when the craft had righted, about 400 to 500 yards off the beach.

Swain, who was next to give evidence, remarked that the small vessel had been driven ashore at 1.15 p.m.

Henry Lang, Chief Officer of the Worthing Coastguard reported to the inquest that some wreckage had come ashore from this boat: a sea anchor and a 16 foot mast fitted with a span of three inch manilla rope.

In summing up the Coroner said the inquest had brought home to them more vividly than usual the dangers and perils of the deep, for in ordinary cases the facts were not so closely scrutinised.

Going over the evidence, he said that even if Swain had acted differently, it may still have been to no avail, but he would not have known that at the time. If he had not done his utmost he was surely to blame because it appeared that he had been more interested in making a salvage claim than in rescueing the person in the boat.

It had been suggested that the lifeboat authorities had not prepared, but the Coroner was of the opinion that that accusation had been disproved this day, even if not at the lifeboat inquiry the previous day. The evidence clearly showed that the lifeboat was in the proper place, the lifeboat house, and the crew ready for emergencies; and the Coroner concluded that there was no doubt that if a report had reached the lifeboatmen they would have launched their boat immediately.

The Jury retired to the ante-room and returned after a short while, the foreman announcing that they had reached a decision: "That these men were part of the crew of the steamship *Zadne;* that they were found drowned; and that no blame could be attached to the Worthing lifeboat or coastguard."

The Coroner entered the verdict accordingly and the inquest on the 11 sailors closed.

As yet, two of the 14 hands from the *Zadne* had not been recovered.

On Saturday 24 November, two days after the inquest, two boys playing on the beach discovered two gruesome corpses: Charles Hide, of 14 Cranworth Road, found one at 11.30 a.m. on the beach near Selden Gap, about ¼ mile west of the *Half Brick;* the other was discovered by William Burden, of 30 Gloucester Place, at 1.30 p.m. while he was shrimping opposite the coastguard flagstaff.

They each reported their finding to the police, who removed the revoltingly distorted bodies to the mortuary in High Street. The Coroner was again called and a final inquest was held at the *Anchor Inn,* near the mortuary, two days later on Monday 26 November.

The same jury, as used in the previous inquest, was again called and the same foreman chosen. To satisfy the requirements of the law, the jurors had to view the ghastly remains before hearing formal evidence.

The Coroner in summing up said that there was no doubt that these two men were the remaining crew of the *Zadne;* the Jury agreed and the Coroner returned a verdict of 'found drowned.'

The following day, the funeral of these last two unfortunate sailors took place with a cortege starting from the Mortuary at 2.30 p.m. and moving in the direction of the cemetery in South Farm Lane (now South Farm Road). It had been decided to dispense with a church service.

Again the Salvation Army Band headed the procession playing the Dead March. The two coffins, draped with Union Jacks, borne on a small carriage were followed by Coxwain Lee and his lifeboat crew, together with the coastguards.

Several hundred people witnessed the service at the cemetery, where the sailors' comrades graves had been well looked after: flowers which had been very neatly arranged covering each one, still retained some of their bloom. Prominent among the wreaths was one under glass from the Worthing lifeboat crew which was placed on Thomas Farrell's grave, the captain of the lost *Zadne.*

As with the previous mass burial, many wreaths, mostly from the fishing community, were laid upon the two graves. Those bearing cards had the following inscriptions: Mrs. G. Read; J. Barnett; Frances and Alice Collier; T.R. Wingfield and family, two; a sailor's mother, two; Mrs. C. Belton; Misses A. and E. Barnett; Thomas and Rachel Wingfield; Mr. Mrs. A.C. West; a fatherless Boy; Mr. C. Belton; and Mrs. F. Lelliott.

And so the last of the 14 crew of the fated *Zadne* were laid to rest.

The events of this bizarre tragedy were commemorated in a beautiful yet pathetic momento of five photographic views on a single large card. On the top were the words 'In memoriam S S Zadne'; in the four corners, a view of the ship's lifeboat washed ashore, the beach where some of the bodies were picked up, Broadwater Church where the first burial service was held, and the entrance to the cemetery where the sailors are interred; whilst in the centre was a photograph of the wreath-covered graves, and the words 'Their last enchorage.' This beautiful work of art was appropriately encircled by oars and entwined ropes, with floral tributes associated with God's acre. It was issued by Mr. Francis Tate, stone mason of North Street (the firm is still there today), to raise funds for a monument over the graves by setting aside a third of the 2s. retail price.

Each 8d. went towards a public appeal, launched to raise £62 0s, 10d, for the design and erection of the monument, and £52 11s. 0d. funeral expenses. Thanks to the warm generosity of Worthing citizens the target of £114 11s. 10d, was surpassed, a total of £127 19s. 3d. being raised. After printing and postage expenses of 9s. 8d. the balance £12 17s. 9d. was divided in two: £2 17s. 9d. was sent to the relations of the sailor buried at Swansea, South Wales; and £10 went to the Mayor of Tynemouth, home port of the *Zadne,* to be added to a distress fund raised in his district.

Lifeboat supporters in Worthing were interested to learn that in the year ended 31 December 1894, R.N.L.I. lifeboats were launched 398 times, resulting in 625 people being rescued. The long list of services included much valuable property being saved, 33 vessels having been rescued from total or partial loss, besides which scores of fishing boats returning from the fleets would have been unable to make harbour and would probably have been wrecked had it not been for the important assistance of the lifeboats. Lifeboat crews assembled on a further 41 occasions, but in the event their services were not required. Rewards were also granted by the institution for the saving of 141 lives by shore boats, bringing the total number of lives saved during the year which could be attributed to the R.N.L.I. to 766, and to 38,621 since 1824.

On Saturday afternoon, 11 May 1895, a little boy about four years old, the son of Mr. Mrs. Burgess of Park Road, Worthing, had a close escape from drowning through falling off a groyne at the end of the Parade (Splash Point) opposite the Amateur Boat Clubhouse. A lady visitor who was walking along the Parade at the time, ran into the sea to help, but the water was too deep for her. She ran to the clubhouse and told Mr. R. Isted, a member of the Worthing Swimming Club. He rescued the unconcious boy from the water and carried him to the clubhouse where he recovered after being given artificial respiration by a Mr. C. Grinstead.

Two months later, on Saturday 20 July 1895, a ship was in danger of being blown onto Worthing beach during a fierce S.S.W. force 10 gale. At 2 p.m. the vessel was spotted by both the lifeboat chairman Mr. Hargood and Charlie Lee the Coxwain, but the brigantine showed no distress signal in the changeable conditions, and no immediate danger was apprehended. But when about two miles east of the Pier, the brig grounded.

Chief Coastguard Officer Lang was taking no chances and immediately fired the black static lifeboat cannon, on the Parade opposite the lifeboat station, to summon the lifeboat crew. At 2.35 p.m., the horses, which had been in readiness all morning at the stables belonging to Councillor Butcher, the lifeboat signalman, were sent for; while the tall wooden doors of the lifeboat house were drawn open and folded back to expose the *Henry Harris* on its carriage.

The black static lifeboat canon on the Parade opposite the lifeboat station. Between the canon and the coastguards' flagmast can be seen one of the R.N.L.I. pillar boxes for donations. The lugger on the beach is opposite Western Place

Having heard the familiar sound of the maroon, people rushed excitedly to the seafront, where a massive crowd of several thousand spectators speedily collected.

Six powerful horses were harnessed to the carriage containing the lifeboat. It was drawn out of the boathouse, taken a short distance along the Parade, and launched opposite West Street in the turbulent water, assisted by many volunteers. The time was 2.45 p.m. It was launched only 10 minutes after the first gun was fired: a remarkably short space of time; and the boat was actually being launched when the second gun fired.

Despite the heavy sea and the roaring wind which was abeam, the courageous and hardy lifeboatmen rowed rapidly eastwards. Beyond the large crowd of residents and visitors who had flocked to the beach, there were hundreds of daytrippers to whom the spectacle appeared quite novel. People gathered on the front between the Pier and Warwick Buildings, and soon the sands were densely covered for a considerable distance by interested onlookers, determined to gain the best view of the wreck.

At 3.15 p.m. the lifeboat reached the grounded vessel and the lifeboatmen could only see one solitary occupant, the master, on the distressed ship, the French Brigantine *Halcyon* of St. Nazarre. To assist in hauling the lifeboat in to meet the 160 ton ship broadside, the bowman threw a heaving line to Captain Rivvel on the deck of the French craft. But the poor fellow, wearing only shirt and trousers, was so exhausted that he could not take the line, and so the lifeboat crew had to manouvre their rescue boat alongside the listing brig without assistance. Coxwain Lee then ordered two of his men to board the stricken vessel and make the lifeboat fast themselves by tying the two boats together with rope.

This done, Captain Rivvel was lifted out of his ship, by the two lifeboat men, in only a few minutes, and transferred to the lifeboat. The Second Coxwain, Harry Marshall, then searched the boat, which was half full of water, until he was satisfied that no one else was aboard.

At 3.45 p.m. the *Henry Harris* cast off from the floundering craft and returned to shore, beaching some distance east of the *Half Brick*, half an hour later.

As they walked up the shingle, a euphoric cheer from high-spirited onlookers greeted the lifeboatmen, and the rescued Frenchman acknowledged the welcome by shouting "Vive la Reine."

Councillor Butcher helped him to change into some dry clothes, while a light horse-drawn van, belonging to Mr. F. Stubbs, a fishmonger, was driven along the sands to be used as an ambulance. Two townsmen, Councillor Captain Fraser and Mr. G.A. Ralli, who had a knowledge of the French language, conversed with the foreigner as they were driven back along the sands to the pier, up South Street and along Warwick Street to the infirmary.

The translated conversation revealed that the five sailors aboard the French brig had been taken off by a Newhaven pilot boat at 10 o'clock that morning.

Meanwhile the lifeboat was returned by road to its station, arriving there at 4.45 p.m., amid cheers of congratulations from well-wishers on the success of their prompt mission.

The wrecked brigantine remained visible from the Parade and the Pier for some time, but the rough sea continually broke over her and, at 6.30 p.m., she keeled over and sank.

Capt. Rivvel recovered and was discharged that evening to Worthing College, in the care of Mr. Hemingway and Monsieur A. Bonefant, where he stayed for the remainder of the weekend.

The Captain, who had a wife and five children back home at Plonezec, near Pimpol, Cote de Nord, stated that his ship had left St. Nazaire some days earlier with, not only his regular crew, but also an English sailor, from another shipwreck, who had been working his passage home.

The crisis had begun during the gale which had started on Friday 19th, when the brig, which had been bound for London with a full load of slate, had sprung a leak somewhere near the stern.

After daybreak the following morning she had appeared to be foundering and the crew had decided to abandon ship. They had signalled to a passing pilot cutter to come alongside, whereupon the French crew had left the ailing vessel, leaving the Captain, with all his personal belongings, instruments and papers, on board.

His hope to steer the vessel, with sails set, into Shoreham harbour had looked for a time as though it would be successful, until, when only about two miles off Worthing, the violent gale had ripped away all the sails except the foretopmast staysail. His brave, but over-optimistic effort at sailing the large vessel single-handed had been in vain. Now that he had no means of controlling the ship he could only let her run before the gale and eventually struck land.

The captain, speaking to hosts, was of the opinion that had his crew remained, as he had wanted them to, and helped him man the pumps and manage the ship, he could have sailed her to the safety of Shoreham Harbour.

On Monday morning the shipwrecked captain left Worthing for Newhaven where he met the French consul and made arrangements for the safe return of his crew to their motherland across the channel. Whilst there, Capt. Rivvel arranged with the Newhaven Coastguard to try and save some of the cargo and belongings from the wreck of the *Halycon*, which was occasionally visible, although fast breaking-up.

The lifeboatmen whose rapid actions rescued Capt. Rivvel were: veteran Coxwain Charlie Lee, Second Coxwain Harry Marshall, Fred Marshall, Mark Marshall, Arthur Marshall, Bill Blann, Steve Wingfield, T. Wingfield, F. Collier, G. Benn, G. Belton, F. Wakeford and S. Bacon; and each was rewarded with 15s. for their brave services.

A large number of helpers, involved with the launching and hauling up of the *Henry Harris,* were paid 5s. per man. The signalman, Councillor Butcher, received an allowance of 10s. for his duties and a further sum of £4 4s. 0d. for the hire of the six horses. The cost of cabs, telegrams and sundries amounted to 6s, making a total expenditure of £25 15s. 0d. for the lifeboat service to the *Halcyon,* which was paid out by the Hon. Sec. Mr. G. Piggott.

The only casualty of this service was a broken rowlock on the lifeboat, which was immediately replaced by a spare whilst another was being made.

The fearless Worthing lifeboatmen were proud to chalk-up this *Halcyon* service on their station's scoreboard, especially after the disproved accusations made against them eight months earlier over the *Zadne* affair. An episode where the sea-going community had stood firmly together, side by side, to protect their reputations and their own self images.

Four years later, Chief Worthing Coastguard Officer H. Lang R.N., who by then had retired, was chosen by the French authorities to receive some well-earned honours on behalf of Worthing's maritime rescue services, in recognition of their humanity and kindness to the captain of the French schooner *Halcyon*.

The Chevalier Lumley, C.H., Delegate General of the French National and Royal Belgian Life Saving Services, and of the Society of the Nievre, for Great Britain, wearing full official uniform and the crosses of the Orders of St. Jean Baptiste d'Espagne and the Redeemer of Jerusalem presented Mr. Lang with the Diploma of Honour after a short address.

A special distinction was reserved for Chief Officer Lang. The Chevalier requested Madame la Comtesse de Morin (Hon. President of the ladies' section of the French National Society and of the societies of the Nievre, the Cote d'Or, and of Belgium) to decorate Mr. Lang with a medal and badge from the Departmental Society of the Nieve.

An irony of the *Halcyon* calamity is that the literal meaning of the word halcyon, derived from the Greek language, is a kingfisher that was fabled to have a floating nest on a calm sea.

An anchor, thought to have come from the *Halcyon,* can be seen in Worthing Museum.

Footnote Ch. 15

[1] E. Edwards – one of the Edwards family that was involved in the *Lalla Rookh* saga.

Ch. 16

Rescues From Land and Sea. 1895 – 6

The Annual Worthing Regatta was held on Wednesday 14 August 1895, having been postponed from the Monday before due to inclement weather. Although there was a stiff westerly breeze the fine weather attracted many people, thronging the Pier and the seafront with spectators. Rough sea prevented pleasure boats from putting out, and apart from competing craft there were very few boats afloat. The judges took up a position on the landing stage leaving the starter as the only official on the water.

Two bands were engaged to add to the gaiety of the occasion: Mr. Wright's performed on the Pier; and Mr. Binstead's on the Parade.

Out of the 14 rowing and sailing races planned for the afternoon one was for coastguard galleys and three were exclusively for Worthing fishermen and boatmen, most of whom, as usual, were also lifeboatmen.

The sailing boat race for Worthing watermen in craft not exceeding 17 feet was an exciting one. Rules permitted any rig, but not a false keel or centre-board; a time allowance of one minute per foot was given.

As the competing boats rounded the first spot boat in a group, Mark Marshall's *Dawn of Day* was just in the lead. Going out to sea George Wingfield's *Lancashire Lass* came out in front and passed round the south spot boat well ahead of the others. Then came E. Bacon in *Adela*, followed by Bill Blann in *Never Can Tell*, with T. Wingfield in *Dolly* holding fourth position at this stage.

Things soon changed in the second lap when *Here We Are* piloted by J. Hutchinson took third place and remained there over the finish. But there was still no serious contender to *Lancashire Lass*, which won easily; *Adela* was still second, but a long way in front of *Here We Are*. The *Dawn of Day* was a close fourth, relegating *Dolly* to fifth position. Bill Blann's *Never Can Tell* was unplaced at the finish, as was E. Bacon's *Ellen & Margaret* and F. Collier's *Princess May*.

The next race for Worthing watermen was for first-class pair-oared Boats. T. Wingfield in *Arawa* easily beat Mark Marshall in *Oruba*, winning by 30 lengths; with C. Wingfield in *Daisy* coming third.

The last of the three races for boats belonging to Worthing fishermen and boatmen was for second-class three-oared boats. The contenders were C. Wingfield's *True Blue*, George Wingfield's *Olive Branch*, Charlie Lee's *Rapid*, H. Browning's *Gladys*, and Mark Marshall's *Pansy*.

Four galleys, from Southwick, Shoreham, Worthing and Black Rock, took part in the coastguards' race.

Prizes were awarded at the conclusion of the sports by the Mayoress. Afterwards Captain Rivvel presented Charlie Lee, the Worthing lifeboat coxwain, with a portrait of himself as a mark of gratitude to the lifeboat crew for having rescued him from his grounded brig *Halcyon* three weeks earlier.

To complete the season, two illuminated boat processions were staged in September, watched by thousands of people. In the latter procession Mr. G.B. Simpson's boat, decorated and manned by the Worthing Coastguard, won fourth prize of 5s.

Sunday 1 September was Lifeboat Sunday in Worthing. Sermons in 10 local churches, praising the good work of the R.N.L.I., were warmly received by the various congregations who contributed thus: Holy Trinity £10 14s 0d, Christ Church £8 18s. 5d. St. Botolph's £8 5s. 0d. St. Andrew's £7 3s. 4d. St. George's £5 17s. 6d. Congregational Church £5 17s. West tarring £2 19s. 6d. Broadwater £2 13s. 2d. Sompting £2 8s. 9d. Ferring 15s. A Sacred Concert held in the Pier Pavilion raised a further £5 9s. 8d. making a total of £61 1s. 4d.

Worthing's first autumn storm of 1895, on Thursday 3 October, was a particularly violent one. A large number of people accumulated on the seafront to watch several boats, riding at anchor, being battered by enormous waves. One boat, the *Clythe* owned by a Mr. J.M. Lawton, was completely destroyed. The powerful sea tore two others from their anchors and the screaming wind drove them both ashore.

When one of them, the *Eclat* belonging to Harry Blann, my great grandfather, came in, a number of men were ready for it and hauled it up the beach, clear of the crashing breakers. The other, owned by a Mr. H. Browning, sustained a little damage when it struck the beach because there was no one at that spot to pull-up the boat.

About noon, in the midst of the gale that had been raging for some hours, the signal gun of the lifeboat station was heard throughout the town. Word quickly spread and hundreds of people rushed to the seafront opposite the lifeboat house, thinking that the lifeboat was being called out to a vessel in distress, but they were reassured that the *Henry Harris* was only to be set afloat for the customary quarterly practice for the crew.

Holy Trinity Church in Shelley Road

Councillor Butcher's powerful horses were attached to the carriage, which was drawn a short distance to the east of the station and lauched swiftly under the direction of the lifeboat chairman, Mr. H. Hargood.

In accomplishing the launch the crew encountered a tremendous sea which drenched them. To capitalise on the situation, the 2nd crew forced their way through the dense crowd of onlookers, accepting coins in their R.N.L.I. collecting boxes as they went.

For an hour they practised their manouevres in these true-to-life conditions.

On their return towards the beach, the lifeboatmen noticed two boats, being dangerously buffetted by the storm, as they rode at anchor to the west of the pier. Coxwain Lee ordered some of his crew to board these two boats, the *Britannia* and the *Skylark*, both belonging to Mr. F. Stubbs the fishmonger, and to steer them to safety.

Second Coxwain Harry Marshall was particularly proud of the crew on this successful mission, as he felt that no other craft but the lifeboat could have reached these endangered yachts in such a potentially destructive sea. So what was intended to be a routine quarterly practise turned into a dramatic errand of mercy.

On Tuesday 3 March 1896, when the *Henry Harris* and crew were summoned for their next quarterly practice, the sea was again very rough. The *Henry Harris* was pulled out of the boathouse and drawn eastward along Marine Parade by Councillor Butcher's horses, with driving rain behind them.

To the excitement of the crowd watching from the Parade and about 300 spectators on the Pier, who braved the howling wind, a quicker and safer method of launching was tried for the first time from the east side of the pier. A towline, fixed to the bow of the *Henry Harris,* was pulled by about 20 men as they moved along the pier; and once the lifeboat had passed the pierhead it was reliant on the crews' oarpower once more.

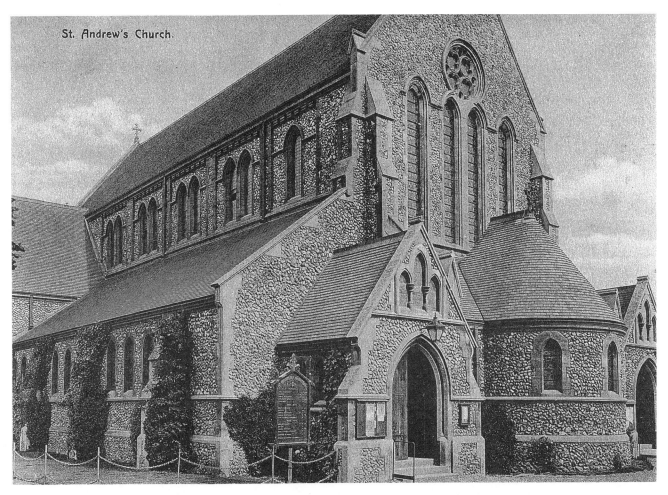

St. Andrew's Church, situated about $^1/_4$ mile North West of Worthing's Christ Church

The structure had acted as a breakwater, giving the *Henry Harris* partial protection from the prevailing wind and raging sea. Under these conditions the lifeboat and its gallant crew had been tested fully and, furthermore, the experiment was a complete success.

At these quarterly practises, as with any other event connected with the lifeboat, crewmen in their strange garb were a familiar sight collecting donations, for the R.N.L.I., in traditional collecting boxes.

At the height of summer, many lifeboatmen competed in boat races for Worthing watermen, organised as part of Worthing Festival Week.

The first of the races, held on Monday afternoon 20 July, was the first class three-oared event for Worthing watermen in licensed boats. After a false start the six boats got away on level terms, and there was nothing to choose between them on the westward leg of the course, but two boats gained a slight advantage in rounding the buoys. By the time they had reached the pier again, the race hotted-up between five of the competitors, the *Elsie* having abandoned the race soon after reaching the western spot.

Passing beneath the pier, Jo. Street in the *Pansy* was only just in the lead, with F. Stubbs' (fishmonger) *Rapid* close behind almost level with H. Browning's *Gladys,* which was on the outside berth.

On the last leg from the eastern buoys to the finish at the pier, spectators became excitedly animated as the crew of the *Pansy* continued to push ahead and finally won by a few lengths.

There was a capital contest for second position between three boats, *Rapid* being the victor in this case. *Gladys* was third. Two Wingfield boats, Charlie's *True Blue* and George's *Olive Branch,* finishing unplaced.

The second race for Worthing watermen in licensed boats was the pair-oared event, for which 10 entries had been received, but four of the pairs were non-starters. Once more, lifeboatmen dominated the event.

Having started from the pier, the first to round the western buoys was George Belton's *Florrie* which maintained its appreciable lead for the whole race to win first prize. Many lengths separated it from George Wingfield's *Trown* which came second, well ahead of the others.

As F. Collier's *Mabel* relinquished the contest, there was a struggle for third place with Tom Wingfield's *Arawa* beating F. Searle's *Tanai* to a close finish. Charlie Wingfield's *Violet* was unplaced.

The final event for Worthing fishermen and boatmen was the single sculls race in licensed pair-oared boats. Once more 10 had entered but this time seven contested the course.

There was a somewhat ragged start, but the race soon shaped itself with F. Collier's *Mabel* being far more successful this time and going into the lead on the eastward leg, followed a few lengths behind by two craft belonging to George Belton, *Florrie* and *Ethel*, almost level with each other.

Collier reached home first by four lengths, but less than a length separated George Wingfield's *Trown* which finished second and George Belton's *Florrie* which ended third. Tom Wingfield's *Arawa* was the only other boat to complete the gruelling course, as another of George Belton's boats, *Ethel*, had dropped out, as did both of Charlie Wingfield's craft, *Daisy* and *Violet*.

This was the extent of Worthing watermen's involvement in Worthing Festival Week, and now the next competitive opportunity they were looking forward to was the Worthing Regatta.

It was held on a showery Wednesday afternoon, 2 September. The slight sprinkling of rain, however, did not interfere with the aquatic sports. Even when the gentle rain fell, from behind banks of clouds floating above the town, the sun could be seen casting its genial rays upon distant places. This enjoyably fine weather produced a beautifully clear view of Brighton, and even here spectators experienced bright and pleasant intervals.

Worthing Regatta spectators on the beach, the pier, and some afloat in boats

The number of people paying for admission to the pier, 3,483, exceeded the previous year's figure. More people were on the pier but the crowds of spectators on the Parade, either side of the Pier, had not increased.

The first event on the programme was for sailing boats not exceeding 17 feet belonging to Worthing watermen.

The clear winner was George Wingfield's *Lancashire Lass,* with Hutchinson's *Here We Are* taking second place, followed by A. Beck's *Marquis of Salisbury* and Jo. Street fourth in *Gold Tip.*

E. Bacon's two entries, *Ellen & Margaret* and *Adlar* were unplaced, as was Fred and Harry Marshall's *Jolly Sailor,* Harry Blann's *Curlew,* H. Browning's *Irene* and F. Collier's *Princess May.*

The next race which fishermen and boatmen entered was for first-class pair-oared boats of Worthing watermen in which G. Belton's *Florrie* had an exceptionally easy win. Tom Wingfield's *Arawa* struggled to take second place from F. Collier's *Grace Darling,* and George Wingfield's *Rose* came in fourth.

The last of the races for boats belonging to Worthing watermen was the second-class three-oared event which was won by George Wingfield, in *Holly Branch,* who beat Frank Burden in *Rapid* by several lengths. Third place was a struggle for Jo. Street, in *Pansy,* who was only just ahead of Harry Browning's *Gladys* when the gun fired.

The last event of the day, the coastguards' race, drew much excitement from the crowd. Shoreham won easily, but, as second place was hotly contested, frantic appeals from supporters urged their respective crews on, as the galleys neared the finish.

The day's proceedings finished with the presentation of prizes in the Pier Pavilion during the evening. Another exciting and eventful occasion involving Worthing fishermen and boatmen was over for another year.

Those watermen who also served as lifeboatmen were summoned by signal rockets for their quarterly practice on Saturday afternoon 12 September 1896. Once they had assembled, the *Henry Harris* was drawn, on its carriage, eastward along the marine road and launched near the pier under the command of Coxwain Lee. The crew were accompanied on this trip by the honorary treasurer John Roberts, who wanted some first hand experience of the lifeboat in action. Manouvres took place for more than an hour in the heavy rolling sea, watched with considerable interest by a highly-charged crowd on the beach.

Two months later, on Tuesday 17 November, Mr. Kepple Foote, District Inspector of the R.N.L.I. came to Worthing for the periodical inspection of the local crew and station. He had been due a week or two earlier but a family bereavement had compelled him to defer his visit.

The crew were summoned to their positions by the signal gun, the carriage was horsed by the signalman, Councillor Butcher, and the lifeboat was launched opposite the lifeboat house at about 10 a.m. Mr. H. Hargood J.P., local chairman, was present at the launch and the return, but did not on this occasion accompany Coxwain Lee and his crew.

As the sea was very calm, the practice was divested of some of its interest; but during the two hours that the boat was on the water, the inspector put the crew through various tests to see how efficient they were in handling their craft. Coxwain Lee did well, although he must have been under some emotional stress as his wife had suddenly fallen ill and died 30 days earlier.

With the tests completed, the lifeboat was landed on the beach, a little to the east of the Pier, and Mr. Kepple Foote expressed his complete satisfaction with the station and crew; adding that he was pleased with the smartness of the crew, and also with the way in which the boat had been horsed.

This inspection and the quarterly practice two months before had set the lifeboat crew in good stead for an emergency.

At the beginning of December terrible gales attacked the South Coast, and the lifeboatmen stood by awaiting that familiar sound of the maroon.

On Friday 4 December a particularly bad storm arose which increased in violence to such an extent that the Chain Pier at Brighton swayed to and fro, before finally collapsing into the sea.

Worthing boatmen, apprehensive of the danger, drew their boats off the beach to the comparative safety of the Parade.

By Saturday morning the seafront was in a desolate state: a wilderness of boulders, shingle, seaweed, wreckage, refuse which had accumulated at the top of the beach, corks and shells strewn everywhere. The road along the front looked like a second beach. A lake of sea water remained in front of York Terrace (later the Warnes Hotel), in the midst of which stood young trees, recently planted at the edge of the footpath, almost dragged out of the earth by the wind, looking very pitiful in their half-drowned leafless state. At Splash Point, part of the Parade itself had been undermined and swept away.

Fishing luggers beached opposite Western Place had narrowly escaped being sucked into the sea and engulfed. A large portion of the beach on which their keels rested was found to have been scoured from under them, leaving half of each boat extended without support over the resulting drop. Gaunt and dangerous the luggers' sterns looked, for a little higher sweep of the tide and the boats would have fallen an easy prey to the waves which lashed the beach with such fury.

ROUGH SEA. WORTHING   240.

The seafront was in a desolate state: a wilderness of boulders, shingle and seaweed

As soon as the precarious position of the fishing craft was discovered many hands were engaged in securing the boats against another devastating tide.

By Saturday afternoon the wind had abated; but as the sun went down, there was an ominous apprearance to the south of huge masses of black clouds rolled up on the horizon. They soon spread themselves over the sky; the wind freshened and then blew stronger.

As the tide rose the wind increased, and at midnight the coast was swept by another gale, accompanied by heavy, blinding rain.

As dawn broke, on Sunday 6 December, a vessel was seen labouring in the heavy sea, flying distress signals and running for the shore.

Her signals were answered by coastguards from Worthing, Lancing and Shoreham. Chief Officer McGregor of the Lancing Coastguard, and his counterpart at Shoreham, Mr. Murphy, immediately contacted the coastguard station at Worthing and the lifeboat station at Shoreham respectively.

At 8.11 a.m. Chief Officer Lang of the Worthing Coastguard ordered out the Worthing lifeboat and the signal gun was fired to summon the crew. The report of the gun startled many residents from their sleep and in their excitement several hurried down to the beach without finishing their toiletries. Very soon the seafront in the vicinity of the lifeboat station became animated with hundreds of eager spectators.

With the promptness that characterised the lifeboatmen, they were ready to start on their important errand of mercy within a few minutes of the alarm being sounded; and with equal briskness Councillor Butcher brought out his splendid horses for the lifeboat carriage.

By now the distressed ship, a barque, was close to the shore at Lancing but as the Lancing Road was impassable, due to breaches made by the invading sea, it was decided to launch the *Henry Harris* from Worthing, using the pier as an effective breakwater.

Although the high tide had not yet peaked, the breakers were sufficiently strong to hamper the launching, but after two attempts the gallant crew were afloat, at 8.30 a.m., in their rescue craft, amid loud cheers, which could only just be heard above the howling S.S.E. gale, from the large crowd on the shore.

Lifeboat volunteers, together with onlookers, then set out for Lancing, some in vehicles and some walking. The chairman and secretary were the first to leave in a horse-drawn cab.

Coxwain Lee's crew pulled through the very heavy sea until they got beyond the breakers, where they hoisted the sail.

The stranded *Ophir* whose crew had earlier cut down the mainmast and the mizzen to prevent her from keeling over in the strong gale. Reproduced from a lantern slide

Meanwhile, the Shoreham lifeboat was not so fortunate, for as the crew vainly tried to put to sea, the craft was struck by a large wave and beaten back; the lifeboatmen on the lee side having their oars snapped.

Sailing skills of the Worthing lifeboat crew were fully tested in earnestly battling through the gale. They did not gain the wreck until 10 a.m., an hour and a half after leaving Worthing beach, whereupon they dropped anchor.

The grounded three-masted barque, which proved to be the *Ophir*, was now off the beach in front of the common, just to the east of the *Three Horseshoes Inn*. She had lost her battle with the ferocious elements and the 410 ton ship was now in a disastrous state.

The *Ophir's* 10 crew had earlier cut down the mainmast and the mizzen to prevent her from reeling over in the strong gale. But as they had been unable to get them clear of the rigging the result was a mass of tangled wreckage floating near the stern of the barque.

It would have been easier for the lifeboat crew to rescue the stranded crew from the stern, as was done with the grounded *Capella* in 1891, but Coxwain Lee was compelled to veer the *Henry Harris* round to the windward side of the wreck.

The lifeboatmen established some sort of communication with the shipwrecked Norwegian crew and endeavoured to bring them off using life-lines. They threw ropes across the heaving swell to the crew of the *Ophir*, and the Norwegians fastened them to their ship.

Together, they rigged-up a breeches buoy between the two vessels – a sling suspended from a life-line that could be used to carry the shipwrecked sailors across, one at a time.

At great risk to themselves, the brave rescuers succeeded in hauling two of the barque's crew – the exhausted steward, who had apparently been ill for many weeks, and the mate – through the surf.

But then, the wreck was driven by the surging sea, away from the lifeboat and among the breakers within 100 yards of the beach. Three more times the *Henry Harris* approached the windward side of the wreck, and each time they had to pull away lest their comparitively little craft should have been dashed against the *Ophir*.

Meanwhile, the Shoreham coastguards had arrived with some rocket apparatus which was placed on the beach opposite the wreck. It was quickly prepared and a rocket was fired, with a life-line attached, from the shore, but the shot missed its mark, as did a second one, carried off target by the strong wind.

This was the point where intense excitement displayed by the enormous crowd of onlookers was at its highest.

There were still eight men on board, hoping to be rescued from the battered wreck. Although the coastguards worked as quickly as humanly possible, there was still some delay before a third line was fired. The rocket sped clean over the vessel, and the success was greeted by loud cheering.

But it was short-lived, and anxiety intensified when it was seen that the line had either broken or was too short.

The fourth rocket, however, also cleared the vessel, and this time the intact life-line was immediately secured; then further resce work began. The lifebelt was hauled along the line to the wreck, and one at a time the distressed and thoroughly exhausted sailors were dragged along the line to the beach. Cheer after cheer went up from the excited crowd as each rescue was effected, and ready hands were there to conduct the unfortunate men to a place of refuge. Almost breathless excitement prevailed as anxious and willing helpers assisted with the ropes, and men rushed into the sea to rescue their fellows as they were hauled in.

Some of the sailors were so fatigued that they had great difficulty in holding on: some were repeatedly turned upside down; while others were carried on the crest of a wave which threw them forcefully onto the beach.

One of the crew slipped from the breeches buoy in which he was being hauled ashore. The poor fellow, numbed with cold and suffering from exposure, hung face downwards, his hands fouling the travelling pulley block, and one turn of the 'whip rope' was round his throat.

L. Davey, Commission Boatman of Worthing Coastguard, and William Dart, Boatman of Lancing Coastguard, regardless of their own lives, rushed into the crashing breakers and freed the man from what would have been certain death by strangulation, if not from drowning, had the rescue been delayed by even a minute. Their prompt action stimulated spectators to show their recognition of this brave deed.

As they were brought ashore the exhausted, shipwrecked sailors, none of whom could stand without assistance, were conducted by willing helpers to the *Three Horseshoes Inn* nearby, where they were attended by Mr. F. Parish, a surgeon. Lodgings were arranged for them at the Inn by Chief Officer Lang of the Worthing Coastguard, who was also the local agent for the Shipwrecked Mariners' Society.

While the coastguards and helpers on the beach were engaged in bringing the eight remaining sailors ashore, the *Henry Harris* stood off from the vessel, ready to render assistance in the event of the ship breaking up during the rescue. When the last man had reached the beach, loud jubilant voices could be heard above roaring wind and the noise of the breakers crashing on the beach stones.

The lifeboat crew rowed back to Worthing with the two sailors they had rescued when first on the scene – the mate and the steward, who was now delirious. Thousands of people had gathered on the Parade at Worthing to watch the return of the lifeboat with avid interest. The craft gallantly bestrode the waves, handled in faultless style by her brave crew. At times she was hidden in the trough of the sea, and when she reappeared, her blue and white bow was seen rising over the mountainous and white-topped waves, and then descending as if to be engulfed in the fearful hollow which was left after the passing of the huge, angry billow.

It must have been a grand sight to witness such a frail boat gaining victory after victory over the waves which continuously threatened it with destruction, as it met and overcame its enemy at every stroke of the oars.

During the return of the *Henry Harris*, despite the apalling conditions, the sun shone brightly through a gap in the clouds and enhanced a wildy picturesque scene.

Foaming breakers dashed with a deafening roar on the beach, and increased the havoc they had already made at the eastern end of the Parade.

A flock of gulls, some of which delighted in settling on the sea and riding triumphantly over the big waves, aroused interest with the huge crowd of onlookers; but the centre of attraction was the lifeboat, which, by now, was battling with the waves about 300 yards from the beach.

The tide was at its height and owing to the short distance between the groynes it was impossible to land on the beach in such a sea.

The condition of the steward, who had been in the lifeboat for more than three hours, was becoming much worse and giving cause for increased alarm.

With great difficulty Coxwain Lee attempted to land him on the landing stage of the Pier, but the high sea continually broke over it, forcing him to abandon the bid.

The Coxwain then decided to wait for a while, hoping that the storm would abate, and instructed his crew to anchor the lifeboat near the pier head.

In the meantime even more people, mainly those who had been to Sunday church services, hurried to the beach to watch, for the news had spread early in the day that the lifeboat had departed on a noble mission of mercy.

Excited onlookers thronged the beach, and when the *Henry Harris* was seen making for the pier head once more, there was a rush of people to the structure, men running at top speed in order that not a moment be lost should assistance be required.

The efforts of the lifeboat crew to get alongside the landing stage were watched with feverish anxiety, and as the boat neared the structure, people wondered how the sick steward was to be landed safely as the waves threatened to dash the boat against the pier.

On board the lifeboat the apprehensive crew had bound the delirious steward with rope after he had behaved like a madman.

At the appropriate moment, as the *Henry Harris* neared the landing stage, eager hands plucked the steward from the boat and drew up the bound, sick man.

Mr. Parish, the surgeon, who had travelled from Lancing was waiting to tend the steward, who was placed in a bath chair and wheeled to the pier entrance, where the suffering mariner was put in a waiting fly.

Mr. Parish mounted the box with the driver, who made his way to the infirmary, where the invalid received the best possible attention.

The other shipwrecked sailor, the mate, remained in the lifeboat until it was able to come ashore an hour later at 2.30 p.m., when the force of the tide had moderated sufficiently to allow the crew to land with comparative safety. The mate was then taken to the *Three Horseshoes* to be reunited with his Norwegian comrades.

The horses were taken into the surf to recover the lifeboat, but in doing so one of the heavy beasts, knocked over by a large wave, trod on one of the carters, necessitating a doctor's medical attention.

The *Henry Harris* was eventually returned to its house at 3 p.m., having been on service for 6½ hours. Everyone was delighted with the admirable management of the lifeboat and its 13 brave crew – Coxwain Charlie Lee, 2nd cox Harry Marshall, Arthur Marshall, Fred Marshall, Mark Marshall (four brothers), Bowman Steve Wingfield, George Wingfield, Fred Collier, George Belton, Fred Wakeford, Bill Blann, George Benn, and J. Elliot, who all performed the service at great risk to themselves.

They each received 15s. from the institution's funds; 46 helpers were rewarded with 4s. 6d. each for assisting to launch and haul-up the *Henry Harris;* Mr. Butcher, the signalman was allowed 15s, in addition to £3 for the hire of six horses over a distance of six miles. Other expenses were 4s. 6d. for a Light man, 15s. for a cab and 4s. for messengers; making the total expenditure £25 0s. 6d. for this service.

During the afternoon an immense number of people went to look at the wreck; the coast road, from Worthing to Lancing and from Shoreham to Lancing, was full of pedestrians and vehicles picking their way through the quagmire of mud and accumulated beach shingle which was strewn across the roadway. By now the gale had decreased and the sun shed warm rays, enabling the very old and the very young as well as the robust middle-aged to venture out and view the *Ophir*.

On the shingled beach, beyond the waste of waters which covered the low-lying green, a cluster of spectators stood watching the vessel, which was facing out to sea, swayed by the wind and sea, for the full force of the gale had not even then completely subsided. The disabled vessel remained upright on the sand. There was no sign of human life on the ship but no one was allowed to go on board and investigate.

Then, to their amazement, onlookers saw a dog running around on deck, and a goat, and someone else saw a cat.

The wreck provided a little competition between two well-known local businessmen. Mr. Aldridge, who had an art firm in Warwick Street, went along and sketched the scene, whilst the photographer, Walter Gardiner, took a photograph. It was a race between the two to see who could get the picture in their shop window first. I understand that Mr. Aldridge probably did.

The next day a continual stream of sightseers visiting the wreck could see a lady artist, seated in a boat, painting a picture of the stranded barque, and various people photographing the *Ophir* for posterity.

As soon as the tide had receded on this Monday morning the Lancing coastguards, accompanied by Capt. Olsen, boarded the *Ophir* to collect the animals, the sailor's belongings, together with the ship's instrument's and books.

Examination showed that considerable damage had been sustained by the barque, which was embedded about 5 feet deep in the sand. Its cargo of bulk salt had all been washed out and the hole had filled with sand.

On returning to the inn, the Captain expressed his deep gratitude to the landlord, Mr. G.N. Prideaux, for his hopitality; and as a token of appreciation gave the goat to Mr. Prideaux as a gift, asking him to look after the dog and cat until they could be found a permanent home.

Some people took home flotsam from the beach, but the coastguards were vigilant in their suppression of illicit wreckers. In one instance a stocky officer raced on his bicycle to accost two men who were on the beach loading their bags with spoils which had been washed ashore from the wreck. After examining the contents of the bags he apprehended the elder of the two and took him to the coastguard station to be dealt with.

Mr. J. Ellman Brown, Norwegian Vice Consul at Shorehem, travelled to Lancing and interviewed Captain Julius Olsen of the *Ophir* at the *Three Horseshoes* where he and his crew had made their temporary residence in an upper room, in which a window commanded an uninterrupted view of the Channel. The captain, who was a comparatively young man, with a fair, pointed beard and a long moustache, was dressed in a neat blue serge suit.

The *Three Horseshoes Inn*, Lancing, where a window in an upper room overlooked the Channel; viewed from Lancing Common, adjacent to the sea

He spoke excellent English, and the information gleaned from the Captain showed that the *Ophir*, a very stoutly constructed craft, was owned by a Mr. Pettersen of Arendal, Norway, and was bound from Trapani for home with a cargo of salt. It appeared that the steward had been ill with "something in the head", as the Captain put it, when the vessel left Sicily, but he had wanted to get back to his home in Norway, and accordingly shipped with his comrades when they began the return voyage. The barque had left the Sicilian port on 28 September, but owing to severe weather, a voyage which would normally have taken 30 days had already been extended to 78 when the vessel came to grief at Lancing.

The crew had managed to steer the ship to the Owers light off Selsey Bill on Saturday night, but it was not until just before 8 o'clock the following morning that the master had found that the *Ophir* was too close to the Worthing coast. Attempts, by the Norwegian sailors, to manoeuvre the ship into the wind, had proved impossible faced with the ravages of the gale.

As the vessel was taking in water, Captain Olsen had decided, after consulting his fellow crewmates, to beach her in preference to drifting ashore at the mercy of the violent winds and lashing sea.

They had gone in under close-reefed topsails, and as it happened, the Lancing beach was one of the better places to beach a vessel.

When the captain and his crew had first seen land, 2½ – 3 miles distant, they had been cheered by the coastguard signal, "We are coming to your assistance".

After the shipwrecked sailors had been picked-up, they stayed at the inn until Friday, when the mate and seven of the crew left for London to be shipped home to Norway, while the captain remained at the *Three Horseshoes Inn* pending the sale of the vessel.

The *Ophir* was auctioned on Thursday 17 September, 10 days after being wrecked, sold to a Mr. Read, from Worthing, for just £34, probably for firewood. The barque's four boats and five sails fetched £2 each; while very few people had the heart to bid against Capt. Olsen for the chronometer, which he successfully purchased for £4 10s.

Meanwhile, the sick steward remained in the care of the infirmary until Christmas, when he was well enough to return to Norway with Captain Olsen.

The rescue of the crew of the *Ophir* was another instance of the gallantry of the lifeboat crew. High opinions were expressed regarding the promptness with which the lifeboatmen had responded, only 19 minutes elapsing between the summons for help and the actual launching of the *Henry Harris*. It was with great difficulty that the lifeboat had got away in the heavy sea; and a great risk had been run at the scene of the disaster, complicated by loose wreckage being flung around in the violent sea.

I firmly believe that in every respect the lifeboatmen fully demonstrated their capacity for undertaking such a dangerous and noble task, making them so proud of their latest entry on the station's 'scoreboard'.

Praise was also due to the Coastguards and the innumerable voluntary helpers for their excellent services. To me, deeds such as those seen on this occassion forcibly illustrate the inherent heroism of Worthing's sea-going community.

The name *Ophir* itself lives on: a street off the seafront at East Worthing, Ophir Road, was named after the wreck.

Only eight days after the *Ophir* had stranded, another ship ran aground, this time at West Worthing. At 5.55 p.m., an hour before high tide, on Monday 14 December, a vessel was seen with burning tar barrels on deck – a form of distress signal used during the hours of darkness to attract attention.

The Coastguard acknowledged five minutes later by firing the maroon to muster the lifeboat crew. Coxwain Lee, 2nd cox Harry Marshall with his three brothers Mark, Fred and Athur, George Wingfield, George Benn, Wm. Collier, F. Collier, J. Elliott, J. Bridger, Frank Burden and Bill Blann, hastily assembled.

Councillor Butcher, who was also the lifeboat signalman, hurriedly brought his horses from the stables and hitched them to the lifeboat carriage. Hundreds of people, from all over the town, rushed to the seafront to watch the *Henry Harris* being pulled out of its house and westward along the coast road. Just past Heene Terrace the array of lifeboat on carriage, 13 crew, 11 2nd (reserve) crew, 30 helpers and uncountable onlookers, scrambled down the beach, and the *Henry Harris* was launched at 6.15 p.m., just 15 minutes after the signal gun had been fired.

Even though there was still a heavy surf on the beach from the previous night's gale, a favourable, moderate N.N.E. offshore wind assisted the oarsmen propelling the *Henry Harris* towards the strange-looking small craft which was about a ¼ mile off Grand Avenue, or the Ladies' Mile as it was more popularly described. In the deepening gloom of this December evening, with the moon now obscured behind the gathering clouds, the crowds of eager spectators which had grown to thousands by now, strained their eyes to follow the course of the lifeboat.

Twenty minutes after launching, the lifeboat reached the distressed craft, which was pointing seaward. The lifeboat bowman threw a grapnell and line up onto the schooner and hauled the lifeboat alongside. Coxwain Lee ordered some of his crew to board the stricken vessel and spread the sails. This attempt at mobilising the stranded craft was soon abandoned and the five crew were taken off. At this point Harry Marshall discharged a green-coloured rocket to convey to the signalman on the beach that the lifeboat was about to return. This signal was in turn answered by Councillor Butcher, who fired a coloured flare.

As the *Henry Harris* returned, a bright, clear light burning for'ard, added picturesqueness to the scene, besides demonstrating that the shipwrecked crew had been rescued and were being brought ashore.

When they beached at 7.15 p.m., the traditional cheer went up from the thronging crowds. It took a further half hour for the helpers to haul-up the *Henry Harris*, and transfer her back on to the carriage to be drawn back to the boathouse.

As the lifeboat crew returned, they were greeted by assembled onlookers with a vigorous cheer as an acknowledgement of their extreme readiness in the moment of necessity. The service had been so smartly and expeditiously managed that the crew were absent from the boathouse for only 1½ hours. The lifeboat itself had performed very well and was undamaged, but a grapnell and line had been lost.

From the rescued shipwrecked sailors it was learnt that the marooned vessel, the *Flora Emily*, a schooner of 99 tons burden, had been bound from Montrose to Shoreham with a cargo of potatoes.

It appeared that the crew of five hands, who had been making for Shoreham Harbour had mistaken the lights on Worthing front for those at Shoreham. The first indication that something had been seriously amiss had come when the master, Mr. Masson, who had heard waves breaking on the beach. At once he had ordered the vessel to be put about, but it was too late, and she had run aground.

Signals had then been made to attract the attention of the coastguard; and the response had been so prompt that the skipper and his men soon found themselves in conversation with Chief Officer Lang at the coastguard station.

Mr. Lang, together with four of his men, manned the pumps on the leaking *Flora Emily*, and early next morning the schooner, owned by a Mr. Morrison of Burgehead, Morayshire, N.B., was successfully towed off the beach by Shoreham harbour's powerful tug *Stella*.

At 9 a.m. the marine convoy reached Shoreham Harbour, where the Worthing coastguards were replaced by Shoreham men; and the *Flora Emily*'s cargo of potatoes was unloaded using the railway company's steam crane.

Costs, authorised by the Worthing lifeboat honorary secretary to be paid out for the service to the *Flora Emily*, were as follows: for their fast and courageous services the 13 Lifeboat crew each received 30s. (the R.N.L.I. scale of payment at this time for winter excercises was half as much again as for those in the summer); each of the 11 standby crew were compensated with 3s.; and 30 volunteers were rewarded with 2s. per man. The signalman, who did special service with horses and helpers, was paid £2 5s. for the hire of his six horses. One man who rendered special service at the launching was rewarded with 5s. The only other expense was that of 2s. for firing the gun which made a total expenditure of £27 5s. for this service.

This second successful service, within little more than a week of the previous one, warranted yet another entry on the stations 'scoreboard'. I am in no doubt as to the popularity of our maritime saviours: on both occasions hordes of Worthingites (Worthing residents) had rushed out in their thousands to support their lifeboatmen and partake of the highly-charged air of suspense and thrilling excitement surrounding the *Henry Harris*.

All expenses connected with wreck services were met by R.N.L.I. H.Q., as were any special requirements, such as the new transporting carriage, which had recently been supplied.

The Worthing Branch was very sound financially at this time: Maintaining a steady average of £104 in annual subscriptions, and the Parade and Pier contribution boxes together producing about £8 a year. The local committee were able to send £40 to head office after paying working expenses. Expenses which included about £8 a year for Coxwain Lee who was in charge of the boathouse and £2 annually for 2nd Cox Harry Marshall.

Ch. 17

A Change Of Coxwain. 1897 - 9

A carnival atmosphere enthralled Worthing residents when royalty came to the town to officiate at the opening of a new waterworks at the foot of the Downs.

On Monday 26 April 1897, his Royal Highness the Duke of Cambridge was welcomed by the Mayor, Worthing Corporation officials and various military officers at Worthing Railway Station. It was adorned with, among other decorations, pretty-coloured bunting and shields painted with coats of arms; whilst in the wide open space beyond the station, pretty garlands and flags hung between Venetian masts.

The Duke of Cambridge arriving at Worthing Railway Station

Assembled in the wide roadway facing the station (Approach Road), were a contingent of 10 Coastguards under the command of Chief Officer Lang and a detachment of the Royal Sussex Regiment in scarlet tunics and white helmets.

After inspecting the troops, on this brilliantly sunny day, the Duke entered his Royal carriage to the strains of the National Anthem played by a military band.

A procession led by seven carriages of Corporation Officers, Town Councillors and Aldermen was formed. The eighth was the Royal carriage containing the Mayor as well as the Duke.

The cavalcade proceeded along Approach Road (now Railway Approach) and on to the Railway Bridge. A great cheering crowd of onlookers had gathered on this vantage point to get a splendid view of all that was passing.

A further 12 carriages conveyed various local dignitaries in the procession which made its way past Broadwater Church, where the bells rang out a joyful peal.

The last leg of the route to the new waterworks, up a road which became known as Waterworks Lane (now Hillbarn Lane), yielded a magnificent view of the fine new plant, which stood beyond a corn field.

The new waterworks was powered by two steam engines. These were started by the royal visitor who named them the Victoria and the Cambridge.

After the ceremony the procession reformed and drove back to Worthing. Thousands of people lined the route as the cavalcade passed through the town, along the seafront, and ended in front of the Town Hall in South Street. The carriages drew up at the municipal offices where the Duke was to be guest of honour at a reception. A small detachment of the 1st Sussex Artillery Volunteers from Shoreham, and the Worthing Coastguards formed the guard of honour, while the *Henry Harris*, appropriately hung with flags, and manned with a crew under Coxwain Lee, looked very colourful on its carriage in the background.

The Duke, joined at this point by Mr. H. Hargood J.P. , chairman of Worthing Branch R.N.L.I., walked towards the lifeboat to inspect the crew. His Royal Highness was evidently pleased with the appearance of the men, and remarked that he had read in the papers of the services rendered by the crew, and especially by Coxwain Lee.

After inspecting more troops, the Duke walked up the Town Hall steps, lined with men of the Borough Fire Brigade, to the sounds of martial music played by military bands. A celebratory luncheon followed.

The seafront along which the procession passed

The procession ended here in front of the Town Hall in South Street

A small detachment of the 1st Sussex Artillery Volunteers and the Worthing Coastguards forming the guard of honour. The *Henry Harris* is just out of view on the right but some of its flags can be seen

The lifeboatmen themselves, together with the coastguards, fire brigade and soldiers, were entertained to lunch in a large marquee erected in the grounds of Warwick House.

Events such as this inauguration of the new Water Works provided Worthing residents with interest as well as entertainment and excitement. Another excuse for more fun and revelry came two months later in the form of Queen Victoria's Diamond Jubilee.

This festive celebration began with a procession from Shelley Road, headed by the coastguards marching with the Union Jack, about 2,400 school children grouped in their individual school colours, and marching bands.

No carnival procession was complete without the lifeboat. There she was, mounted on her polished carriage, pulled by six horses, supplied as usual by Councillor Butcher. He himself, as Signalman to the crew, occupied a position in the *Henry Harris*, on this carnival occasion, with the veteran Coxwain Lee.

Another event which drew excited crowds was the quarterly practice of the lifeboat crew. In September 1897, the maroon, which was fired to alert those fishermen and boatmen who doubled as lifeboatmen, could be heard all over the town. On hearing the signal, hundreds of people of all ages and from all walks of life rushed to the seafront to watch the *Henry Harris* being launched on the east side of the pier. The crew rowed out past the pier head and hoisted canvas in a strong south westerly wind, which tested the sailing capabilities of the boat.

Hundreds of people of all ages and from all walks of life rushed to the seafront to watch the *Henry Harris* being launched from the beach on the east side of the pier

Mock rescues were carried out on several members of Worthing Swimming Club, who swam from the pier head in order to be picked up by the crew. I understand that one sporty member of the club, who was as much at home in the water as out, amused onlookers by embracing a lifeboatman trying to 'save' him so vigourously that he dragged him out of the *Henry Harris* and into the sea with him.

This same month two watermen died within 36 hours of each other in unrelated incidents.

A startling discovery was made on a Friday evening by a boatman by the name of West who was in charge of a pleasure party of ladies and gentleman. West saw a small fishing boat, which appeared abandoned, some distance from the pier. He rowed to the boat, found George Goble slumped on his lobster pots and brought him ashore, leaving him in the charge of some other watermen, James Davis, Albert Street and Edward Bacon, who took him to Mr J. D. S. Nodes, a surgeon. But 59 year old Goble, who was separated from his wife, was dead.

He had been living at 17, Field Row with his married sister, who told an inquest that for the past two years he had been very ill with a dreadful cough, and had received treatment at the infirmary where they thought "he had freezed his wind over the other side," when he had been fishing way out in the Channel during very severe weather.

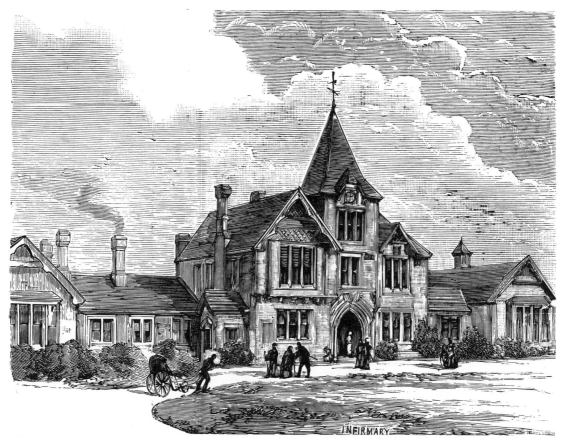

Worthing's Infirmary (now part of Worthing Hospital in Lyndhurst Road)

Ironically, Edward Bacon, one of those who removed Goble's body from the beach, was himself found dead in a boat on Sunday morning. Edward Blaker, of Buckingham Road, found his body, still warm, lying face downwards in a boat under the pier. Although Bacon, of 12, Paragon Street, had been susceptible to epileptic fits, the 44 year old man's death had been caused by heart failure through physical exertion.

Several small sailing boats, laying at anchor off the town, were damaged during a violent storm on Sunday 5 September. A heavy downpour of rain was accompanied by a high wind which whipped up huge waves, furiously lashing the tiny vessels. The *Albatross* belonging to a Mr. Browning, had her side stove in and sank. Another boat, the *Medora* broke from her moorings and drifted as far as Shoreham, where she was driven ashore and extensively damaged.

Having a boat wrecked was one of the hazards faced by our fishermen. Their livelihood itself brought them into close contact with nature.

One could stand on the beach early on a November morning with the waves gently lapping breaking on the shore and hearing the piercing screams of seagulls overhead. Out of the mist over the sea, small fishing boats, loaded with their catches, would silently come shoreward after being out all night.

Fishing boats and lobster pots on the beach opposite Library Place

The fishermen would jump out of their boats to haul their craft in, with their long boots dripping with wet and weed, their oilskin overalls reaching below their knees, and their peaked cloth caps covered with herring scales, I would say that they must have looked the very picture of perennial hardiness. Unloading their boats and fetching basket after basket of fish up the beach, while communicating with each other in deep low voices punctuated by hearty laughs was an indication, I am sure, of their fine British manhood.

The fish piled at the top of the beach in silvery heaps were mainly herrings because, towards the end of October, herrings migrated from the deep waters of the ocean to spawning grounds closer to land. The movements of the herring were very uncertain: in some years it came to our shores in such enormous numbers that the catches exceeded consumption to such an extent that it was used as manure; while in other years numbers were so small it had a devastating effect on our fishermens' livelihoods, resulting in their poor families going hungry.

When the herrings were all landed, the fish salesman took his place beside the pile, and the buyers or hawkers encircled him. The fish were sold by Dutch auction: that is the salesman named a price higher than the normal value of the fish; which usually met with a chorus of laughs and jeers. Then he would drop his price until a hawker thought it was worth his while to buy, when he would cry out and the fish was his. The remarks and quips passed by the buyers at these sales often caused a lot of fun, as these fellows were full of noisy humour.

As soon as the sales were over, the hawkers went off to dispose of their fish to consumers. Streets in the town echoed and re-echoed with the cry: "Fish ho! All alive ho! All fresh this morning!" as cats trotted out and rubbed around the hawkers' legs in anticipation of a tasty meal.

Fishermen were not given to many words, but in a yarning mood could be very amusing. Jolly fishermen, full of manliness and pluck, were always ready to lend a helping hand in an hour of danger.

Those fishermen who subsidised their income by acting as lifeboat crew were summoned to the lifeboat station on Thursday morning, 2 December. It was the periodical inspection by Lieut. Keppel-

Foote, one of the R.N.L.I. inspectors. Horses drew the lifeboat on its carriage from the Parade, down the sands opposite the lifeboat house and the *Henry Harris* was launched in a calm sea shortly before 11 a.m., assisted by the Chief Coastguard Officer. The veteran Coxwain, Charlie Lee, and the full compliment of crew exercised the boat for an hour and a half until the inspector was completely satisfied.

Harry Marshall, pictured centre wearing a flat cap, and other fisherman with their boat. The piece of equipment in the boat (visible on the right of the picture) is a dan, used for marking the position of fishing nets in the sea

The *Henry Harris* was launched just once on active service during 1897. It was Thursday 16 December when a steamer, the *Paroo* of London bound for Brisbane with 1600 passengers, was in trouble off the town.

At 8.15 a.m., when the large ship was sighted by the coastguard with her hull down, they kept her under observation for the next few hours as she was gradually being driven towards land by a southerly force six wind, despite attempting to bear south.

By 11.30 a.m. she was just 5 miles off Worthing, when her crew unsuccessfully attempted to draw her off against the strong breeze, under sail.

Extremely concerned for her safety, the coastguard signalled her in the overcast squally conditions, asking if she was in need of assistance. These messages were ignored until about 1.30 p.m., when she was only about three miles south of Worthing Pier.

In response to a signal, from the ship, that she was disabled, the *Henry Harris* was launched in the rough sea 45 minutes later at 2.15 p.m.; the lifeboat crew having been on hand since 8.30 that morning.

Our tough little lifeboat tacked against the headwind, eventually reaching the steamship 2¾ hours later at 5 p.m. when it was quite dark. The Captain of the *Paroo*, owned by the British India Steam Navigation Company, informed Coxwain Lee that they had managed to repair a broken cylinder in the steam engine and would now be able to veer away from the coast under their own steam.

As the services of our lifeboatmen were no longer required, they headed back for the shore. With the wind behind them the return journey was quicker, taking only 2 hours. At 7 p.m. the *Henry Harris* landed and just 15 minutes later it was back in the boathouse.

The 13 courageous Lifeboatmen, Coxwain Lee, 2nd cox Harry Marshall and his brother Fred, bowman Steve Wingfield, T. Wingfield, F. Collier, Wm. Collier, Frank Burden, J. Bridger, Bill Blann, Lelliott, Cousins, and George Belton, who had all been on duty for 10½ hours, were paid 30s. each. Twenty three men, who had helped to launch and haul up the lifeboat, were rewarded with a total of £5 15s. Walter Butcher, the signalman, received 7s. 6d. as well as £3 for the hire of 6 of his horses to pull the carriage. A sundry cost of 6d. for a telegram made the total cost £28 14s.6d. for this abortive mission risking the lives of our brave lifeboatmen.

This service to the *Paroo* was the final one for Coxwain Charlie Lee, veteran of 14 lifeboat rescues. On his retirement in January 1898 after 26 years in the lifeboat crew, 19 of those years as coxwain, he was awarded a bar to his silver medal, and granted a pension of £11 10s.

Harry Marshall was promoted from the position of 2nd coxwain to replace Charlie; while Bill Blann moved up, replacing Harry to become 2nd Coxwain. The new Coxwain proudly led his crew in a fund-raising exercise at Balham, on Tuesday 15 March. The Worthing crew, who were stationed in a different lifeboat being drawn through the streets in a carnival procession, proved very popular with the crowds; returning in the evening with very pleasant memories of a highly interesting and enjoyable outing in a good cause.

During the previous year, 1897, the lifeboatmen around the British coast, as well as saving 30 vessels, rescued 534 people, making a total of 40,000 lives since the R.N.L.I.'s inception.

At Worthing's quarterly lifeboat practise on Wednesday 6 April, unusual interest was taken in the proceedings. In addition to the large gathering of hundreds of spectators which were always attracted on these occasions, a 'moving picture' syndicate arrived to take special views of the launch and return of the boat, and of a demonstration of artificial respiration on a 'drowning man.'

Two months later on Friday 3 June, Mr. Keppel-Foote, on behalf of R.N.L.I. H.Q., inspected the lifeboat house and the equipment once more. Then, in front of a large number of excited spectators, the *Henry Harris* was launched near the pier.

But, during the excercise, Coxwain Harry Marshall got the hook of a grapnell into his hand, severely lacerating it. Although the courageous coxwain was willing to continue with the work, the inspector insisted on landing him at the pier to have his injury attended to.

The wound, which was dressed by Dr. Collett, turned out to be not too serious, but I would still regard this as the kind of typical tenacity that a lifeboatman displayed in not wanting to leave his post and fail his fellow crewmen.

Lifeboat crewman Harry Blann, while attending his fishing boats on the beach, on Tuesday 26 July, rescued a man from drowning. The man, a West Worthing dairy proprietor named Osborne, had waded into the sea in a drunken stupour and dived under. Harry rushed in and fished him out. The police arrived, handcuffed him and took him to the cells. But as there was not sufficient evidence to charge him with attempted suicide, a charge of drunk and disorderly conduct was preferred against him at the Petty Sessions.

Another fisherman had an experience of a different kind, the likes of which hadn't happened here for the past 20 years. On Wednesday morning 8 June, Mr. Searle caught a massive sea thresher 11' 6" long whilst mackerel fishing 11 miles off Worthing. It got entangled in his net and, half throttled, was hauled on board but it quickly expired. On bringing it back to Worthing, the monster fish was displayed in a make-shift tarpaulin tent on the beach. The thresher was a deadly enemy of the whale, which it often attacked with tremendous blows from its flexible tail and, with the aid of the swordfish, killed.

Mr. J. Belton, a well-known boat-builder and relative of George Belton the lifeboatman, completed two pleasure yachts among his other constructions in 1898. One, for Capt. Fred Collins of Brighton, was just under 24' long and was launched in July.

The other was the 41' 6" yawl-rigged *Narcissus* built for a Mr. Pocock who spared no expense in having the fittings made of teak and satin wood. The four berths in the cabin and three in the fo'castle were upholstered in 1st rate quality by Messrs. Jordan & Gray.

After the launch, Mr. Pocock generously invited Mr. Belton and his workmen, and the new yacht's crew to dinner at the *Spaniard Hotel* on Wednesday evening 15 June. Among the 30 guests present, W. J. C. Long, J. Haslett, Wm. Paine, Newman and Charlie Lee provided the best entertainment with their appropriate renditions of some excellent songs.

Sailing matches in the annual regatta were held in somewhat unfavourable conditions. Originally scheduled for 6 August and postponed due to bad weather, it took place in rainy conditions with a strong south westerly breeze. Lifeboatmen were prominent in the races exclusively for Worthing boatmen and fishermen.

A view of Worthing from the sea showing part of the pier on the left and featuring a pleasure yacht

S. Bacon, dressed in whites, in *Adelaide* won the race for sailing boats not exceeding 17 feet belonging to Worthing watermen. George Wingfield, in his red colours, took 2nd place with *Lancashire Lass*; while F. Stubbs, in green and white, came third with *Victoria*. Seven other boats were unplaced: T. Belton, blue, *Empress*; George Belton, green, *Ina*; Wm. Wells, yellow, *Little Jack*; G. Street, black, *Gold Tip*; Bill and Harry Blann, red and white, *Never Can Tell*; A. Beck, blue and white, *Marquis of Salisbury*; T. Wingfield, yellow and white, *The Dolly*.

In the rowing race for first-class pair-oared boats for Worthing watermen, George Belton in his whites took first prize in *The Florrie*, with T. Wingfield in his red colours coming second in *Lily*; and another of George Belton's boats, *The Weattie* was third. Four other boats were unplaced: F. Collier's *Mabel*; Marshall's *Bertha*; Wm. Wells' *Lady Annie*, and T. Wingfield's *White Rose*.

The last of the 10 boat races, the one for coastguard galleys, was cancelled. Prizes were presented at the conclusion of the events by the Mayor and Mayoress.

The lifeboat crew journeyed to Croydon, on Wednesday 6 July, to take part in a demonstration for R.N.L.I. funds. Unfortunately, soon after arriving, Steve Wingfield slipped off a kerb when avoiding a ladder on the pavement, fell and broke a bone in his foot. He was treated in Croydon Hospital and remained incapacitated for some weeks, unable to work and support his wife and children.

Fund raising in Worthing culminated in Lifeboat Sunday on 28 August, when the R.N.L.I. appealed to the generosity of the public to support the 295 lifeboats now on our coast. Collections were made at St. Botolph's, Pier, Holy Trinity, St. Andrews, Christ Church, Baptist, Angmering, Salvation Army, Broadwater, Parade Boxes, Ferring, Primitive Methodist, Sompting, West Tarring and the Congregational Church; and the substantial sum of £73 14s.8d. was sent to R.N.L.I. H.Q. by John Roberts, the

Worthing branch honorary secretary.

One Saturday morning at the beginning of December the *Henry Harris* and crew were inspected by Lieut. Keppel-Foote R.N. for the third time. The lifeboat was launched under the direction of the new Coxwain, Harry Marshall, opposite Grand Avenue. The proceedings, watched by Chairman H. Hargood, John Roberts and Alderman Fletcher, proved satisfactory to the inspector.

Beltons the boatbuilders - 2nd from left J. Belton junior, 3rd from left J. Belton himself, and 4th from left Jack Dowds wearing a bowler hat

On 27th of that month, when a strong S.S.W. gale was howling and a heavy sea was battering the beach groynes, the crew were summoned for the real thing. About 8 a.m. the coastguard had seen a two-masted steamer anchored, to weather the storm, about four miles S.S.W. of the lifeboat station in a very dangerous situation, threatened by huge waves. Two hours later, when it appeared unlikely that the vessel would be able to hold on, with the sea breaking over her and the steamer sheering badly, the lifeboat crews and volunteers were assembled.

The first Worthing crew were ordered to put their lifebelts on and be prepared to start at a moment's notice; and the helpers were also instructed to remain available in the boathouse.

At 3.45 p.m. a telegram was received by Coxwain Harry Marshall from Littlehampton, stating that the Littlehampton lifeboat and a tug had been out to the steamer, *Linfield* of London, and were returning. Consequently, the 13 Worthing crew and 13 permanent helpers were dismissed after being on duty for nearly six hours, and paid 6s. and 4s. each respectively.

Walter Butcher received his signalman's allowance of 4s. and was paid £3 for keeping six of his horses in reserve most of the day. Six carters were paid 4s. each, making a total cost of £10 18s. for this lifeboat standby, even though it was never launched.

The crew were Coxwain Harry Marshall, his brothers Mark and Fred, 2nd Cox Bill Blann and his brother Harry, Bowman Steve Wingfield with his two relatives George and Tom, Wm. Cousins, George Benn, George Belton, Steve Bacon, and Wm. Collier.

A boat under construction at Beltons' yard

Two weeks later, on Thursday 12 January 1899, another gale ravaged Worthing. At midnight, when the tide was at its highest, the sea came up and over the Parade in places, bringing with it large quantities of shingle, seaweed and a large fish that was said to be a shark. It lay where it was washed ashore - an object of curious interest - until it was carted off by Corporation workmen.

Despite the late hour, the combination of the wild elements of the weather and sea attracted a number of excited people to the seafront, some of whom were enlisted by fishermen and boatmen in hauling their boats up out of danger's way.

Shortly before dawn the next morning, the wind dropped dramatically, but not before stripping a large sheet of lead from the roof of a shop in South Street. In one place the beach stones had been hurled up in great bulk, covering part of the Parade near the R.N.L.I. collecting box.

The annual meeting of the Worthing Branch R.N.L.I. was held a few weeks later on Wednesday afternoon 8 February. At the meeting, in the Council Chamber, Lord Henry Thynne was re-elected president of the branch, while the committee was re-appointed en bloc. It was revealed that the last year's income was £282 0s.1d., while the expenditure amounted to £206 8s. 4d., leaving a balance in hand of £75 11s.9d., enough to cover most emergencies.

The next emergency occurred some 12 days later, on 20 February, when a small schooner ran aground about ¾ mile from the shore. Local experience had repeatedly shown that popular interest was never more effectively aroused than by some incident connected with the sea. It was not surprising therefore that despite the absence of dangerous weather elements or weird scenes that had been so typical of these occurrences, the interest and curiosity of the townspeople were still largely stimulated.

At 2 p.m., when it was low tide, the schooner, *Prince Llewellyn*, was sighted two miles east of Worthing Pier, having run aground after tacking up the Channel towards Shoreham Harbour.

The watching lifeboatmen could see no distress signals being hoisted but continued to keep her under observation. As the tide would now be rising it was at first thought that the vessel would float off, but this proved not to be the case, for as the water got deeper the vessel went shorewards, until it was only a few hundred yards from the beach opposite the Esplanade at East Worthing.

THE PIER,   WORTHING.

Worthing Pier between high and low tides

At 5 p.m., with the E.S.E. wind increasing and the 91 ton schooner being buffetted by the sea which was becoming rougher, the Worthing Lifeboat Committee decided that assistance was imperative. The lifeboat crew and Walter Butcher's horses had been on standby for some time, and within 30 minutes the *Henry Harris* was pulled along the Marine Road and launched, when the tide was half flood, from the beach to the east of the Esplanade with the aid of a competent band of willing helpers, and vigourously cheered by a large muster of spectators.

In the meantime a waterman named C. Stubbs had put off in a small boat and brought one of the shipwrecked crew ashore. While landing at the pier head, Stubbs and his companion had a dangerous experience: a large wave caught the boat, dashed it against the ironwork and swamped it, but not before the occupants had managed to get out.

Having realised that the rising rough sea and the strong E.S.E. wind could drive her into the pier, Mr. Belton, the piermaster, had sent a telegram to Shoreham, which had the effect of bringing the harbour tug *Stella* onto the scene. At about 6 p.m., the same time as the *Henry Harris* reached the *Prince Llewellyn*, an attempt was made to tow the unfortunate schooner into deeper water.

This proved unsuccessful however, and tension amongst the crowds that lined the beach and the pier increased when they saw the tow rope snap under the strain.

Several efforts were made to fix a new line but these proved futile; and on making what proved to be the final attempt a huge wave caught the tug as she was passing under the schooner's stern, and dashed it against the latter vessel, smashing away the stern rails. The tug returned to Shoreham Harbour alone with a damaged paddle-box.

All this time the schooner had been drifting westward, until at 7 p.m. when the tide had turned, she was seen in the darkness scarcely 100 yards from the pier.

Notwithstanding his former experience, Stubbs rowed another boat out to the schooner, which had been bound for Shoreham from Port Madock in Wales with a cargo of slate, and rowed back with the information that the crew had at last consented to be taken off in the lifeboat, which had been standing-by all evening.

At 9 p.m. the four remaining hands were removed to the *Henry Harris*, which then returned to shore and beached opposite West Street at 9.45 p.m. The shipwrecked crew joined their colleague and were introduced to Chief Officer Lang of the Coastguard, who represented the Shipwrecked Mariners' Society and who provided them with lodgings at the *Rambler Inn*, West Street.

The schooner *Prince Llewellyn* stranded east of the pier

Assisted by a large number of helpers, 32 in all, the *Henry Harris* negotiated the beach which was in a difficult state after the recent gales, and was eventually returned to the boathouse at 10 p.m.

The patient crew, many of whom had been on the scene for eight hours, were Coxwain Harry Marshall, his brothers Fred and Mark, 2nd Coxwain Bill Blann, his brother Harry, Bowman Steve Wingfield, his relatives George and Tom, Fred Wakeford, George Benn, George Belton, Steve Bacon and newcomer William Curvin. They were very proud to chalk up yet another rescue on their station's 'scoreboard'.

Each of the 13 crewmen received 30s.; 32 helpers 5s. each; 7s.6d. for the signalman; and £4 10s. for the hire of six horses made a total expenditure of £32 7s.6d. for this service.

Captain Humphrey Roberts whose father, Edward, owned the schooner thought that there would be little difficulty in getting her towed off the next morning. With the aid of Mr. Butcher's horses the vessel was lightened by removing the cargo of slates, which were subsequently stacked in Walter Butcher's yard in West Street.

During the afternoon a large number of onlookers went onto the sands and gazed up at the wooden hull, while several climbed onto the deck. No fewer than five anchors had been put in position to prevent the schooner from drifting into the pier.

At 8 p.m. the *Stella* returned and after about an hour's pulling managed to pull the schooner to face east, but just as a refloating attempt seemed likely, the tow rope again snapped and the tug returned alone once more to Shoreham.

At this time the tide had only just begun to turn, and almost before the tug was out of sight, the *Prince Llewellyn* of Carn turned back to its original position and drifted a little closer in shore.

On the Thursday the Newhaven steamer, *Nelson*, arrived here accompanied by the *Stella*. A brilliant moonlit night favoured operations, and a large crowd of spectators assembled on the beach and pier to see what success was to reward this latest undertaking.

About 10 p.m., when there was no wind and the sea was calm, the *Nelson's* powerful machinery succeeded in pulling the schooner off southwards, but then, for some reason, the steamer went shorewards and collided with the pier, striking one of the iron columns with sufficient force to cause the deck to shake perceptibly, with alarmed spectators fleeing from the spot.

The only way out of the difficulty was for the Captain to go astern with the risk of running aground. The spectators saw the ludicrous aspect of the situation and were highly amused by the difficulty into which the steamer having come so many miles to render help had itself been plunged. It was now the *Stella's* turn to prove her usefullness, and with some willing helpers on the pier a tow rope was fixed to the *Nelson* and she was speedily extracated from her undignified position.

No further time was lost. The Newhaven boat once again directed itself to the task of getting the Welshman away. This was soon accomplished and it was towed into deeper water to the cheers of assembled onlookers.

But the most exciting moment had yet to come, for as the three vessels started away to the east, a report was heard, as though the towrope had snapped yet again, and the schooner immediately changed course, heading in an oblique direction directly for the pier.

It was felt that there was no hope for the structure now, and the eager ones who had hastened to the pier head to see the last of the departing craft were amazed to see it apparently bearing down on them at terrific speed.

They rushed down the pier in a state of panic, but happily their fears were unfounded. The tow rope was still holding and had simply slackened and, just in time, the rope tightened and the nose of the troublesome little Welsh trader was turned in an easterly direction.

The two tugs and the liberated schooner were seen at 10.30 p.m. pursueing a safe course eastwards concluding this thrilling adventure for hundreds of excited onlookers.

Ch. 18

A Fruit-Filled Finale. 1899 - 1901

A Worthing fisherman had a narrow escape from drowning on Thursday 4 May 1899. Tom Bridger, of 25, Gloucester Place, was one of the crew of the Worthing fishing smack *Happy Return*, which was lying in the Camber at Portsmouth. At about 10 p.m. when Tom was about to return to his vessel he slipped from the quay into the water.

Some time elapsed before his cries attracted attention. He was eventually rescued by a party of fishermen, who hauled him out. Tom, in a pitiful state, was successfully treated by two police constables, and recovered sufficiently to rejoin the smack.

Exactly one month later, on Sunday 4 June, a French cutter grounded on the sandbank just off Worthing Pier. The *Voyager*, which had been bound from Barfleur to Newhaven with a cargo of potatoes, came too near the shore and grounded at about 11.30 a.m. During the day, curious onlookers who put off in a number of boats from the beach to view the vessel at close quarters, felt that the *Voyager* did not appear as imposing as its name. The craft was compelled to stay there with its crew of four Frenchman until the tide was half flood at 4.30 p.m., when she refloated and continued her voyage.

3. The Pier, Worthing.

The east side of Worthing Pier. A French cutter grounded on the sandbank just off here

The R.N.L.I.'s periodical inspection, now six-monthly, of the Worthing Lifeboat Station was carried out on Friday 2 June by Lieut. Keppel-Foote R.N. He examined the boathouse and equipment first, before the *Henry Harris,* with a full crew under Coxwain Harry Marshall, was launched from the sands opposite West Buildings.

It was at the inspector's request that the launch took place at low water; and after performing several manoeuvres taking an hour, the lifeboat was beached. The customary collection, for R.N.L.I. funds, was taken among the spectators.

During the regular quarterly lifeboat practise on Tuesday 19 September, the somewhat high wind experienced was most favourable to the full crew headed by Coxwain Harry Marshall. The launch, watched by a large number of spectators on the seafront and the pier, took place to the east of the pier shortly before midday superintended by the lifeboat chairman, Mr. H. Hargood J.P., and the honorary secretary, Mr. John Roberts.

The lifeboat being beached after manouvres

At the R.N.L.I.'s twice yearly inspection, on Saturday 25 November, the usual collection, instead of being devoted to the Lifeboat Institution, was given to the Mayor's War Sufferers' Relief Fund, for soldiers returning from the Boer war with horrific injuries.

After the boathouse had been viewed, the *Henry Harris* was drawn onto the sands by Councillor Butcher's horses and launched from a point opposite Augusta Place. The full crew, under Coxwain Harry Marshall and Deputy Coxwain Bill Blann, exercised the lifeboat watched by a large number of people from the Parade and the pier.

On Sunday, in addition to the collection made the previous day, money placed in the R.N.L.I. pillar boxes was also handed over to the Mayor's fund for veterans of the Transvaal war.

Six months later, on Wednesday evening 6 June 1900, when the inspector returned on his routine inspection, patriotism prevailed among a large crowd of sightseers assembled in the vicinity of the pier to witness the launch of the *Henry Harris*. Just before the lifeboat was drawn into the sea the spectators, at the invitation of the Mayor, Alderman F. Parish J.P., joined in singing the national anthem to the accompaniment of Mr. G. F. Wright's Brass Band. As the boat, manned by a full crew under Coxwain Marshall and Second Coxwain Blann, took to the water, three cheers were given for the crew.

Regular practises took place in March, August and November. On each occasion Harry Blann acted as second coxwain to Harry Marshall, the coxwain. The most notable one was the summer launch, when the sound of the lifeboat gun on a Friday afternoon brought a large number of residents and visitors running to the seafront, thinking that the very high wind and consequently rough sea had resulted in a ship of some sort getting into difficulties. A rough day was of course preferable as then the lifeboatmen would exercise under conditions that could prevail in a real emergency; and it was seldom that the committee was so fortunate in the selection of such a day. Councillor Butcher's horses were, as usual, employed to draw the *Henry Harris* from the boathouse to be launched from the beach to the east of the pier, watched by hundreds of people on the pier itself as well as on the seafront.

Lifeboatman George Belton was related to Alfred Belton, one of four fishermen who were prosecuted in June for possessing immature fish. Three of the defendants, Henry Saunders, John Tester and Richard Munnery, were shown to have varying numbers of crabs, 'each of which measured less than $4\frac{1}{2}$ inches across the broadest part of the back;' while Alfred possessed several lobsters, 'each of which measured less than eight inches from the tip of the beak to the end of the tail when spread as far as possible flat.' The proceedings were taken under the Act of 1877, and Mr. H. F. Gates of Brighton, who was prosecuting on behalf of the Fisheries Committee, said the law was well known, and it was time the Act was enforced. The Bench fined each fisherman 10s. including costs.

Two months later, at a meeting of the Sussex Sea Fisheries Committee at the Royal Pavilion in Brighton, a new bye-law was discussed to the effect that after 30 April 1901, 'no person shall in fishing for sea fish use any seine or draft or tuck net having more than 30 rows of knots to the yard, measured when wet, except that during the months of May, June and July in any year, a person can use a net having not more than 36 rows of knots to the yard, measured aforesaid.' The Clerk explained that the Committee would shortly have a report from the Board of Trade dealing with the question of the use of the kettle 'net at Eastbourne, and an amendment was agreed deferring the matter until the next quarterly meeting, so that the proposed bye-law could be considered in conjuction with the report.

Alfred Belton, fined for catching young lobsters, was notorious for his drinking habits. Before the Bench, in December, on a charge of being drunk and disorderly in Lyndhurst Road, he pleaded guilty. He had been so drunk that the landlord of the *Selden Arms* refused to serve him. But in his defence, Police Superintendant Bridger reported that the man had not been before the Bench for the past five years.

The beach opposite J. Belton & Sons boatbuilding yard in Library Place

Alfred was related to J. Belton, whose firm Messrs. J. Belton & Sons, built four boats for the Naval Cruising Club of Brighton this year. The last one was almost square, 10 feet long with a 7 feet six inch beam, half-decked with a dagger centre board. Her mast was 21 feet high, with a topsail-yard setting six feet across the mast. Her bowsprit was eight feet outside the stern, and her main boom 16 feet long, giving her a total overall length of 28 feet from bowsprit to the end of her boom. Mr. Belton said at the time of her maiden launch that the *John Dorcy*, as it was called, "sails like a bird."

One evening at the end of June, Charles Paine conducted a sale of used rowing and sailing boats on the beach opposite Montague Place. A rowing boat was purchased by a Mr. Moore for £5, while Worthing fishermen, F. Stubbs, Wakeford and Wingfield snapped up other bargains.

George Wingfield, a lifeboatman, came second in the Worthing watermens' sailing boat race in the annual regatta of 1900, and won the greasy pole competition on the same day, taking home £1 5s. from the former and a leg of mutton from the latter.

The beach opposite Montague Place where Charles Paine conducted a sale of used rowing and sailing boats

In November, 50 years since the *Lalla Rookh* tragedy, the son of one of the victims recalled that fateful day. Stephen Newman of Germiston, Westcourt Road wrote: 'I was one of those fatherless children, my father being the late Henry Newman, whose age was 47 years, and my dear mother was left with eight of us children to mourn his loss; and what made it more sad was we never saw our dear father again, as he was one of those who were never found.'

Stephen's late elder brother, G. H. Newman, used to speak of an occurrence where he met Captain Haines, formerly of the barque *Lalla Rookh*. He was walking on the Front one day, many years after the sad event, and saw a gentleman talking to a man. Just before he reached them the man turned and said to the gentleman, "This is the man you want, sir."

The gentleman came up to him and asked him to allow him to shake hands with a son of one of the brave men who lost their lives in attempting to save his, expressing his deep sorrow at the tragic loss of life and his admiration for the heroic spirit which had prompted the 11 men to venture in an open boat in such a sea to save the lives of those who were in distress.

Explaining that his duties had prevented him coming before, he went on to say that he had always wished to visit Worthing and stand on the shore and try to picture that courageous scene.

Old George Newman had been a youth of 18 on that dreadful, dramatic, November day in 1850. He had been standing beside a gentleman who was looking through a telescope, and who saw the boat go over and the poor men struggling in the water. And when he had heard him say they were all drowned George had collapsed on the beach with such stunning shock that it caused a deafness with which he was ever after afflicted.

To augment lifeboat funds a sacred concert was given in the (southern) pier pavilion one Sunday in 1900. Over 1400 people paid for admission to the pier that evening, and the pavilion itself was packed, with many having to stand. Several vocalists sung to the pier orchestra and the proceeds amounted to £8 13s.2d.

On another Sunday evening £2 15s. was collected for the R.N.L.I. when the Worthing Salvation Army band played in the bandstand.

Following Queen Victoria's death in January 1901, St. Paul's church was chosen as Worthing's venue for its official mourning service, where Worthing townspeople unanimously expressed visible sorrow at the loss of a popular sovereign who had reigned over them for so many years.

It was Saturday afternoon 2 February, the day she was buried in London, when a long procession formed at Worthing Town Hall. Marching with the bands, soldiers, local dignitaries and officials was the lifeboat crew under the command of Coxwain Harry Marshall and Deputy Coxwain Harry Blann (standing in for his brother Bill). Ex-Coxwain Charlie Lee was also present. They all entered St. Paul's for an hour-long service which terminated with Beethoven's and Mendelssohn's funeral marches as they left the building.

At the annual meeting of the Worthing Branch R.N.L.I., held in the council chamber during the week following the memorial service, the chairman, Mr. H. Hargood J.P., moved the following address:

To his most gracious majesty King Edward VII, president of the National Lifeboat Institution.

'We, the subscribers of the Worthing Branch of the Royal National Lifeboat Institution, together with the coxwains and crews, at our annual meeting held on Thursday 7 February 1901, hereby record our sense of the irreparable loss which your majesty, your august family, and the empire have sustained by the lamented death of our beloved Queen, her most gracious majesty, Queen Victoria, for 63 years patron of this national institution; and we also humbly offer to your majesty, to her majesty Queen Alexandra, and other members of the royal family, an expression of our sincerest sympathy. At the same time we most respectfully beg to be permitted to recognise the interest your majesty has taken in the life-saving work of the institution as its president, and to assure our most gracious majesty of our unswerving loyalty and devotion to your throne and person.'

Alderman Parish seconded the motion, and the chairman mentioned that the coxwain and crew wished to be associated with it.

All stood while the proposition was formally put to those present, and the chairman, declaring it to be unanimously carried, concluded with the words, "God save the king!"

During the course of the meeting a speaker referred to the ceremonial launch of the *Henry Harris* which had been one of the principal events of the Worthing jubilee celebrations in 1887. It was also mentioned that Worthing had been chosen by R.N.L.I. H.Q., when his present majesty, then the Prince of Wales, had requested, as president, to be furnished with animated photographs of the launch and return of the lifeboat.

The committee's annual report set forth that the *Henry Harris* had happily not been called out on service during the past year; and that the branch had made satisfactory financial progress, enabling £100 to be forwarded to H.Q., the largest ever made by this branch out of its ordinary receipts.

The report included confirmation that a new improved lifeboat was being built for Worthing to replace the 14 year old *Henry Harris*. It was explained that the (national) Committee of Management had agreed to the unanimous request of the coxwains and crews for a new boat fitted with all the modern improvements. The new, self-righting 35 feet long lifeboat, which was to be the liberal gift of a Mrs. Birt-Davies-Coleman, should be ready by the summer.

Among other matters contained in the report was the statement that since Worthing had been made an official station of the institution, 49 lives had been saved by the two successive lifeboats, the *Jane* and the *Henry Harris*, without any loss to the crews.

The balance sheet, which accompanied the report, read by Mr. Roberts, showed that the financial year began with a balance of £105 12s.; subscriptions received represented a sum of £126 13s.; and with other items the total available income was brought up to £275 13s.9d. The expenditure for the year amounted to £144 10s.8d. which left the Branch with a balance of £131 3s.1d., out of which the grant to the parent institution was made.

Some general comments on the present position of affairs were made by the chairman, who showed how well prepared they were, by means of telephonic communication between the various stations, to deal with any emergency that might arise. He also illustrated the additional facilities for launching and claimed these to be a tribute to the efficiency and economy of the branch, and also an indication of the generosity of the town. The meeting then closed.

The lifeboat was urgently needed three weeks later on Friday 1st March. Conscientious Coxwain Harry Marshall had been on duty all night, ready for any demand on his crew, as a strong S.S.W. gale had been gusting since the previous evening.

As daylight approached a large steamer was observed about three miles south of the lifeboat house.

About 7.30 a.m. it became obvious that all was not well: she was very low in the water and pointing shorewards. Since no distress signals of any kind were received from the ailing ship, the coastguard signalled her, but these went unanswered.

Chairman Mr. H. Hargood hurriedly consulted Harry Marshall and Mr. Lester, the chief coastguard officer, resulting in a determined decision to launch the lifeboat.

Most of the crew had already made their way to the beach opposite the station by the time the lifeboat gun was fired. The *Henry Harris* was taken out of the boathouse and drawn westward by six of Councillor Butcher's horses and wheeled down the beach in the vicinity of the Hotel Metropole (now Dolphin Lodge) on the corner of Grand Avenue.

Once off its carriage and in the thundering surf, the lifeboat was at first stubborn in refusing to go any further. The lifeboatmen's repeated attempts to row their heavy craft into the surging breakers were continually hampered. Their sheer muscle power and nerve were extended to their extremities, and it was only their grim determination and tenacity that enabled them to overcome the mightiness of the roaring wind and sea, and successfully launch at 7.55 a.m.

With the gale being so forcefully violent they dare not hoist the sail, and lashed by driving rain the lifeboatmen rowed for more than 1½ hours, reaching the sinking vessel at 9.30 a.m.

The sea was breaching over her superstructure, and, although her funnel had gone, the name *Indiana* was still visible. There was no sign of the crew and it was obvious from the position of the davits that the ship's lifeboats had been lowered and launched.

Anxious watchers on the beach glimpsed the *Henry Harris* on the horizon circling the ill-fated vessel,

The lifeboat *Henry Harris* returning from service to the *Indiana*, photographed from the pier. Standing in the bow is Steve Wingfield (bowman) and standing in the stern are Coxwain Harry Marshall and 2nd Coxwain Bill Blann.

which had only her bow and masts visible by now, twice and then return.

Meanwhile, oranges and lemons began washing ashore in their tens of thousands. The news spread through the town like wildfire. Costers came with their horse trolleys; professional men as well as tradesmen were seen piling the fruit into baskets; hundreds of children, instead of going to school, went down to the beach and filled sacks, bags, and buckets with fruit, necklaces and nick-nacks from the general cargo washed up from the *Indiana*, a large British steamer; and all were busy frantically gathering this unanticipated but welcome harvest of the sea.

Large numbers of unbroken cases washed ashore. Whilst some of these were stacked at the top of the beach, others were carted away by the more ambitious folk or broken open where they were found on the beach to remove their citrus contents. Police later visited homes, demanding that undamaged cases be taken to the police station for safe-keeping.

As the lifeboat approached the shore, people left their pleasant task of gathering up fruit and dashed towards the pier to watch the boat being beached. Highly-spirited citizens welcomed their lifeboatmen ashore with a tumultuous cheer at 10.30 a.m.

The spectators learnt from Coxwain Marshall that the *Indiana* of Hull had been abandoned by Captain F. Kershaw and his crew, and as it was mostly submerged the cause of the disaster could not be ascertained, but it was surmised that a collision had occurred.

While the *Henry Harris* was being hauled up the beach, a telegram was received from the Littlehampton station asking if their lifeboat should be launched. A reply was cabled to the effect that it would not be necessary.

While the *Henry Harris*, repositioned on its carriage, was being drawn towards the boathouse, a messenger, from Messrs. J. Howard & Dartnell, brought news that there was a small boat about a mile off the *Half Brick Inn* with, what appeared to be, some men in her.

"Alright, we'll launch her again!" insisted Coxwain Marshall amidst fervent "hear, hears!" from the rest of the crew.

The lifeboat carriage was turned around, taken back to the pier and relaunched at 10.50 a.m., with the same crew, once more on an errand of mercy.

It was not until after the lifeboat had been launched that a second messenger arrived, confirming that there were two men in the boat.

It drifted close in shore, about mid-way between the town and Lancing, anxious eyes straining to glimpse the supposed occupants.

Suddenly, a large wave swamped the craft and into the water fell a plank. It must have been fixed in an upright position giving every appearance of being a man.

Gaining on the boat was the *Henry Harris*, which had been making good speed under sail. When it reached the waterlogged boat, which proved to be one of the boats from the S S *Indiana*, Harry Marshall found two detached air tanks floating in the boat which probably added to the impression that men were on board.

With no shipwrecked sailors to rescue, the *Henry Harris* beached at Lancing at 11.45 a.m. The return trip by road to Worthing took some time, and it was not until one o'clock in the morning that it was rehoused.

While this was happening, Boatman Clark of the Lancing Coastguard swam out and brought ashore the *Indiana's* damaged lifeboat, containing a compass lashed to the bottom and other signs of earlier occupation.

A great deal of fruit, from the submerged freighter, washed up on the beach to the west of the pier. But gradually, entrepeneurs moved further east, beyond Splash Point, where the water was simply one mass of oranges, each golden crested wave bringing in more and more, carpeting the beach in all directions.

Women went into the sea and lifted up their skirts to make hammocks to carry the fruit. Great quantities of it were immediately carried off, but there was a lot trampled on which turned into a messy pulp. A constant stream of men boys, women and girls was seen, all wending their way home, heavily laden with their spoils, but returning again and again for more.

The Lifeboat crew: Coxwain Harry Marshall, his brother Mark, 2nd Coxwain Bill Blann, his brother Harry, Bowman Steve Wingfield, his relation George, George Newman, Wm. Wells, Jo. Street, George Benn, George Belton, Frank Collier and Wm. Cousins were paid 15s. per man for each of the two services.

Twenty seven men were paid 7s.6d. each for assisting in launching and hauling-up the Worthing lifeboat. Walter Butcher, the signalman, was allowed 5s. for each service and was paid £6 10s. for the hire of six horses, seven on the 2nd service because one became disabled and had to be replaced by another. The cost of a messenger in connection with the first service was 2s.6d., which brought the total expenditure to £36 15s. for both services, excluding the cost of replacing a broken oar.

Considerable speculation ensued as to the cause of the disaster, and it was not until late that afternoon that particulars of the accident reached the town.

At approximately 5 a.m., during a thick fog, the *Indiana*, homeward bound from Sicily, had been rammed slightly aft of amidships, off the Owers lightship, by the German cross-Atlantic oil steamer, *City of Washington*, on her way to New York. The 23 crew of the former had been taken onto the Hamburg ship, but had subsequently returned and the *Indiana* taken in tow. But when the hawser broke, another vessel, the *Simla* went alongside, took off the crew and took her in tow. However, she listed heavily and eventually ended up grinding to a stop on the sea bed S.S.W. of Worthing Pier in comparatively shallow water. The *Simla* continued and landed the crew at Newhaven.

The 2,225 ton *Indiana* had been used for trading between Hull and Adriatic Ports, and and on this occasion was shipping a general cargo for her owners, Bailey & Leatham.

In the position where she had sunk she was almost completely submerged at high tide, but at low water about ¾ of her length was still visible.

It's cargo continued to wash ashore as far west as the Goring Coastguard Station and as far east as Brighton. As well as boxes of oranges some lemon essence in copper tanks cased in wood washed up on the beaches. For some time to come, people from miles around would be making marmalade.

This loss of cargo had a serious effect on the fruit market. The following paragraphs appeared in Messrs. Plumbridge & Son's price list.

'Oranges - The market is deficient of 6,000 cases of valencia this week, which were coming forward by the *Indiana*, now lost off Worthing.

'Lemons - are also some thousands of cases short, in consequence of the afore-mentioned disaster,

High-spirited youths on the deck of the wreck of the *Indiana* at low tide

and the prices are a little firmer.'

I think it is interesting to note that a street opposite West Worthing Railway Station, Valencia Road, was developed about this time.

The enormous amount of flotsam strewn along the coast was not surprising for, when the 277 foot long wreck was inspected, a 30 foot hole was found in the main hatch.

Two weeks after the steamer had come to grief, some of its cargo, collected from the beach, was auctioned by Chief Coastguard Officer Lester acting on instructions from the Trinity Corporation in London. About 400 cases and 21 casks of oranges and lemons went under the hammer, together with between 600 and 700 bags of sumac (ground leaves used for tanning and dyeing).

Two months after the disaster, divers were still busy removing the remaining cargo from the *Indiana*; and on 9 May another public auction of salvaged cargo was held, this time at the Kingston Wharf at Shoreham, by Messrs. Vidler & Clements of Hastings. It was well-attended and very good prices were realised: 200 bales of hemp fetching between 62s.6d. and 95s. a bale; while £32 was offered for the patent steam steering gear. A surprising feature of the sale was the prices secured for boxes of bead and shell necklaces, between 8s. and 54s. a box, the latter being far more than the original shipping cost to purchasers. Whisks fetched from 4s. to 5s. a bale, making the total proceeds from the sale £1,000.

The summer that year was warm and boatmen did plenty of business taking sightseers out to what later became known as 'the wreck' to generations of Worthing folk.

Some time after, a fisherman decorated his 'box' on the beach, opposite what is now the Berkley

Four young men on the deck of the wrecked Indiana. The one in the middle is Charlie Deadman, whose stepson Ted Baker lives in Worthing

Hotel, with a varnished name plaque from the *Indiana*. He was an ex-navy man named Smart, nicknamed Admiral Smart by children who went to play on the beach. One of those children, Derek Marshall Churcher, now grown up and living in Worthing, remembered it well. Smart owned a 27 foot long sailing boat, a typical size of a beach boat at the turn of the century, called *The Pearl*, licensed to carry 15-20 people.

Being a potential navigation hazard the wreck was eventually blown-up. Its remains are still there today, about two miles from the pier in about 40 feet of water, and are famous as the home of giant

The wreck of the *Indiana*, still visible at high tide, before being blown-up

conger eels which were popular with local fishermen.

It has also proved to be popular with local divers who have recovered various relics. Worthing Museum has custody of the hub from her wheel and a porthole rim; while the Marlipins Museum at Shoreham has her brass steam whistle. In 1983 a condenser plate was retrieved; and the following year a $3\frac{1}{2}$ cwt. brass pump was discovered. At one stage a bathroom in the old cargo steamer was revealed – marble bath with brass taps, china wash basin with lead taps, and brass door hinges were all visible.

The lifeboat's service to the *Indiana* was the last time that the *Henry Harris* was seen on an active call of duty. It was soon to be replaced by a new, improved boat.

The *Henry Harris* had been initiated into the town as a most conspicuous spectacle, around which Queen Victoria's jubilee celebrations in Worthing had been centred, in 1887. Her reign continued until her sad death.

Now the *Henry Harris* had come to the end of its term as a prime lifeboat. A lifeboat with a history of 10 service launches to vessels in distress when 37 lives had been rescued, making a total of 43 lives saved in 21 services since the R.N.L.I. had taken over the Worthing Station.

The following lifeboatmen - 'Stoner' Overington, 'Johnny' Tyler, 'Commodore' Parkes, Hutchinson, Alfred Dean and Charlie Lee - had all been coxwains of the Worthing Lifeboat Station. A station which had always been regarded with particular favour and was held in high esteem by the authorities at R.N.L.I. headquarters.

The following facts illustrate this point: it had been due to a representation from the Worthing Branch Committee that the appointment of a Bowman had been universally adapted throughout the service; Mr. Hargood, Worthing Branch Chairman, had at one time been chosen to give evidence before a House of Commons committee; and Worthing had been specially selected by headquarters when the Prince of Wales required some animated photographs of actual lifeboat work, for exhibition at the Imperial Institute at the time of Queen Victoria's Diamond Jubilee celebrations.

Worthing was proud to possess such an agency for the preservation of life off our coast, and with such an excellent record there was no need to fear as to the readiness of our brave lifeboatmen to respond to the sound of the maroon – the call of duty. They exercised vigilance in times of storm and stress, ever conscious of the supreme significance of their grand motto:

"Ready! Aye Ready!"

Second Coxwain Bill Blann and Coxwain Harry Marshall, worthy representatives of British lifeboat stalwarts, had been associated with the Worthing service since they had been old enough to volunteer.

Seated upon the boat in which he took an inexhaustible pride, Harry was asked about his worst experiences. With becoming modesty he disclaimed all idea of heroism, but his story is well worth repeating.

"On 11 November, 1891," he said, "we were called out by signals of distress from a schooner lying helpless about a mile from the shore. The wind was blowing a hurricane, so much so that the boat was blown out of her carriage as we hurried to the launch. However, after great trouble we got off, and succeeded in reaching the wreck and saving the seven lives on board.

"Hardly had we returned when we were summoned again, this time to a barque three miles off. The wind had increased, and our task was a dangerous one. Reaching our objective, we cast anchor, but it would not hold, and we were swept helplessly by. Wearing round again, by good luck we managed to lay hold of a buoy which was thrown to us, and after very great difficulty took on board all the crew, another seven lives."

This reproduction from a cracked lantern slide features the *Henry Harris* on the seafront road outside the lifeboat house, part of which can just be seen on the right of the picture with the doors open. Both the regular and reserve crews are shown here on a festive occassion, with Coxwain Harry Marshall 2nd from left in the lifeboat.

"We had been at it all day, but would have gone out again had we known. For next day we learned that there had been a wreck at Aldrington, further up the coast, in which all hands were lost. The gale had destroyed both telephone and telegraph wires, and unfortunately no message could be got through to us."

"Yes, it's hard and dangerous work sometimes, but we never mind so long as we can do good. And I'm thankful to say that in all our history as a station we have never had a casualty on the water, and I hope we never shall."

During the 50 year period covered by this book, the enormous number of casualties around the coasts of our great maritime nation was in excess of 150,000. Thirty thousand lives had been lost through shipwreck, but our lifeboats had successfully saved more than 33,000 people.

1892 Local Regatta –
Results of Worthing Watermen's Races

Sailing Race for Dandy Rig and Standing Lugs:

Sea Gull	J. Hutchingson	1st prize £4
Ellen & Margaret	E. Bacon	2nd £3
Lancashire Lass	G. Wingfield	3rd £2
Dolly	T. Wingfield	
Lucy	W. Collier	
Petrel	F. Wakeford	
Dawn of Day	M. Marshall	
Here We Are	W.J. Hutchinson	
Moss Rose	J.G. Davis	
Young Skylark	F. Collier	
Lady Brassey	C. Lee	

Pair-Oared Boats

Rubie	M. Marshall	1st prize £3
Daisy	C. Wingfield	2nd £2 10s.
Thistle	H. Marshall	3rd £2
Snowdrop	G. Wingfield	4th £1
Lady Annie	G. Belton	5th 10s
Mabel	F. Collier	
Edith	A. Beck	
White Rose	J.G. Davis	
Fred	C. Lee	
Water Lily	E. Bacon	
Young William	T. Wingfield	

First-Class Three-Oared Boats

Lizzie Annie	E. Bacon	1st prize £3 10s.
Coquet	C. Lee	2nd £3
Kathleen	F. Wakeford	3rd £2
May Flower	C. Wingfield	4th £1
Mary Rosamond	W. Collier	5th 10s.
Marian	A. Beck	
Mildred	J. Freeman	

Quarter Boats

Lily	M. Marshall	1st prize £3
Lily of the Valley	H. Marshall	2nd £2
Young Ted	J. Belton	3rd £1
Myrtle	C. Wingfield	4th 10s.
Union Jack	E. Bacon	
Cosby	G. Belton	
Lillian	A. Beck	

Second-Class Three-Oared Boats

True Blue	C. Wingfield	1st prize £3 10s.
Pansy	M. Marshall	2nd £3
Beatrice	T. Wingfield	3rd £2
Mabel	F. Collier	4th £1
Rapid	C. Lee	5th 10s.
Alcey	G. Belton	6th 5s.
Olive Branch	G. Wingfield	

1893 Watermen's Regatta Results:

Sailing Race:

Lancashire Lass	George Wingfield	1st prize £3
Southern Cross	H. Reed	2nd £2
Here We Are	T. Hutchinson	3rd £1
Never Can Tell	Harry Blann	4th
Marquis of Salisbury	A. Beck	
Princess May	F. Collier	
Petrel	F. Wakeford	

Licensed Quarter Boats:

Myrtle	C. Wingfield	1st prize £1
Lily	Arthur Marshall	2nd 10s.
Lily of the Valley	Harry Marshall	3rd 5s.
The Union Jack	E. Bacon	

The race resulted in an easy win for the *Myrtle*, which had the advantage of some three or four lengths at the finish. For second place the contest was keen, only about half a length separated the Lillies when the gun was fired by the judge.

Sculling Race:

Oruba	Arthur Marshall	1st prize £1
Moss Rose	C. Wingfield	2nd 15s
Daisy	C. Wingfield	3rd 10s
Thistle	Harry Marshall	4th 5s
Mabel	F. Collier	
Olive	F. Collier	
Grace Darling	C. Collier	

The winner held the lead throughout, though the distance that separated him from the other competitors was considerably diminished after returning from the eastern buoys. The *Daisy* was a good third.

Pair-Oared Boats:

Oruba	Arthur Marshall	1st prize £1 10s.
Arawa	H. Reed	2nd £1
Rosie	Arthur Marshall	3rd 15s.
Daisy	C. Wingfield	4th 10s.
Olive	F. Collier	5th 7s.6d.
Dorothy	G. Wingfield	
Shamrock	Harry Marshall	

The contest was a good one, as all the boats kept well together, though the winner's position was never assailed. There was a near finish for both third and fourth places.

Three-Oared Boats:

Olive Branch	G. Wingfield	1st prize £2
Rapid	C. Lee	2nd £1 10s.
Pansy	Arthur Marshall	3rd £1
Rose	Harry Marshall	4th 15s.
True Blue	C. Wingfield	

From the eastern buoys the race promised to be a close one, but the *Olive Branch* pulled ahead and won by about a length and a half, there being a race between second and third.

Rescue Race:

Oruba	Arthur Marshall	prize £2

Glossary

Athwart	— Across vessel.
Ballast	— Heavy material put in hold of empty cargo ship to keep it stable.
Barque	— Three-masted ship with fore and main masts square-rigged.
Barquentine	— Vessel with foremast square-rigged, main and mizzen fore-and-aft rigged.
Beam	— Ship's breadth.
Beating Windward	— Tacking.
Bow	— Fore end of vessel.
Bowsprit	— Spar projecting from vessel's bow, usually almost horizontal, to which the foresail stays are fastened.
Breeches Buoy	— Rescue equipment rigged up between a shipwreck and land with a lifebuoy on a hawser.
Brig	— Vessel with two masts, both square-rigged.
Brigantine	— Two-masted vessel, square-rigged on foremast only.
Bring to	— Manouevre a vessel to come alongside another.
Bulwarks	— Sides of vessel that are above deck.
Capstan	— Upright cylinder, usually of wood, revolved by horse or manpower, to draw boats up the beach.
Coxwain	— Head of lifeboat crew.
Cutter	— Small-masted type of sailing vessel.
Fore	— Bow.
Foremast	— Mast nearest bow.
Foresail	— Largest sail on foremast.
Fore-topmast	— Mast above foremast, carrying fore-topsail.
Fore-topgallant-mast	— Mast above fore-topmast, carrying fore-topgallant-sail.
Galley	— low, flat one-decked vessel propelled by oars.
Go about	— Turn a sailing vessel to travel in the opposite direction, involving sail repositioning.
Guano	— Dung of sea fowl.
Guernsey	— Thick jersey.
Gunwhale	— Upper edge of vessel's side.
Hands	— Seamen working on board a vessel.
Hawser	— Thick rope or cable.
Helm	— Where the helmsman stands to control the tiller or wheel.
Jib	— Triangular sail at vessel's bow.
Jolly Boat	— Small boat carried by ship.
Lee	— Shelter, side (of ship, etc.) away from wind.
Leeward	— Towards the lee.
Lifebuoy	— Buoyant ring to support person in the sea. Normally thrown to person who has fallen in.
Lugger	— Small vessel with two or three masts and lugsails.
Lugsail	— Square sail bent on an equally slung spar hanging across mast.
Maroon	— Signal rocket with loud report, fired to summon the lifeboat crew.
Mizzen	— Lowest sail on mizzen mast.
Mizzen mast	— Aftermost mast when there are three.
Neap tide	— Tide at beginning of moon's 2nd or 4th quarter, when high water is at its lowest.
Port	— Left side of vessel looking forward.

Reef	— Part of sail that can be rolled up to reduce area.
Rowlock	— Device on gunwhale in which an oar works.
Rudder	— Flat piece hinged to stern of vessel below water, to steer by.
Salvors	— People who saved a vessel or cargo from peril of sea.
Schooner	— Fore-and-aft rigged vessel with two or more masts.
Scull	— Light oar pulled with one hand or oar used in stern like a propeller.
Sheet	— Rope at lower corner of sail for working it.
Sieve net	— Fishing net with a very fine mesh.
Sloop	— One-masted fore-and-aft rigged vessel like cutter.
Smack	— Small fishing boat, sloop.
Spar	— Pole or beam usually forming mast.
Starboard	— Right-hand side of ship looking towards bow.
Stern	— Back part of vessel.
Tacking	— Sailing obliquely against the wind on a zig-zag course to enable the wind to catch the sails from alternate directions.
Tiller	— Handle or spar for turning the rudder.
Watermen	— Fishermen and boatmen.
Windlass	— Machine for hoisting or hauling with rope wound on a cylinder.

Acknowledgements

I am indebted to Eric Cockain for his inspirational guidance, moral support and encouragement.

For their help, advice and photographs I would like to thank the following:

My father, Bill Blann.

Jeff Morris, Honorary Archivist of the R.N.L.I. Enthusiasts Society.

Derrick Marshall Churcher.

The Royal National Lifeboat Institution and staff.

Mrs. Arthur Wingfield and Alan Wingfield.

Worthing Reference Library and staff.

West Sussex County Council Library Service.

West Sussex County Records Office and staff.

Beckett Newspapers.

West Sussex Gazette.

Worthing Museum and staff.

Mrs. Gena Wilmshurst.

Mrs. Lynn West.

Ted Baker.

Mrs. Stevens.

The National Maritime Museum.

Terry Child.

Mrs. Mabel Foggett.

Fred Bashford.

Mrs. Freda Kiernander.

David Nicholls Photography and staff.

Arthur Chandler.

Walter Gardiner Photography and staff.

Ken Jakes.

And above all to my wife, Josephine, for putting up with me during the times when I spent countless hours researching and word-processing for my book.